MORE HEROES OF THE ALBERT MEDAL

MORE HEROES OF THE ALBERT MEDAL

Civilian recipients who did not survive to receive the George Cross

By

Allan Stanistreet

2015

First Published in Great Britain 2015
by
Token Publishing Ltd,
Orchard House, Duchy Road, Heathpark, Honiton, Devon EX14 1YD
Telephone: 01404 46972   Fax: 01404 44788
email: info@tokenpublishing.com   Website: http://www.tokenpublishing.com

British Library Cataloguing in Publication data:
A catalogue for this publication is available from the British Library
ISBN: 978 1 908828 22 4

Printed in Great Britain
Short Run Press, Exeter

Acknowledgements

A s before, I have to acknowledge the not inconsiderable contribution made by many friends and correspondents over many years. My first thanks must go to the families of so many of those featured in these pages, without whose invariable kindness and generous assistance it would be impossible adequately to chronicle the lives of their forebears. I am always touched by their pleasure at having their ancestors' gallantry brought to public attention.

Next, I must mention the relatively small coterie of people with an interest in this rare award and its recipients. Their names appear alphabetically.

Dave Carpenter (for assistance with Welsh recipients)
Jonathan Collins, ARRC
Sarah Dyson
Chris Fagg (Australia)
Lieutenant-Colonel (Retired) Maxwell Macfarlane
The late Bob Mansell (for assistance with Welsh recipients)
John D. O'Malley (USA)
Joe Murphy (for assistance with Irish recipients)
Phillip O'Shea CNZM, CVO (New Zealand Herald of Arms Extraordinary)
Anthony Staunton (Australia)
Paul Xuereb (Malta)
The Registrar, The Royal Archives, Windsor Castle
John Mussell and the Staff at Token Publishing Ltd
Her Majesty's Stationery Office (for London Gazettes)

Special thanks are due to Paul Street (Australia), who is indefatigable in his research in obscure places and most generous in sharing the results of his labours; to John Wilson and Bob Scarlett for kindly scrutinising the manuscript and making many helpful comments and suggestions; Alan & Christine Hammond for the help with proof checking. Last but by no means least, I must pay tribute to my wife, who endures my endless hours in front of the computer screen with amazing patience and good humour.

Once again, I am grateful to Mrs Margaret Purves GC for kindly consenting to write a Foreword to this book.

All errors and omissions are solely down to the author.

Books by the same author

The Malayan Railway—Keretapi Melayu

'Gainst All Disaster—Gallant Deeds Above and Beyond the call of Duty

Brave Railwaymen

Portrait of the West Somerset Railway—25 Years of Preservation Progress

Heroes of The Albert Medal

Foreword

When I wrote the foreword to *Heroes of the Albert Medal,* I little realised that Allan would continue to discover yet more tales of extreme bravery which would be lost forever without his persistence in searching for the human stories as he has done.

The failure of the Home Office over the years to keep a log of civilian awards of this medal has amazed many people, but with this volume the otherwise forgotten deeds of valour are recorded for posterity.

When Queen Victoria instituted the Albert Medal she did so to create a civilian award equal to the Victoria Cross. The Victoria Cross is still accepted as the nation's highest award for valour, but somehow over the years successive monarchs and politicians have changed the goal posts and some important medals have been cast into history.

Margaret Purves

Preface

*A*lthough the history of the Albert Medal was summarised in the first book, it may be convenient to reiterate it here.

Representations were made to Queen Victoria in 1864 that a medal should be created for award to individuals "for acts of daring" performed by civilians, as opposed to military personnel in conflict situations, and for whom the Victoria Cross (VC), Conspicuous Gallantry Medal (CGM) and Distinguished Conduct Medal (DCM) already existed. After some correspondence between Her Majesty and the Home Secretary, the Albert Medal was instituted by Royal Warrant dated March 7, 1866. Named after the late Prince Consort, this Warrant only allowed for the award in one class and only one medal was awarded under it: to a farmer in Devon.

By the next year, it was felt that the award should be expanded into two classes: First in gold and Second in bronze. Accordingly, a new Royal Warrant was issued, dated April 12, 1867, containing revised regulations for the award of the medal. For about the first forty years of the medal's existence, both classes were manufactured by Phillips of Cockspur Street, London, whose particulars appear on the reverse of the crown surmounting the medal and for the first ten years the medal was only awarded for gallantry in saving, or attempting to save, life at sea.

In 1877, there was a terrible disaster at the Tynewydd pit in the Rhondda, South Wales. As a result of the great gallantry displayed by many of those involved in the rescue operations, it was decided to extend the scope of the Albert Medal to those who performed acts of gallantry in saving life on land, so a third Royal Warrant was issued, dated April 30, 1877, which had this effect. Like most awards for gallantry intended for what might be termed civilian situations, the Albert Medal of both types and classes was also awarded to service personnel in situations where purely military honours were not considered appropriate and it was so awarded on many occasions, particularly in the First World War.

During its currency from 1866 to 1971, 571 awards of the Albert Medal were made. These are broken down as follows: 25 Gold Sea; 45 Gold Land; 211 Bronze Sea and 290 Bronze Land. Until the institution of the George Cross in September, 1940, the Albert Medal was regarded as the civilian VC and was awarded very sparingly indeed. Amongst its civilian recipients were a boy of eight and a man of sixty-seven. Two boys of ten were awarded it and several teenagers. Its award was not confined to the male sex and sixteen ladies received it, four of these being nurses during World War One. As may be imagined, merchant seamen feature prominently among the awards for service at sea.

Contents

Albert Medal First Class (Gold)
for Sea Service.

Albert Medal Second Class (Bronze)
for Sea Service.

Albert Medal First Class (Gold)
for Land Service.

Albert Medal Second Class (Bronze)
for Land Service.

Introduction

*H*eroes of the Albert Medal was published in 2002. It listed members of the three Services who had been awarded the Albert Medal but had not survived to exchange it or be eligible to exchange it for the George Cross in October, 1971. Those who had survived to do so were dealt with in the book *'Gainst All Disaster'* by this author and published by Picton Publishing in 1986.

This volume will list those civilian recipients who did not survive to exchange their medals. Out of the total of 571 medals awarded between 1866 and 1971, when the award of the AM was discontinued, almost half (249) went to service personnel, while there were 322 awards to civilians, including members of the Merchant Navy.

Readers will no doubt appreciate that while service personnel can be relatively easy to research, it is exactly the opposite with civilians, although some, such as Merchant seamen, police officers and doctors, are easier than others. There are several reasons for these difficulties. Even during its currency, the Albert Medal was a little known award. Few had heard of it and even fewer had ever set eyes on one or its recipient. For the first half-century of its existence, communications were haphazard and unreliable, meaning that its award and the recipients were poorly chronicled, if at all, albeit all awards save four appeared in the contemporary *London Gazette*. However, the *London Gazette* was not widely read by the general population, many of whom were, in the early days in any event, illiterate.

Furthermore, photography was still relatively in its infancy in the mid-1860s and only the more well-to-do could afford studio portraits of themselves and their relatives. So likenesses of medal recipients tend to be few and far between in the early days. Nevertheless, Queen Victoria commanded that a photographic record of recipients be made and there exists a highly decorated album of these individuals in The National Archives, the contents of which are as follows (although there are some gaps):

Photograph No. 1	Samuel Popplestone
Photograph No. 2	Samuel Lake
Photograph No. 3	William Halse Millett
Photograph No. 4	Rev. Charles Cobb
Photograph No. 5	John Batist
Photograph No. 6	John Donovan
Photograph No. 7	Charles Sprankling
Photograph No. 8	James Hudson
Photograph No. 9	Theophilus Jones
Photograph No. 10	Allen Thompson Shuttleworth
Photograph No. 11	John Ricketts
Photograph No. 12	E. B. March

Photograph No. 13	Lionel Audros de Sausmarez
Photograph No. 14	James Crowden
Photograph No. 15	Capt James Beautine Willoughby R.N.
Photograph No. 16	William Simpson
Photograph No. 17	Capt Edward Giles I.M.
Photograph No. 18	Lieut William Balfour Forbes R.N.
Photograph No. 19	Augustus Raymond Margary
Photograph No. 20	John Dodd
Photograph No. 21	Missing
Photograph No. 22	Missing
Photograph No. 23	Lieut Alfred Carpenter R.N.
Photograph No. 24	John Summers
Photograph No. 25	Ernest W. Owens
Photograph No. 26	Sub-Lieut Robert James Archibald Montgomery R.N.
Photograph No. 27	Not included
Photograph No. 28	Not included
Photograph No. 29	Not included
Photograph No. 30	Pte Anthony Gerrighty R.M.
Photograph No. 31	John Summers
Photograph No. 32	Capt Peter Sharp

Publicity relating to the early Albert Medallists was hampered by the fact that after the death of the Prince Consort in 1861, the Queen seems to have shunned investitures and quite often Albert Medals were presented on social occasions in the locality of the recipient's residence by some local dignitary. This tended to denigrate the importance of the deed, the recipient and the occasion.

Those listed in *Heroes of the Albert Medal* appeared in alphabetical order. Since there were a few occasions when more than one award was made, this did not turn out very satisfactorily from a presentational point of view, so it has been decided that the list in this book will be chronological. The result should be much neater in appearance.

There were a number of occasions in the later days of the Albert Medal when it was awarded to more than one person but not all survived to become a holder of the George Cross. As far as civilian recipients were concerned there were four such occasions and this will be brought out in the text.

Sixteen ladies were awarded the Albert Medal, all save two being civilians. Two of these civilian awards were posthumous and five subsequently became GCs. Other categories of civilian recipients are as follows:

Police officers / Fireman -	5/2
Railwaymen	15 (?18 [1])
Doctors	6 [2]
Merchant seamen	44 [3]
Fishing boat crews	8
Coastguards / Lifeboatmen	9/2
Dockyard workers	7
Miners	56
Others	167

1) There were three others, all servicemen, who may have been railwaymen in their civilian occupation.

2) 14 doctors were awarded the AM but 8 of these were in the services.

3) One was also a doctor; he has been counted with those.

It is, perhaps, worthy of note that the youngest person ever to receive an official award for gallantry (the AM) was an eight-year-old boy, Anthony Farrer. Until the award of the George Medal to 72-year-old Mrs Eva Helen Dickson in New Zealand in 1992, the oldest person to receive an official decoration, albeit posthumously, was Henry Charles Morris AM, aged 67, in 1950.

The demise of the Albert Medal was rather sad and extremely protracted. It is a somewhat complicated story. In September, 1940, upon the institution of the George Cross and George Medal, there then existed six official awards for gallantry not displayed in the presence of an enemy; nine if both versions of the Albert, Edward and Sea Gallantry Medal were to be included.

This presented something of a dilemma to officialdom when attempting to decide which medal to award in certain circumstances. The fact that there was also a world war raging at the time did not help matters. Accordingly, it was decided that the Empire Gallantry Medal would be subsumed into the George Cross, despite the fact that it had always been considered a junior award to both the Albert and Edward Medals. It is not known by what process of logic this decision was reached; suffice it to say that it was probably by someone with little or no knowledge of the history and development of gallantry awards, nor the process of their award.

Thus, overnight, as it were, all living holders of the EGM and the next-of-kin of posthumous awards subsequent to September 3, 1939, were obliged to hand in their medals and henceforth become GC holders. Not all EGMs were handed in, however. No consideration appears to have been given at the time to holders of the AM and EM, so to paraphrase a biblical expression, "Those who were first shall be last and those who were last shall be first".

In 1956, the centenary of the institution of the Victoria Cross was celebrated. Ten years later, in 1966, it occurred to the late Instructor Commander David Hywel Evans AM MA RN (Retired) that it might be appropriate to celebrate the centenary of the institution of the Albert Medal similarly, so he set about finding as many surviving holders of the decoration as he could by advertising through various media, including the BBC. He eventually recruited 73 members to the Albert Medal Association, which held an annual gathering every year in London from 1966 to 1972, when it was absorbed into the VC and GC Association.

It was very soon realised that no living person had been awarded the AM since the end of 1949 and it was thought that there was a lack of awareness among the general public of the status of the decoration and those who had received it. Although the members had no desire for the matter to become political, it was inevitable that politics would enter the arena when they began lobbying for the recognition they felt was their due. Many distinguished people were to campaign on their behalf, firstly achieving the grant of an annuity to recipients in 1968 and finally, in 1971, parity with holders of the GC.

Although no brief was ever held for recipients of the Edward Medal, always considered less prestigious than the AM, the former was also included in the exchanges. Unlike in the case of the EGM over thirty years before, holders of both AM and EM were not compelled to exchange their awards and might elect to retain the original medals. In the case of the AM, out of 64 persons eligible to exchange, nineteen elected to retain their original award, though all would be considered to be holders of the George Cross. Of the four survivors at the time of writing (September, 2015), two still wear their Albert Medals (in both cases for Sea service).

For the sake of the record, some photographs of subjects in the first volume came to light after the publication of *Heroes of the Albert Medal* in 2002. These photographs are included at the back of this book. Further information on any of the subjects of both books is always welcomed by the author via the publisher. Apart from minor editorial amendments, the *London Gazette* citations which follow are given verbatim.

Awards of the Albert Medal to Civilians

1866

SAMUEL POPPLESTONE

Date of Deed: March 23, 1866
Date of Gazette: June 15, 1866

The Spirit of the Ocean, a barque of 557 tons, with a crew of 18 and 24 passengers, was wrecked on the rocks 400 yards west of Start Point, in the county of Devon, on 23rd March 1866. The mate and one of the crew were saved by Samuel Popplestone, unaided, and at the imminent risk of his own life.

Samuel Popplestone

The circumstances under which this very dangerous service was performed by Mr Popplestone are as follows, viz.:

The vessel, with a part of her crew sick, and the mates and passengers assisting in working her, was caught in a strong gale from the south-west; and on Friday, the 23rd March, she was off the Start, in a very dangerous position. Mr Popplestone observed the peril of the vessel, and knew that if she failed to weather the rocks she must inevitably be lost, and every soul lost with her, unless assistance could be rendered from the shore. He therefore despatched a messenger on horseback to Tor Cross, to rouse the villagers, and another messenger on horseback to give information to the Coast Guard. The vessel had by this time struck on the rocks and had begun to break up rapidly.

Mr Popplestone took a small coil of rope, and, alone and unaided, proceeded over the shore from rock to rock until he got near to the vessel. The wind at the time was blowing at force 11, that is, a storm, nearly equal to a hurricane, accompanied by rain, and a very heavy and dangerous sea. Whilst Popplestone was standing on the rock nearest the vessel, endeavouring to effect a communication with the vessel, he was washed off; but, by a great effort on his part, and by the help of a returning sea, he regained his footing, and from this perilous position he succeeded in saving the lives of two persons, and conveying them beyond the reach of danger.

This, the first award of the Albert Medal was to a farmer, Samuel Popplestone, who farmed at Start Farm, Start Point, Devon. Not much is known of Mr Popplestone, who was born circa 1831. He was a bachelor at the time of his heroic act with a large and successful farm, which still exists. In 1867 he married Sarah Anne Lidstone (born in Loddiswell) but they had no children. Samuel Popplestone died in the middle of 1914 in Plymouth, aged 83. His wife died in 1931, aged 86. His medal is now in the care of Plymouth City Museum, having languished in a drawer for many years, its historical importance not having been previously appreciated.

Note: This was the only award of the Albert Medal made under the original Royal Warrant of 1866. There was only one class of award at this time, that in gold and of course, this was the Albert Medal in Gold. It was also the only gold award to have the original blue and white ribbon of five-eighths of an inch in width.

1867 – 1877

As a result of representations made to the Queen, by Royal Warrant of April 12, 1867, the Albert Medal was divided into two classes, the First Class being a medal in gold and the Second Class being in bronze, for acts which were deemed not to come up to the standard which merited the gold medal but which nevertheless merited official recognition. All the awards in the following section were for sea service.

CHARLES SPRANKLING

Date of Deed: June 11, 1866
Date of Gazette: June 28, 1867

On the 11th June, 1866, the fishing boat containing five men ran for the beach at Burton. As she touched it, a heavy sea struck her and threw her upon the crew. CHARLES SPRANKLING, a Commissioned Boatman, of the Burton Coast Guard station, who was near the spot, managed by great exertion and at some risk to himself, to raise the side of the boat which was washing backwards and forwards in a heavy surf, and thus enabled three of the men to get from under her.

The other two men, who had been injured by the gear in the boat, drifted into deep water, when SPRANKLING, who is a good swimmer, rushed into the sea and succeeded in bringing first one and then the other to land, but apparently lifeless. He then followed the directions given for treating the apparently drowned, and when the men had somewhat recovered sent them to their homes, and sent also for medical attendance.

In rendering this service SPRANKLING was unaided, as the men who succeeded in getting from under the boat were too exhausted to render him any assistance.

Charles Sprankling was awarded the **Albert Medal of the Second Class.** He was also awarded the large Board of Trade Medal in Bronze and this award is now in a private collection. Sprankling was born in 1828, the son of Robert and Elizabeth (née Lake). He married Margaret McMullen on January 6, 1852 at Burton Bradstock and they had three sons and two daughters. After retirement from the Coastguard Service, he was employed as a lodge keeper at Arundel Castle, the seat of the Duke of Norfolk. He died in 1909.

SAMUEL LAKE and WILLIAM HALSE MILLETT

Date of Deed: June 20, 1866
Date of Gazette: June 7, 1867

The ship "Diamond", of Calcutta, from Jeddo for Calcutta, having on board the master, his wife, the mate, and another European, a crew of 47 Lascars, about 400 passengers (Mahommedan pilgrims), and a cargo of salt, experienced bad weather, and being dismasted, bore up for Bombay. About noon on the 20th June, 1866, she was observed passing the Bombay lighthouse, but as it was blowing heavily, assistance could not be given to her, and she drifted on to the rocks at Breach Candy. A heavy sea was breaking over them at the time, the place being quite exposed to the force of the south-west monsoon.

Samuel Lake

Image: www.bythedart.co.uk

Attempts were at once made by people on the spot to render assistance, which were not then successful; but on the two following days they were renewed, and by the unceasing exertions of those who took part in rendering assistance, the whole of the passengers and crew who remained on board (some having jumped overboard and swam ashore, or reached it by means of spars, &c., and some having lost their lives in the attempt), were safely landed.

The rescue of the shipwrecked persons was attended with much difficulty and danger, as, in consequence of the heavy sea breaking on the beach, several of the boats were capsized and damaged.

Amongst a large number of persons who rendered much valuable assistance on this occasion, two gentlemen, viz., Messrs. S. LAKE of the Bombay Reclamation Company's Works, and W.H. MILLETT, Third Officer on board the Peninsular and Oriental Company's steam-ship "Emeu", made themselves conspicuous by their gallantry. Mr. LAKE took command of the first boat that put off to the wreck on the 20th June. The boat was capsized, but the crew were saved by clinging to her. He also formed one of the crew of another boat which made an attempt to board the wreck on the following day, but which became waterlogged and unmanageable, and was driven on shore where she was stove. The boat was repaired, and Mr. LAKE again went in her. This time she succeeded in reaching the wreck. Mr. LAKE volunteered to go on board for the purpose of giving confidence to the shipwrecked people. He went on board and rendered great service in assisting the almost helpless passengers into the boats. When it became dark he swam ashore, promising to go on board next day. At daybreak he went off again in a surf boat, and remained for some hours exerting himself in putting the passengers over the ship's side, until all had left the wreck.

Mr. MILLETT was in command of a lifeboat sent overland to the scene of the wreck by the Superintendent of the Peninsular and Oriental Company at Bombay. Upon her arrival, on the 21st June, Mr. MILLETT, accompanied by Mr. H.B. Greaves, the Company's Dockmaster, and a crew of 123 Chinamen, proceeded in her to the wreck, and in two trips brought ashore some of the passengers. On the following day he made seven trips, and succeeded in landing in safety altogether 120 people.

During the time he was engaged in this service the sea was very heavy, and the boat was continually filled with water. On two trips Mr. MILLETT was washed out of the boat, and was with difficulty saved, but he continued his work until the last passenger was landed.

Samuel Lake and William Halse Millett were each awarded the **Albert Medal of the First Class**. Samuel Lake was born in 1842 in Dartmouth, Devon. He spent some of his life in India, returning to Dartmouth in 1866. Lake Street in the town is named after him. He died in 1887. William Millett was born in Penzance, Cornwall, on May 2, 1840, the son of John Millett, a solicitor, and Mary Rey, a doctor's daughter. He was also the recipient of the Royal Humane Society's Bronze Medal and the Shipwrecked Mariners' Benevolent Society Silver Medal in 1863. He was drowned on July 15, 1877, when the steamer *Yarra Yarra*, of which he was the Chief Officer, sank entering the harbour of Newcastle, New South Wales. The whereabouts of the Albert Medal of Samuel Lake are unknown but that of William Millett is still in the possession of the family.

JOHN DONOVAN

Date of Deed: November 30, 1866
Date of Gazette: June 7, 1867

Image: Source Unknown

John Donovan

The "Thetis", of 324 tons, with a crew of eleven persons, became embayed in Courtmacsherry Bay during a gale on November 30, 1866.

She had anchored in a dangerous position surrounded by reefs, and had cut away her masts when she was observed by the Coast Guard and Fishermen on shore.

JOHN DONOVAN, Chief Boatman in charge of the Old Head Coast Guard Station, Kinsale, endeavoured to prevail upon the fishermen who lined the shore, to the number of about 200, to launch one of their boats, well adapted for the service, and already on the strand, for the purpose of rendering assistance, but they refused.

DONOVAN then caused the Coast Guard Galley to be dragged across the land a distance of about one and a-half miles, and lowered over a perpendicular cliff about 50 feet in height. When this was done, he and four Coast Guard men launched her and proceeded to the vessel. On getting alongside, the galley was capsized and partially stove, but by good management her crew, who had life jackets on, got on board the barque, where they remained for some hours expecting that she would part her cables, owing to the heavy sea running, and a gale blowing on shore. She however rode till the weather moderated, when the galley was repaired and the crews of the boat and vessel landed in her.

John Donovan was awarded the **Albert Medal of the Second Class**. He was born c1821 at Castletown, Co. Cork, Ireland and joined the Royal Navy as a Boy 1st Class on June 4, 1840. On the books of HMS *Belvidere*, he was on loan to HMS *Gorgon* until 1842. Promoted Landsman on May 23, 1841. He went back to *Belvidere* on February 28, 1842 after serving one month with HMS *Ceylon*. Paid off March, 1845 – character 'Indifferent'. Served HMS *Rodney* 1845-49 and promoted Petty Officer (Captain of the Main Top). Drafted to Coastguard June 8, 1849, at Inverness. Removed September 19, 1849 and transferred to Harwich. Removed from Harwich in 1851 and sent to Poor Head, Queenstown (now Cobh), Co. Cork on August 16, 1851. Drafted back to RN for the Baltic campaign aboard *Royal George* from February 15, 1854 to May 4, 1856. Commissioned Boatman from July 14, 1857 and sent to serve at Ballycronen and later at Ballymena. He received the Royal Humane Society's Medal on October 19, 1862 for the wreck of the *Industry*. Chief Boatman January 15, 1863 and drafted to Ballygeary, Co. Wexford. Chief Boatman-in-Charge there from November 4, 1864. To Old Head of Kinsale Station on November 4, 1864. Discharged April 30, 1872 on books of HMS *Valiant*. His other medals include: Naval General Service Medal 1793-1840 clasp *Syria*; Baltic Medal 1854; St Jean d'Acre Medal; SGM (large) and RHS (large) Medal; RNLI Silver Medal (1862). All his medals, except the RNLI Medal, are now in the Royal Navy Museum, Portsmouth.

REV. CHARLES COBB and JOHN BATIST

Charles Cobb

Date of Deed: January 6, 1867
Date of Gazette: June 7, 1867

The "Courier de Dieppe", of 59 tons, with a crew of four persons in all, drove ashore at Dymchurch, on the morning of Sunday, January 6, 1867.

On the evening of January 5, a strong gale of wind arose, the weather became tempestuous, and the vessel was found to be on the English coast. The next morning, the master failed to get assistance, and ran the vessel ashore. Attempts made to reach her by means of the Mortar Apparatus were unsuccessful; and the master, a cabin boy, and a seaman were washed overboard and drowned.

Soon the vessel parted, and the portion upon which the mate, the only survivor of the crew, had taken refuge, was driven within 50 or 60 feet of the shore.

JOHN BATIST, a Boatman of the Coast Guard Station at Dymchurch, clad in a cork jacket, and having a line attached to him, attempted to reach the vessel, but failed and was dragged ashore. The REV. CHARLES COBB, Rector of Dymchurch, then rushed into the water, made for the bulwarks of the vessel, and, after one or two ineffectual attempts, reached the survivor, who was in the rigging. BATIST followed, and with a line, which he carried with him, the French sailor was dragged ashore, supported by Mr. COBB and BATIST. Mr COBB made this attempt in spite of the remonstrances of the people on the spot, and declined their assistance by refusing to take a line with him.

It was blowing a strong gale from the S. by E., and a heavy sea was running at the time.

Rev Charles Cobb was awarded the **Albert Medal of the First Class** and John Batist the **Albert Medal of the Second Class** for this rescue. Charles Cobb was born on June 23, 1828, one of five children of Thomas and Eliza Cobb of New Romney. He went up to Cambridge in 1848 and was ordained in 1853. After serving as Rector of Dymchurch, he became Vicar of Rainham, Essex and died on March 2, 1918, aged 89. There is, or was, a photograph of him in the vestry of the church at Rainham, where he is wearing his Albert Medal, the RNLI Gold Medal and the RHS Large Silver Medal. The French government also awarded Mr Cobb a Gold Medal and Diploma for his part in rescuing lives from a French ship. The whereabouts of his medals are not known. John Batist, about whom nothing is known, was awarded the Silver Medal of the RNLI for this rescue. His AM is in a private collection.

JAMES HUDSON and THEOPHILUS JONES

Date of Deed: March 17, 1867
Date of Gazette: June 28, 1867

The "Marmion", of North Shields, on the 17th March last, drove from her anchors and was stranded on the Cornish Coast at Gylynvase, near Pendennis Castle, Falmouth. The wind at the time was blowing strong with squalls, - the tide was first quarter flood. At ten A.M. the ship was in the midst of breakers, and often entirely covered with surf, and no communication with the shore appeared possible. The master and one of the crew died on board from exposure and exhaustion.

After an ineffectual attempt had been made to communicate with the shore by means of a line tied to a stool and thrown overboard from the ship, JAMES HUDSON, a youth of seventeen, an apprentice belonging to the "Maid of Orleans", then lying at Falmouth, volunteered to swim off to the vessel. He was at first dissuaded from the attempt, for it was thought that he would lose his life. But he persisted, and the Coast Guard attached to him their life lines and guided him afloat. He had neither jacket nor belt on. He was soon in the midst of a heavy sea, and in a short time got to the stern of the vessel, and after three attempts to reach the deck swung himself on board by the aid of a spar hanging over the side. The line attached to HUDSON effected a communication between the ship and the shore, and six of the crew were rescued by a hawser and running gear then set up.

HUDSON was compelled, by his want of clothing, to return when he had been about a quarter of an hour on board. His distress in returning was great. He expected to have been pulled on shore, but the running gear had fouled and he was obliged to pull himself hand over hand along the hawser to the shore. He was very much exhausted, and without assistance would probably not have succeeded in landing himself upon the beach.

There still remained one man alive on board, but he was too weak to fasten around himself the cork jacket with which he had been supplied. In this emergency, THEOPHILUS JONES, who had a line but no jacket or belt on, threw himself into the sea, and after two or three unsuccessful attempts, reached the vessel, and was lifted on board by the waves and by the aid of a spar which hung over the side.

He succeeded in fastening a cork jacket round the seaman and pushed him overboard, and this man too was saved. JONES was some time in the surf; he was very much benumbed and exhausted when he arrived on shore.

James Hudson and Theophilus Jones were each awarded the **Albert Medal of the Second Class.** Nothing is known about either man, however, Theophilus Jones' Albert Medal is in a private collection.

ALLEN THORNTON SHUTTLEWORTH

Date of Deed: July 22/23, 1866; August 1, 1866;
July 18, 1867
Date of Gazette: December 24, 1867

Allen Thornton Shuttleworth

Image: Illustrated London News

On the 22nd July, 1866, the "Berwickshire" ran on Chawool Kadoo Reef. Mr. SHUTTLEWORTH went to her assistance in a fisherman's canoe, and, for two days' exertions, succeeded in landing six men in one of the ship's boats. Mr. SHUTTLEWORTH again proceeded to the ship with the fishermen in another boat in so dangerous a sea that some of the "Berwickshire's" seamen, who had landed and the coolies of Colaba, to whom a large reward was offered, declined to take a message to her. After rowing for three hours, the boat having twice filled to the thwarts, he reached the vessel, and informed the captain of her true position, and remained on board to give assistance.

On the 1st August, 1866, the "Di Vernon" ran on the Chawool Kadoo Reef, near Alibagh. Mr. SHUTTLEWORTH put off in a boat with ten native fishermen, and by his coolness was the means of averting a greater loss of life than that which unhappily took place. The boat was dashed against the vessel's side and capsized, throwing all her crew into the water, and, while endeavouring to save some of these, Mr. SHUTTLEWORTH was washed overboard. He, however, regained the vessel and was for two hours lashed in the mizen rigging. He refused to forsake the captain and carpenter who were helpless, and eventually succeeded in saving the captain. The carpenter was washed away and drowned.

On the 18th July, 1867, the ship "Terzah" was wrecked about south-east of Kennery. Mr. SHUTTLEWORTH put off in a life-boat manned by fishermen, and succeeded in bringing off the captain and thirteen men out of a crew of thirty-one. Eight others came on shore on pieces of wreck. This service was rendered by Mr. SHUTTLEWORTH and his crew at great peril of their lives. The sea was breaking very heavily all round the ship and washing over her.

Allen Thornton Shuttleworth was awarded the **Albert Medal of the First Class** for these rescues. He was born in Bengal in 1839, the son of Edward and Elizabeth Shuttleworth. He was educated at Woolwich and accepted for service in the Indian Marine in 1855 as a Captain's Clerk. He served for eight years, during which he was awarded the India General Service Medal 1854-95 with clasp *Persia*. After his service with the Indian Marine, he was appointed to a position with the Forest Department of the Bombay Presidency, where he performed the acts of gallantry described above which resulted in his being awarded the Gold Medal of the Shipwrecked Fishermen and Mariners Royal Benevolent Society, Lloyds Medal for Saving Life at Sea in Silver and the large Bronze Medal of the Royal Humane Society, in addition to his Albert Medal. Retiring to England in 1902, he died at Walmer, Kent in January 1915, leaving a widow and five sons, all of whom served as officers, four of them in the Indian Army. Mr Shuttleworth's medals are now in a private collection.

EDWARD BERNARD MARCH

Date of Deed: December 7, 1867
Date of Gazette: February 28, 1868

Image: Pro

Edward Bernard March

On the night of the 7th of December last, the French ship "Nouveau Caboteur" was cast on shore in the Bay of Zurriola, on the north coast of Spain, during a gale of wind. The sea at the time was running so heavily that no boat would venture to put off. There was also a general belief that it was impossible for a boat to be of any service.

At this crisis, the British Vice-Consul at San Sebastian, Mr. E.B. March, after unsuccessfully entreating some of the bystanders to accompany him, plunged into the sea, swam to the vessel, and succeeded in bringing a rope to land. The rope was then secured, and one of the crew came safely to shore along it. The second, however, (a lad), lost his hold, dropped into the sea, and sank.

Then Mr. March, though benumbed with cold, at the greatest personal risk, again swam to the vessel, dived under her keel, recovered the lad, and brought him safe to land.

The remainder of the crew (which consisted of six men in all) got safely to land.

Mr. March was for a time completely prostrated from the effects of his exertions and the intense cold; but by care and attention he was restored – a result scarcely to have been expected under the circumstances.

Edward Bernard March was awarded the **Albert Medal of the Second Class** for this rescue. Little is known of Mr. March, save that he was also awarded the Silver Medal of the Royal Humane Society, the Order of Beneficencia, 1st Class (Spain) and the Imperial Gold Medal Sauvetage (France) in addition to the Albert Medal. His medals are now in a private collection.

JAMES CROWDEN

Date of Deed: December 21, 1868
Date of Gazette: April 16, 1869

Image: Family

James Crowden

The schooner "Kinloss" was wrecked at Scatraw Creek, a mile and a half from Muchals, on the 21st of December, 1868.

Mr. JAMES CROWDEN, the Chief Officer at Muchals Station, proceeded with his boat's crew to Scatraw, and found the ship breaking up fast. The fishermen of the place had succeeded in getting a rope from the vessel, by which it was hoped that the lives of those on board would be saved.

Mr. CROWDEN ventured out on to a rocky point and endeavoured to fasten a life-belt to the rope in order to send it out to the ship, but without success. While striving to perform this operation Mr. CROWDEN was several times washed off into the sea. Once a heavy sea swept him off and carried him about 100 yards towards the wreck, and it was thought that he was lost; but after a few minutes struggling he was carried round a point by a violent run of the sea, and thrown upon the rocks with such violence, however, that he became insensible and received a severe contusion of the left knee.

When he recovered his senses Mr. CROWDEN succeeded in getting a coble launched and was the first to jump into it. He and his men (4 in number) hauled off to the ship by the rope and succeeded in taking four men from the mast and bringing them ashore.

On being informed that there was still another man on board, Mr. CROWDEN and his crew hauled off again to the wreck; but the man was dead or dying, and in such a position that it was impossible to extricate him.

A very heavy sea was running at the time of the rescue, and the coble might have been dashed upon the rocks at any moment.

Mr. CROWDEN was fourteen days upon the sick list in consequence of the injuries received by him in being washed off and dashed against the rocks.

This is the fourth time that Mr. CROWDEN has been instrumental in saving life from shipwreck, and including the present instance, he has aided in the rescue of thirteen lives.

James Crowden was awarded the **Albert Medal of the Second Class** and the Silver Medal of the Royal National Lifeboat Institution for this rescue. James Crowden was born at Plymouth Dock (now Devonport) on December 17, 1814. He was educated at Greenwich Hospital School from 1824 – 1828. He joined the Royal Navy in August 1828 aboard the *San Josef* at Devonport, subsequently serving aboard the *Bombay*, *Druid* and *Endymion*. He had three 3-year commissions during his RN service before joining the Coastguard and his Coastguard Service was at Looe, Lulworth, Lossiemouth, Buckie and Muchals.

He was married in Plymouth on May 18, 1841. He died at Buckie on August 3, 1888. The whereabouts of his Albert Medal are unknown.

WILLIAM SIMPSON

Date of Deed: September 13, 1869
Date of Gazette: February 8, 1870

During a very heavy gale on the 13th September, 1869, the ship "Avonmore" was wrecked on the coast of Cornwall, near Bude, and the Second Officer and six other members of the crew were drowned.

The rocket apparatus from Bude was taken to the spot and under the personal direction of WILLIAM SIMPSON, Chief Boatman in charge of the Coast Guard Station there, nine of the crew were saved by it.

Six of the crew still remained on the wreck, one of them with a broken limb, lying jammed amongst the debris on the vessel's deck, SIMPSON saw that these six men could neither save themselves nor be saved by the apparatus unless additional assistance was rendered from the shore.

Although the ship was expected to break up momentarily, SIMPSON determined to reach the deck himself, if possible, by means of the gear.

While being hauled to the wreck the line became fast in the block and the gear was for a time rendered useless.

In consequence of the failure in the gear SIMPSON was hauled through the water under the stern of the ship amongst floating wreck, and it was not without difficulty and perseverance and much risk that he succeeded unaided in reaching the deck.

The ship was on her beam ends, masts had gone by the board. The decks were swept by the sea, and the leeside was under water.

When on board the wreck, SIMPSON saw that the gear, which had become choked by drift oakum, must at once be cleared. This he set himself to do with his teeth whilst he held on to the wreck with his hands.

When the rocket gear was restored to working order and got clear of all obstacles, four other volunteers were handed on board from the shore to assist, and under SIMPSON 's direction the wounded man was extricated from the debris, and the whole of the six remaining members of the crew were saved.

SIMPSON was the last to leave the wreck.

William Simpson was awarded the **Albert Medal of the Second Class**. Nothing else is known of this gallant man, save that he was also awarded the Baltic Medal, 1854. His AM is now in a private collection.

AUGUSTUS RAYMOND MARGARY and JOHN DODD

John Dodd

Image: Unknown

Augustus Raymond Margary

Image: Unknown

Date of Deed: August 9, 1871
Date of Gazette: October 29, 1872

During the raging of a very violent typhoon, which burst over the north coast of Formosa on the 9th August, 1871, the schooner "Anne", of Hong Kong, and the French barque "Adele" were amongst the vessels blown from their anchorage and driven on the rocky shore of Ke-lung Harbour. The night was very dark, with a blinding rain, and great quantities of wreck were floating in the water and being washed ashore in the surf; but, by the aid of a brilliant light of burning camphor, the position of the ships was made out from the shore.

MR. AUGUSTUS RAYMOND MARGARY, *Assistant in Her Majesty's Consular Service in China, and MR. JOHN DODD, a British Merchant, at Ke-lung, had a rope fastened to their bodies and went into the surf with a view to aiding the crew of the schooner "Anne", of Hong Kong, the nearest ship that could be discerned. Aiding each other, they waded and then swam a distance of some thirty or forty yards through the surf. The rope proved to be too short, and they were compelled either to throw it away or to return to the shore. They threw the rope off and reached the ship by swimming. They then tried to reach the shore with a rope from the ship, and after making an unsuccessful effort to do this, they persuaded two volunteers to lower a small boat, which was done with great difficulty, in which MESSRS. MARGARY and DODD tried to row back with a rope. Their efforts were frustrated. The boat was turned completely over and MR. MARGARY was for a few moments underneath it. They were, however thrown on shore with fortunately few bruises. The ship was rocking violently from side to side when they left her, but seemed to sustain no damage, and by the advice of the Captain, who appeared confident then of the strength of his ship, they desisted from further efforts, as there were more distressing cases calling for assistance further off. Timber was strewn on the beach and was beating amongst the rocks in such a way that little hope could be entertained of any living thing yet remaining; but an occasional wail of the sufferers in the sea induced MESSRS. MARGARY and DODD to persevere for several hours. They then with difficulty, effort and danger, and in the dark, crawled over sandstone rocks of a peculiarly rugged nature, amidst breakers and wreck, until they arrived to within a short distance of the remains of the French ship "Adele", and by swimming they were able to make a connexion with her by a rope from the shore.*

MR. DODD swam to seize the buoy which the Frenchmen threw over, while MR. MARGARY swam to meet him with the shore rope. They joined the two and immediately gained the deck, which was by this time shattered. With the aid of the rope the greater part of the crew passed safely to shore, when MR. DODD and MR. MARGARY discovered the boatswain lying half under water, with his leg completely broken above the ankle. They raised him and carried him on shore by swimming. They then made repeated efforts to cross the broken back of the ship, to save four men who remained cut off in the bows. These men were helplessly frightened, and could scarcely be got down. MESSRS. MARGARY and DODD in the end succeeded, but both were washed down by a heavy sea, which caused much injury to MR. DODD.

The last thing which left the ship was a black cat, which clung to MR. MARGARY's shoulder in spite of the heavy surf which was rolling over all, and when they left the ship she was actually breaking up beneath their feet.

Augustus Raymond Margary and John Dodd were each awarded the **Albert Medal of the First Class** for this gallant rescue. Augustus Margary was born on May 26, 1846, in Belgaum, India, the third son of Major-General Henry Margary. He was educated in France, at Brighton College and University College, London. He was appointed student interpreter in the British Consular Service in China and served in Peking (now Beijing), Taiwan, Shanghai and Yantai. He was murdered, along with his entire staff, while surveying the overland Asian trade routes on February 21, 1875. A monument in his memory was erected in Hong Kong in 1907 but was removed during the Japanese occupation and has never been replaced. He was also awarded the Silver Medal of the Royal Humane Society for this rescue. His Albert Medal is believed to have been lost at sea. Little is known of John Dodd, save that he was a Scottish merchant trading in China and Hong Kong from about 1860. He was also awarded the Silver Medal of the Royal Humane Society. His AM is now in a private collection.

DAVID WEBSTER

Date of Deed: February 17 – March 20, 1874
Date of Gazette: July 10, 1874

Nothing is known of the next recipient of the Albert Medal, but it surely ranks among the more extraordinary deeds in the annals of the decoration.

The "Arracan", whilst on a voyage from South Shields to Bombay, with a cargo of coals, took fire from spontaneous combustion of her cargo, and on the 17th February was abandoned by her crew, who then took to their boats and endeavoured to make for the Maldive Islands. The boats kept company until 20th, when finding the currents too strong it was agreed to separate after dividing the provisions.

The Master in command of the long boat then made for Cochin, the Mate in charge of the gig, and the Second Mate, MR. DAVID WEBSTER, in charge of the pinnace with four of the crew, viz., three men and one boy, made for the Maldive Islands.

After two days, MR. DAVID WEBSTER's boat was injured by a heavy sea, and could not keep up with the gig, and lost sight of her. From this time the pinnace was kept working to windward until the 9th March, by which day the provisions and water had been consumed.

Shortly afterwards the crew cast lots which of them should be first killed to be eaten, and the lot fell upon the ship's boy HORNER, but WEBSTER, who had been asleep, was awoke in time to save the boy's life. After dark an attempt was made to kill WEBSTER himself, but the boy HORNER awoke him in time to save himself.

On the following day, WEBSTER having fallen asleep, was awoke by the struggles of the crew for possession of his gun, with which to shoot him. Two hours later the crew attempted to take HORNER's life again, but were prevented by the determined conduct of WEBSTER, who threatened to shoot and throw overboard the first man who laid hands on the boy.

The next day one of the crew attempted to sink the boat, but WEBSTER mastered him and prevented further mischief. Two days later the same member of the crew again tried to sink the boat, and expressed his determination to take the boy's life. For this he would have been shot by WEBSTER had not the cap on the gun missed fire. Soon after, putting a fresh cap on his gun, a bird flew over the boat which WEBSTER shot; it was at once seized and devoured by the crew, even to the bones and feathers.

During the next five days the crew were quieter, subsisting on barnacles which attached themselves to the bottom of the boat and on sea blubber for which they dived. The following day some of the men became delirious. One of them lay down exhausted, when another struck him several times on the head with an iron belaying pin, cutting him badly. The blood which flowed was caught in a tin and drunk by the man himself and the two other men. Afterwards they fought and bit one another, and only left off when completely exhausted, to recommence as soon as they were able; the boy, HORNER, during the time keeping watch with WEBSTER.

On the thirty-first day in the boat they were picked up six hundred miles from land by the ship "City of Manchester", HARDIE, Master, by whom they were very kindly treated, and brought to Calcutta.

WEBSTER, by his conduct, was the means of saving the lives of all in the boat.

David Webster, late Second Mate of the barque "Arracan" of Greenock, residing at Broughty Ferry, Dundee, was awarded the **Albert Medal of the Second Class** for his remarkable display of courage and leadership. The ship, of 770 tons, was built at

Bremerhaven in 1856 and was owned by Colin. S. Caird of Greenock at the time. The AM was presented to Mr Webster in Liverpool on January 4, 1875. A binocular glass was presented to the boy, Horner. The whereabouts of Webster's Albert Medal are unknown.

JOHN SKELTON SUMMERS

Date of Deed: August 3, 1876
Date of Gazette: November 17, 1876

On the 3rd of August, 1876, SUMMERS was riding his nets, 35 miles east-south-east from Buchanness, and broke adrift about noon in the height of a violent gale, with a dangerous cross sea running, accompanied with heavy rain. About 15 minutes after getting his close-reefed foresail set, to make for the land, he observed a boat on his weather bow, about a quarter of a mile off, with sail down, and making signals of distress. He hauled up for her at once, and, on nearing, observed she was swamped, and her mast lying over to leeward at an angle of about 45°, rendering great caution necessary in approaching her, for fear of carrying away his own mast, as she rolled so heavily in the trough of the sea.

At the first sweep, close on her port quarter, SUMMERS picked off two men with lines; but he had to wear round and come up to her again five times before he succeeded in getting off the third man; but, nothing daunted, he repeated his manoeuvre nearly twenty times before he got off the last man, who was the master, and who was much exhausted.

SUMMERS first observed the distressed vessel at about 12.30, and it was 4 P.M. before the last man was dragged on board. In consequence of the violence of the gale, he did not reach Peterhead until four o'clock next morning.

The total number of men rescued was six; and there is little doubt that this could not have been effected if SUMMERS had not displayed great coolness and intrepidity, combined with very skilful handling of his boat.

John Skelton Summers was awarded the **Albert Medal of the Second Class**. The whereabouts of his Albert Medal are unknown.

ERNEST WILLIAM OWENS

Date of Deed: August 28, 1875
Date of Gazette: January 2, 1877

The next award of the Albert Medal was the last to a civilian before the institution of the Albert Medal for Gallantry in Saving Life on Land. Once again, it went to a merchant seaman.

On the morning of the 28th August, 1875, the "Compadre" being then off Cape Horn, in a very severe gale, a heavy sea struck the ship, and washed overboard Duncan McKay, an apprentice, who was attending to his duties on deck. MR. OWENS, seeing McKay in the sea bleeding and fainting, immediately jumped

Image: Paul Street, Australia

Ernest William Owens

17

overboard to his assistance, notwithstanding that he was very heavily clothed, and had on his oilskins and sea boots.

A rope was thrown to them from the ship, which MR. OWENS caught with his right hand, and wound round McKay's body, which he was supporting with his left hand. His hands, however, were so benumbed with cold, that he could not make the rope fast, but winding it several times round his own wrist, he held on to it with all his power. Difficulty was experienced in getting them on board, as McKay was quite helpless, and both wore oilskins and sea boots, besides heavy clothing, which was saturated with water. After several efforts, they were taken on board, having been in the water about fifteen or twenty minutes.

Ernest William Owens, Second Mate of the "Compadre" of Liverpool, was awarded the **Albert Medal of the Second Class**. Owens was born in 1854, going to sea as an apprentice when he was 14. He eventually attained the rank of Captain. In 1893, he was appointed as an instructor at Liverpool Technical College. In 1898, he went to London to become a junior examiner of masters and mates for London, eventually becoming chief examiner. He was a keen astronomer and wrote nautical text books, among which was "How to Learn Ashore the Rule of the Road at Sea". He died at Erith, Kent, on August 4, 1915. He was a Fellow of the Royal Astronomical Society. He was presented with his AM by the Lord Mayor of Liverpool on January 10, 1878. This was stolen from his mother's house in 1879 while he was at sea. He applied for a replacement but was refused. However, he applied again on November 5, 1901 and this time he was given a replacement, which was received by him on January 30, 1901. His Albert Medal is now in a private collection.

1877 – 1907

On April 11, 1877, there was a major disaster at the Tynewydd Colliery in the Rhondda Valley, South Wales, which was caused by a sudden inundation of the workings. As a direct result of this and to recognise the gallantry shown by those attempting to effect a rescue of those trapped underground, it was decided to extend the scope of the Albert Medal to acts of gallantry in saving, or attempting to save, life on land. Accordingly, a Royal Warrant was issued on April 30, 1877, promulgating this and establishing the medal in two classes, as before, for such acts.

The medal was slightly different in design from that for sea service, the land award omitting the anchor on the obverse and having a red enamel background to the centre of the obverse, as opposed to the blue enamelling on the sea award. The wording was also, of course, different and the ribbon was red and white instead of blue and white. Like its sea counterpart, it is a jewel, rather than a medal.

No fewer than twenty-five awards of the Albert Medal for Gallantry in Saving Life on Land were made for the Tynewydd disaster; four in Gold and the remainder in Bronze. To save space, the two citations will be amalgamated, since much of the original citation is repeated.

Back row, from left to right; Dr Price, Dr Henry Naunton-Davies, Thomas Griffiths, Charles Oatridge (AM), John Williams (AM), Issac Pride (AM), David Davies, David Minton, Thomas Rees, John Davies, John B Howells, Richard Hopkins (AM), Thomas Thomas, William Morgan (AM), William Thomas, Owen Morgan (Morien).
Middle row, from left to right; David Davies, David Jenkins (Rescued), George Jenkins (Rescued), David Hughes (Rescued), Moses Powell (Rescued), John Thomas (Rescued), William Rawlins
Front row from left to right; John Griffiths, Thomas Jones

GEORGE ABLETT, CHARLES BAYNHAM, RICHARD HOPKINS, RICHARD HOWELLS, CHARLES OATRIDGE, JOHN WILLIAMS, ROBERT WILLIAMS, EDWARD DAVID, WILLIAM MORGAN, DAVID REES, REES THOMAS, DAVID DAVIES, THOMAS JONES, EDMUND THOMAS, THOMAS G. DAVIES, DAVID EVANS, DAVID JONES, HENRY LEWIS, ISAIAH THOMAS, THOMAS THOMAS, WILLIAM THOMAS, DANIEL THOMAS, ISAAC PRIDE, JOHN WILLIAM HOWELL and WILLIAM BEITH.

Image: Unknown

George Ablett

Image: Unknown

Isaac Pride

Date of Deed: April 11, 1877
Date of Gazette: August 7, 1877

On the 11th of April, the Tynewydd Colliery, situate near Porth, in the Rhondda Valley, South Wales, was inundated with water from the old workings of the adjoining Cymmer Colliery. At the time of the inundation there were fourteen men in the pit, of whom four were unfortunately drowned, and one killed by compressed air, leaving nine men imprisoned by the water; of this number four were released after eighteen hours' imprisonment, and five after nine days' imprisonment. It was in effecting the release of these latter five that those distinguished services were rendered which the conferring of the "Albert Medal of the First Class" is intended to recognise.

From Thursday, April the 12th, when the operations for the rescue were commenced, until Friday, April the 20th, when the intervening barrier of coal had been cut through and the imprisoned men released, [the above-named eleven men]* were present at different times, and, while being of valuable service in the rescue, exposed their own lives to the great danger which would have attended an outburst of water and compressed air, or an explosion of the inflammable gas which at different times during the rescue escaped under great pressure and in dangerous quantities.

During the five days from April the 16th to April the 20th [the above-named eleven men] *were at various times engaged in cutting through the barrier of coal separating them from the five imprisoned men, and while exposing their own lives to the great danger which would have resulted from an outburst of compressed air and water and to the danger which actually existed from the presence of large quantities of inflammable gas, continued to perform their work until the five men were safely rescued.*

The rescuing operations consisted in driving through the barrier of coal thirty-eight yards in length, which intervened between the imprisoned men and the rescuers, and kept back a large quantity of water and compressed air. This task was commenced on Monday, April the 16th, and was carried on until Thursday, April the 19th, without any great amount of danger being incurred by the rescuers; but about one o'clock P.M. on that day, when only a few yards of barrier remained, the danger from an irruption of water, gas, and compressed air was so great as to cause the colliers to falter. It was at this juncture that the above-mentioned four men [the four men awarded the AM of the First Class] *volunteered to resume the rescuing operations, the danger of which had been greatly increased by an outburst of inflammable gas under great pressure, and in such quantities as to extinguish the Davy lamps which were being used. The danger from gas continued at intervals until half-past three on the following morning, and from that time the above four men* [the four men awarded the AM 1st Class] *at great peril to their own lives continued the rescuing operations until three o'clock P.M., when the five men were safely rescued.*

Daniel Thomas, William Beith, Isaac Pride and John William Howell were each awarded the **Albert Medal of the First Class (Land)** for their part in this rescue, while George Ablett, Charles Baynham, Richard Hopkins, Richard Howells, Charles Oatridge, John Williams, Robert Williams, Edward David, William Morgan, David Rees, Rees Thomas, David Davies, Thomas Jones, Edmund Thomas, Thomas Thomas, Thomas Getrych Davies, David Evans, David Jones, Henry Lewis, Isaiah Thomas and William Thomas each received the **Albert Medal of the Second Class (Land)**.

Note: James Thomas was originally nominated for the AM of the Second Class but it subsequently transpired that he had not been present and his name was withdrawn, although it appeared in the *London Gazette*.

The majority of those named above were humble miners. Many, if not all, would probably have been illiterate or very poorly educated and consequently we know little or nothing about them. The medals of Isaac Pride, William Beith, Daniel Thomas, Isaiah Thomas, Edmund Thomas and Rees Thomas are now held in the National Museum of Wales and are on loan to the Big Pit Museum at Blaenavon. The medals of William Thomas, George Ablett, Edward David and Richard Howells are known to be in private collections. John Williams' medal is in a local historical museum. The whereabouts of the other Albert Medals are unknown.

Daniel and Edmund Thomas were both colliery proprietors, so came from a rather different background from most of the others. Daniel was born on January 15, 1849, the second son of D. and M. Thomas of Graigddu Cottages, Dinas. He was the proprietor of the Brithwynydd Colliery at the time of this incident. He died while attempting another rescue at Naval Colliery, Penygraig, on January 27, 1884. He also held medals from the Order of St John of Jerusalem and the Royal Humane Society. His brother, Edmund, was the eldest son of D. and M. Thomas, born in 1831. He did well for himself, becoming a magistrate for Glamorgan in 1885 and was also a member of the Board of Governors of Ystradfodwy School Board and Burial Board. He married, in 1851, Catherine (née John) and died at Penarth on October 19, 1887. He was buried at Cymmer Independent Chapel. Isaac Pride died on April 11, 1897 aged 46 and is buried in Lledrddu Cemetery (better known as Trealaw Cemetery). Rees Thomas died in January, 1939, aged 90, and is buried in Glyntaff Cemetery, Pontypridd. Isaiah Thomas died on June 4, 1896, aged

45 and is buried in Cymmer Chapel graveyard. Henry Lewis was the father of Dr Sir Thomas Lewis (1881-1945). Charles Oatridge was born in Pentyrch on July 11, 1846 and died at Llwyncelyn on September 18, 1928.

WILLIAM BUYERS

Date of Deed: July 31, 1878
Date of Gazette: December 10, 1878

On 31st July, 1878, the "Harlaw", when on a voyage from Sydney to Shanghai, struck on the Tung Sha Bank, in latitude 31° 10' N., longitude 122° 15' E., and soon after became a total wreck. The boats were got ready, and WILLIAM BUYERS, Second Mate, was ordered by the Captain into the quarter boat, the dingy (sic), which was to remain by the ship. The steward, four seamen, one of whom was Thomas Lewis, A.B., and three apprentices, got into the boat, in addition to the Second Mate, making nine in all. Owing to the strong tide that was running and the heavy sea, the boat was obliged to be loosed from the ship. The boat was therefore kept near the ship, but to wind. One other boat was seen to leave the ship and run before the wind, and then the ship was shut out from the sight of those in the dingy by squalls of rain.

When the ship was again seen from the dingy, the two other boats had left her, and she was swinging round; and before the dingy reached her she fell over. A box of Indian corn flour was picked up, and the second mate swam on board the wreck, cut the jib sheet adrift and brought it back to the boat.

The dingy was then run before the wind, and at sundown the Gutzlaff Lightship was sighted but they failed to reach it. In attempting to keep the boat's head to the sea, and towards the light during the night she shipped two heavy seas and capsized. The crew in their efforts to clamber up on the bottom of the boat, caused her to turn round like a cask, and one by one the men and boys dropped off her. The Second Mate was seized by the Steward, but managed to extricate himself after being dragged down some depth. When he again reached the boat, he found Lawrie alone. Early in the morning Lawrie was washed off, when BUYERS at great risk to his life swam to his assistance, and with great difficulty brought him back to the boat. They then managed to right the boat and got inside her. Lawrie was, however, washed out of the boat by a heavy sea, but BUYERS again saved his life and pulled him back into the boat by means of one of the boards at the bottom of the boat. Soon after, when close to the light, the two survivors were picked up by a junk, were kindly treated, and landed at Shanghai.

William Buyers was awarded the **Albert Medal of the Second Class (Sea)** and thereafter disappears from history, like so many of his compatriots. The whereabouts of his Albert Medal are unknown. However, he was not entirely forgotten. Issue No. 197 of the *Hornet* comic, dated June 17, 1967, featured his gallant act for posterity, although the ship is called the *Harlow*.

JOHN MITCHELL, WILLIAM STEWART and CHARLES WILSON

Date of Deed: May 9, 1877
Date of Gazette: March 1, 1878

On the 9th May, 1877, the "Conference" and "Avonmore" and twenty-five or thirty other vessels, were lying at anchor off the village of Huanillos, a short distance from the shore, loading with guano. The village itself stands on a platform or ledge of the mountains, about thirty feet above sea-level, and the mountains rise precipitously to a height of 5,000 feet. According to the statement of Captain George Williams, the late Master of the "Conference", at about 8.30 P.M., the weather being dark and gloomy, with a calm sea, a severe shock of an earthquake was felt. The ship trembled so much that the masts and yards seemed to be coming down, and the stern moorings parted. The noise of the earthquake, as it shook the mountains, was very great. Large boulders were rolled down the side of the mountains, and striking against each other, emitted sparks of fire, while the cries of the guano diggers on the mountains, who were in danger of their lives, increased the terror of the scene. The earthquake was followed by three distinct tidal-waves, which rolled in from seawards at intervals of about ten minutes, rising about fifty feet, as seen by the marks on the shore, causing many vessels to break their moorings and drag their anchors, and submerging the village of Huanillos. The first tidal-wave drove two vessels across the bows of the "Conference", and carried away her bowsprit and jib boom. The second tidal-wave carried away her starboard bower-chains; and at the same time the American vessel "Geneva" was driven against the fore-rigging of the "Conference", damaging her severely. She then commenced to drift towards the rocks. The "Geneva" was then carried back, and again driven against the "Conference", cutting the latter down amidships, four or five planks below the covering-board. Then a vessel which afterwards proved to be the "Avonmore", was seen for a moment as she was driven at a furious rate across the bows of the "Conference". Almost immediately her anchor-light disappeared, and the cries of drowning people were heard. It was at this time when, as it is stated, "everything was calculated to destroy the strongest nerves", when ships, out of the power of human control, were ranging about in all directions, the sea confused and turbulent, and the "Conference" herself badly damaged, that the Master called for volunteers from his crew to man the jolly-boat. After some hesitation, JOHN MITCHELL, WILLIAM STEWART and CHARLES WILSON volunteered their services. They rowed away into the darkness, which was then described as so great that objects were invisible at a distance equal to the ship's length, and after some time succeeded in finding and rescuing the Master of the "Avonmore" and his child, the Second and Third Officers, and an A.B. Fortunately there was no further tidal-wave, and when the boat returned to the "Conference" the disturbance of the sea had considerably abated, but the rest of the crew were about to abandon the "Conference" in their other boat, as she was then close on the rocks, with her stern and bows knocked in. Both boats then rowed out to sea. Four vessels, including the "Avonmore" and the "Conference", were totally wrecked that night at Huanillos, five were uninjured from being moored outside of the others, and all the rest were more or less damaged. Numerous lives were lost.

The Board of Trade have further determined to recognize the great bravery and presence of mind shown by Captain Williams of the "Conference", by a suitable present.

John Mitchell, Carpenter, William Stewart, Sailmaker and Charles Wilson, A.B., late of the "Conference" of Bristol were each awarded the **Albert Medal of the Second Class (Sea).** The "Conference", 967 tons, was built in New Brunswick in 1856 and was owned by C. Hill of Bristol. Wilson appears to have been a native of Sweden. Mitchell was presented with his AM at Truro on June 4, 1878; Stewart at Llanelli on October 4, 1878 and Wilson at Guadaloupe in the Leeward Islands by the Vice-Consul. It is not known who made the other two presentations. All three men faded back into obscurity; nothing else is known about them and the whereabouts of their Albert Medals are unknown.

MARK ADDY

Mark Addy

Image: Unknown

Date of Deed: 1853-1878
Date of Gazette: December 17, 1878

The next award of the Albert Medal is probably unique in the annals of that award. It was not given for a single act of gallantry but for an extended period of gallantry in rescuing some thirty-six people from the River Irwell in Manchester over a period of twenty-five years. Even the announcement in the *London Gazette* of December 17, 1878, is remarkable.

THE Queen has been graciously pleased to confer the "Albert Medal of the First Class (Land)" on –

MARK ADDY, of Salford.

"Statement of the case of MARK ADDY, to whom the Albert Medal of the First Class has been granted in recognition of his repeated acts of heroism in saving life from drowning in the River Irwell.

MARK ADDY, a well-known oarsman and sculler, has resided all his life on the banks of the polluted River Irwell; his father and brothers having followed the trade of Boat Builders.

During a period of about twenty-five years, he has, under circumstances of imminent peril, both from the violence of the river and the pestilential nature of its waters, saved no fewer than six-and-thirty lives, several of the cases having occurred subsequently to the date of the creation of the said Order (sic).

For his heroic efforts and conspicuous gallantry, he has, at various times, received the following distinctions:-

The Manchester & Salford Swimmers' Silver Medal.
The Bronze Medal of the Royal Humane Society.
The Silver Medal of the Hundred of Salford Humane Society.
The Gold Medal of the Hundred of Salford Humane Society.
An Illuminated Address setting forth his Badge of Honour from the Salford Humane Society.
A purse of 200 guineas and an Illuminated Address from the inhabitants of Salford."

Mark Addy was born in Salford in April, 1838. He saved more than 50 lives altogether but the total may be nearer 80. His last rescue was on Whit Monday, 1889. At one time, he was the licensee of the Old Boathouse Inn in Everard Street, Salford. He was presented with his AM by the Mayor of Salford, Alderman Robinson on behalf of the Queen. As a result of swallowing several mouthfuls of filthy water performing his last rescue, he contracted tuberculosis and died, after a long illness, on June 9, 1890, aged 51. He was buried in Weaste Cemetery, Salford, where there is a monument in his memory. His portrait hangs in the art gallery in Peel Park and a memorial fund of £100 was invested to provide prizes for swimming to Salford boys (presumably this now includes girls). In 1981, a new public house named the Mark Addy opened on the bank of the River Irwell on the site of the old Nemesis Rowing Club boathouse. The Everard Street footbridge is commonly known as the Mark Addy Bridge. All his medals are now in the Salford Museum and Art Gallery.

PETER SHARP and JOHN MCINTOSH

Date of Deed: November 20, 1878
Date of Gazette: April 4, 1879

Peter Sharp

Image: Strand Magazine

On the 20th of November, 1878, at about 5.45 P.M., a fire suddenly broke out on board the French ship "Melanie", which was lying in the River Adour, at Boucan, near Bayonne, loaded with 500 barrels of petroleum, of which 40 were on deck. A mass of flame shot up from the main hatch and the ship quivered all over from the explosion of some of the barrels. The ship's seams opened at once, and the petroleum pouring through spread a belt of flame around the ship. The master and a seaman then jumped overboard, but the mate remained to try to save his son, who was lying helpless under some heavy objects which had fallen on him. Captain PETER SHARP, Master of the "Annabella Clark", of Ardrossan (which was lying close by in the river), accompanied by a seaman, named JOHN McINTOSH, came at once to his assistance. They rowed their boat through the flames, picked up the seaman who had jumped overboard and took the mate from the blazing vessel.

Captain SHARP and McINTOSH both sustained very severe injuries. It was feared at first that Captain SHARP would lose the sight of one eye, and JOHN McINTOSH the use of his hands.

Both Peter Sharp and John McIntosh were awarded the **Albert Medal of the First Class (Sea)**. Nothing is known of either of these gallant men, although Captain Sharp's Albert Medal is now in the collection of the National Maritime Museum at Greenwich. Sharp was also awarded the French Ministry of Marine and Colonies Medal in Gold for this rescue, while McIntosh received the Medal in Silver. Each man also received the Lloyds' Bronze Medal for Saving Life at Sea. Sharp was presented with his AM by the Mayor of Newport, Monmouthshire, on April 24, 1879 and McIntosh by the Provost of Ardrossan on October 23, 1879.

***

The Mercantile Marine looms large in the number of Albert Medals awarded over the years and is increased still further if one includes the crews of fishing boats.

***

ALEXANDER CHRISTIE

Date of Deed: January 24, 1879
Date of Gazette: May 20, 1879

On the 24th January, 1879, the fishing-boat "Expert", of Stonehaven, was run down by the steamer "Countess of Durham", when off Dunnottar Castle, Kincardineshire. The "Expert" at once sank, and three members of the crew were drowned. The master, Captain CHRISTIE, succeeded in obtaining a buoy, by which he supported himself, and a boat was put off from the steamer to his assistance.

Captain CHRISTIE, although he had been in the water a quarter of an hour, and the cold was so great that the spray turned to ice, refused to be taken into the boat until one of the crew, George Main, who was some two or three boats' lengths off in a state of insensibility, had been picked up.

Captain Alexander Christie was awarded the **Albert Medal of the Second Class (Sea).** It was presented to him on August 16, 1879 at Stonehaven by the Lord Lieutenant of the County of Aberdeen. He also received a purse of sovereigns. Nothing else is known of this man neither are the whereabouts of his Albert Medal known.

During the period under review, which precedes the institution of the Edward Medal for Mines and Industry, over fifty miners were to be awarded the Albert Medal for gallant rescues underground. The next awards were to eight miners for an explosion in the Abercarn Colliery, Monmouthshire.

HENRY DAVIES, JOHN HARRIS, WILLIAM SIMONS, THOMAS HERBERT, MILES MOSELEY, CHARLES PREEN, WILLIAM WALTERS, LEWIS HARRIS *and* CHARLES MORGAN.

Image: Strand Magazine

John Harris

Image: Strand Magazine

Henry Davies

Date of Deed: September 11, 1878
Date of Gazette: August 19, 1879

On the 11th September, 1878, an explosion of firedamp occurred in the Abercarn Colliery, in the county of Monmouth, whereby 260 persons perished, and on which occasion the greatest possible gallantry was exhibited in saving about 90 lives. The force of the explosion was terrific, doing great damage to the roadways and to the bottom of the shaft, and setting the coal and timber on fire in several places. Into this state of confusion and apparent danger to life, these men, without hesitation, descended, and, although they discovered that fires were raging in the mine, and that consequently the chances of another explosion were considerable, they remained at their gallant and humane work of rescue, not re-ascending the shaft until they had satisfied themselves that no one was left alive below.

Henry Davies, after being down the Abercarn Pit all the afternoon, with those recommended for the Second Class Medal, volunteered to descend the Cwmcarn Pit (a shaft two miles distant), with a view of conveying to the explorers, who had attempted to enter the workings from that side, an order from those in charge of the operations to come out, as, in consequence of the fires underground continuing to burn fiercely, and large quantities of gas were pouring out of the workings, a second explosion was deemed to be inevitable, which, had it occurred, would assuredly have killed every man below ground. Henry Davies, after being deserted by two men who refused to accompany him further, and when he must have felt that there was little or no chance of his coming alive out of the pit, pursued his course alone for five or six hundred yards, and heroically accomplished the object of his mission.

John Harris went down the pit with those recommended for the Second Class Medal.

Having descended to a depth of about 295 yards, the progress of the cage was stayed by the damaged state of the shaft.

John Harris got off the cage, and sliding down a guide rope, reached the bottom, where, although he knew well that any moment might be his last, he remained for many hours, until all who were alive (some of whom were badly burnt and otherwise injured) reached the cage by his assistance, and were taken to the surface in safety.

Henry Davies and John Harris were each awarded the **Albert Medal of the First Class (Land),** while William Simons, Thomas Herbert, Miles Moseley, Charles Preen, William Walters and Lewis Harris each received the **Albert Medal of the Second Class (Land).** It would seem that one man's gallantry had been forgotten, so in the *London Gazette* of November 18, the following appeared.

On the 11th September, 1878, an explosion of firedamp occurred in the Abercarn Colliery, in the county of Monmouth, whereby 260 persons perished, and on which occasion the greatest possible gallantry was exhibited in saving about 90 lives. The force of the explosion was terrific, doing great damage to the roadways and to the bottom of the shaft, and setting the coal and timber on fire in several places.

Into this state of confusion and apparent danger to life, Charles Morgan and certain others, without hesitation, descended, and, although it was discovered that fires were raging in the mine, and that consequently the chances of another explosion were considerable, he remained with them at the gallant and humane work of rescue, not re-ascending the shaft until it was certain that no one was left alive below.

Charles Morgan was awarded the **Albert Medal of the Second Class (Land).** Simons', Walters' and Harris' medals are now in private collections, while Davies' is in the Sheesh Mahal Museum, Patiala, Punjab, India. Nothing is known of any of these men or the whereabouts of the other Albert Medals.

HENRY WESLEY

Date of Deed: August 3, 1879
Date of Gazette: February 27, 1880

On the 3rd August, 1879, the brigantine "Harriet", of London, whilst on a voyage from Cape Coast Castle to Jellah Coffee, was wrecked on the bar of the River Volta, about five miles out of Addah. Owing to the heavy surf, the crew were unable to launch any of their small boats, as they would have been swamped, and the men once in the water would have been devoured by sharks, with which the river abounded.

The perilous position of the crew was noticed from the shore, and a surf boat was launched to their assistance, but soon after starting it was capsized and had to return.

The boat then put out again, being in charge of MR. HENRY WESLEY, and manned by thirteen Krooboys, but, owing to the roughness of the surf, she had to go round the vessel six times before the distressed crew could be rescued. They were at length all saved by jumping into the boat as she came under the bulwarks.

The risk being so great, MR. WESLEY had great difficulty in persuading the Krooboys to man the boat.

Henry Wesley, who was the Agent for Messrs. Miller Bros. of Glasgow at Addah, was awarded the **Albert Medal of the Second Class (Sea).** His medal is now in a private collection.

GEORGE WILLIAMS

Date of Deed: March 6, 1881
Date of Gazette: May 6, 1881

On Sunday morning, the 6th March last, during a heavy gale, accompanied by blinding snow and sleet, the Norwegian brig "Ranger", of Fredrikshald, was wrecked at Marywells, on the Uzon Guards, when WILLIAMS, by his gallant conduct, was the means of saving the four survivors of the crew, the master and mate having been washed overboard when the vessel struck on the rocks.

Communication with the wrecked vessel was obtained by means of the rocket apparatus, but the crew did not seem to understand how to use it, so WILLIAMS got into the breeches buoy, and hauled himself out hand over hand. On getting within about twenty yards of the wreck, and finding he was making no headway, he dropped from the buoy on to the rocks, and made his way over them and through the wreckage of the wreck, on reaching which he found the crew quite helpless. By dint of great exertions he managed to get on board and secure the hawser, but the whip (the endless rope by which the breeches buoy is hauled backwards and forwards by the party on shore) was foul among the wreckage. In endeavouring to clear it the whip carried away, leaving one end on board, the other on shore. WILLIAMS then sent one man on shore, but in hauling off, the whip again got foul of the wreckage, and was cleared with great difficulty. Then two more men were landed. One man was then left, with whom WILLIAMS himself intended going ashore, but before he could get into the buoy it was hauled away from him. The lines again got foul, and the man was in great danger of being drowned in the breakers, when WILLIAMS jumped from the wreck, swam to the breeches buoy, and cleared it. They were then both hauled ashore much exhausted. WILLIAMS's hands were greatly lacerated and his back severely bruised, and he has since suffered from the effects of the exposure, and the shock to the system.

George Williams was awarded the **Albert Medal of the Second Class (Sea)** the whereabouts of which are not known.

DAVID LOWSON

Date of Deed: November 12, 1880
Date of Gazette: July 5, 1881

Image: British Medical Journal

David Lowson

We know a little more about the next recipient of the Albert Medal, primarily because he was one of fourteen doctors to be awarded it, six of whom were civilians at the time of their award.

On the 12th November, 1880, DR. LOWSON, of Huddersfield, was called to attend Matilda Elizabeth Higginbottom of that town, who was suffering from laryngeal diphtheria, when he performed the operation of tracheotomy. On the following morning, finding the child livid, and breathing with very great difficulty, and tracing that a large quantity of mucus was accumulated in the trachea, he applied his lips to the wound, and, at imminent risk to his own life, afforded relief by suction. Throughout the day he continued to suck out mucus by means of pipetts. Notwithstanding this display of heroism the child died on the third day after the operation. In the course of a few days DR. LOWSON was seized with a severe attack of diphtheria, followed by other dangerous illnesses, which resulted in his retirement from a lucrative practice.

David Lowson was awarded the **Albert Medal of the First Class (Land)**. He was born in Aberdeenshire in 1850, being educated at the University of Aberdeen and graduating with the degrees of MB and CM. He achieved his MD in 1875. After qualifying, he was appointed Assistant House Surgeon at Pendlebury Children's Hospital. Later he became Resident Surgeon at Huddersfield Infirmary. He settled in Hull c1882. He was Surgeon to Hull Dispensary and later Surgeon at Hull Hospital for Diseases of Women and Orthopaedics. He became a full Surgeon at Hull Royal Infirmary in 1898. He was married with one son. Dr. Lowson died in Wimpole Street, London, on March 15, 1907 and was cremated. The whereabouts of his Albert Medal are not known.

It is of interest that in the same year, Surgeon Henry Grier of the Army Medical Department (see volume one of this book) was awarded the **Albert Medal of the Second Class** for performing an almost identical life-saving operation on a fellow officer. One wonders how those responsible for deciding which class of the medal to award reached their decisions in each of these cases.

WILLIAM HENRY BURT

Date of Deed: August 15, 1881
Date of Gazette: October 18, 1881

At two o'clock in the afternoon of the 15th July last, a fire broke out on the premises of Mr. Ernest Wellings, Italian Warehouseman, Market Place, Devizes. After the fire had been raging some time, and all the inmates of the house had effected their escape, it was reported that there was a certain quantity of gunpowder stored in the shop, and MR. BURT at once volunteered to enter the burning premises and remove the case containing the gunpowder. At this time a great body of flame was distinctly visible on the other side of the shop counter only a few feet distant from the spot where the gunpowder was deposited.

It was under these circumstances that MR. BURT made his way into the shop, effecting his entrance through the window; and eventually succeeded in finding and removing the box containing ten or twelve pounds of gunpowder, thereby preventing an explosion, which might have been attended with serious loss of life amongst those necessarily engaged in dealing with the fire, as well as amongst the crowd of onlookers.

William Henry Burt was awarded the **Albert Medal of the Second Class (Land).** He was presented with his award by the Mayoress of Devizes at the Town Hall on 30 October 1881. Little is known of Mr. Burt. He was born c1841 and carried on a business as an ironmonger at 41 Market Place in Devizes. He died in Devizes on February 22, 1892, aged 51 and lies buried in Devizes cemetery. The whereabouts of his Albert Medal are not known.

We now turn to the first of the sixteen ladies to be awarded the Albert Medal. She was a twenty-three-year-old school teacher from St Helens, Lancashire.

HANNAH ROSBOTHAM

Date of Deed: October 14, 1880
Date of Gazette: December 16, 1881

During a violent gale of wind on the 14th of October last, the stone belfry of the Sutton National Schools was blown down, and fell through the roof into the Infants' School-room (where nearly two hundred children were assembled), causing the death of one, and injuring many others, and filling the room and its gallery with stones, slates, and timber.

Hannah Rosbotham

Image: British Library Reproductions

Whilst others fled for safety, MISS ROSBOTHAM (who at the time of the accident was teaching elsewhere) deliberately entered among the falling mass and cloud of dust; and, while fully conscious of the extreme danger to which she was exposed, remained on the spot until every child had been placed in safety. At the imminent risk of her own life, MISS ROSBOTHAM removed four infants who were partially covered with the debris, and rescued therefrom a little girl who was completely buried, and who must inevitably have been suffocated had not such gallantry been displayed.

Hannah Rosbotham was awarded the **Albert Medal of the Second Class (Land).** Neighbours made a collection of £13 in her honour (a not inconsiderable sum in those days) and she continued to teach at the school after repairs had been effected. She subsequently married and became Mrs James Parr, spending the rest of her life teaching at the same school. She retired as headmistress after 41years. She died on August 15, 1935, aged 77, and is buried in St Nicholas' churchyard, Sutton, St Helens but there is no mention of her award on her headstone. Her Albert Medal is now in a private collection. It is of interest that in one of her portraits she wears her decoration as a pendant.

FRANCIS PITTS

Date of Deed: May 30, 1881
Date of Gazette: January 3, 1882

At about 7 A.M., on the 30th May last, when the "Pleiades" was running before a very heavy south-westerly gale an able seaman was washed overboard. Three life buoys were at once thrown to him, and the engines slowed. Soon after the lookout man reported him to be on the starboard beam, but owing to the tremendous sea that was running the Master deemed it unsafe to lower a boat, and for the same reason it was impossible without imperilling the ship, to turn her in the direction of the man.

The Master then, knowing MR. PITTS to be a fair swimmer, called upon him to attempt to rescue the man by swimming to him with a line. Without a moment's hesitation MR. PITTS jumped overboard with a line, but after going about 300 yards he was obliged to let go the line and swim towards the ship. So great was the force of the waves that he was carried past the ship and was not rescued without much difficulty. When taken out of the sea he was quite exhausted.

Francis Pitts was awarded the **Albert Medal of the Second Class (Sea)** the whereabouts of which are not known.

FREDERICK JAGGERS

Date of Deed: October 14, 1881
Date of Gazette: January 24, 1882

The Norwegian schooner "Atlantic" was wrecked off the South Pier, at South Shields, on the 14th October, 1881, communication with the stranded vessel was speedily effected by means of the rocket apparatus, but as one of the crew was being hauled ashore, the whip – which is an endless line used for hauling to and from a stranded vessel – fouled the rocks. FREDERICK JAGGERS, Coast Guard Boatman, at the risk of his life, went into the surf with the view of clearing the line, but was washed off his feet by a heavy sea, and thrown against the rocks which his head struck with such force as to render him insensible. He was then hauled out of the sea.

For this praiseworthy attempt the Board of Trade awarded F. JAGGERS their Bronze Medal for gallantry in attempting to save life at sea.

On the 26th November last (About six weeks after the wreck of the "Atlantic") the ketch "Ida", of Ipswich ran ashore near the Pier, at South Shields. Between the "Ida" and the rocket apparatus was the wreck of a brig which made communication by rocket difficult. JAGGERS volunteered to be hauled off to the brig, although cautioned of the danger attending such an enterprise, as it was feared her masts would fall, but he reached the brig safely, and from her fore rigging succeeded in throwing a line on board the "Ida" by means of which the crew were saved.

Frederick Jaggers was awarded the **Albert Medal of the Second Class (Sea).** Nothing is known of this gallant man, nor the whereabouts of his medal.

ARTHUR MCKEE, JOHN ADAMS and WILLIAM ROLLESTON

Date of Deed: October 18, 1881
Date of Gazette: February 10, 1882

The "Low Wood", when off the Newfoundland coast, on the 20th October last, fell in with the barkentine "Bend Or" in a disabled and sinking condition, and showing signals of distress. The weather at this time was very bad, and the sea very high, but the "Low Wood" rounded to, and sent a boat manned by five men to her assistance. When about half-way between the two vessels the boat was capsized in a violent squall, and all her crew were drowned.

The "Low Wood stayed by the wreck till the 23rd, and, at about one P.M. on that day, a second boat, manned by ARTHUR McKEE, JOHN ADAMS, and WILLIAM ROLLESTON, was lowered and proceeded to the rescue.

The sea was then as high as on the previous days, and the risk greater, as the boat was smaller than that which was capsized.

The smaller size of the boat also made it necessary to make two trips to the wreck, and in returning the second time to the "Low Wood" it was almost swamped. At last, after much difficulty and danger, the rescue was safely accomplished.

Arthur McKee, John Adams and William Rolleston were each awarded the **Albert Medal of the Second Class (Sea)**. The "Low Wood" was out of St John's, New Brunswick, Canada and was of 1091 tons burden. The "Bend Or" was of 216 tons burden and was built at Appledore, Devon. The five men lost were George James, Second Mate; John Smith, George Russell, Eugene Pottier and John Hamilton, all seamen. Pottier came from Havre, France, while the others were British. Rolleston's medal was presented to him on March 29 1882, McKee's on September 5, 1882 and Adams' on June 1, 1885. Rolleston's medal is now in the Glenbow Museum, Calgary, Canada but the whereabouts of the others are not known.

JAMES CARNEY

Date of Deed: July 10, 1881
Date of Gazette: March 21, 1882

On the 10th July last, a Native shunting porter was coupling up the wagon of a train that was moving through the Station at Dinapore at the rate of two or three miles an hour. A sudden movement of the train knocked the native down, and he fell half stunned between the rails and underneath the train.

The man's convulsive struggles threatened every moment to throw him under the wheels of the moving wagon. MR. JAMES CARNEY, who was at the time on duty at the Station, jumped down from the platform without hesitation, rushed under the train which was still in motion, and grappling with the injured man, held him down until the train had passed over the two struggling men. In doing this MR. CARNEY narrowly escaped being struck upon the forehead by the axle-tree of a pair of wheels as it passed over him.

But for this act of gallantry, the Native, in all human probability, would not have escaped with his life.

James Carney was awarded the **Albert Medal of the Second Class (Land).** He then passes back into obscurity, since nothing is known of him. His Albert Medal is now in a private collection.

WILLIAM HINTON

Image: Strand Magazine

William Hinton

Date of Deed: January 13, 1881
Date of Gazette: March 24, 1882

On the 13th January, 1881, a fire occurred on the premises of Mr. John Booth (an Ironmonger residing at Halesowen), in the basement of which a large quantity of oil was deposited.

A crowd of three or four hundred people had collected in front of the shop, and a rumour was current that gunpowder was stored therein.

MR. HINTON having been informed of the locality in which the powder was placed, at once entered the burning premises, amidst dense volumes of smoke, and succeeded in removing therefrom a drawer containing several canisters of gunpowder.

On being told that a large quantity of blasting-powder was also within the building, MR. HINTON, at imminent risk to his life (for the fire was at this time raging fiercely) again entered into the shop, and returned with twenty-five pounds of such material.

The outside of the canister containing the powder was hot and blistered by flames, which were then in actual contact with it, and the heat was so intense that solder was melted on a number of articles which were at a greater distance from the fire than that at which it was found by MR. HINTON.

Those acquainted with the locality of the blasting-powder would not approach it; and had not MR. HINTON, by this conspicuous act of gallantry, rescued it from the premises, in all human probability an explosion would have occurred, destroying a block of three buildings, and causing a great loss of life amongst those assembled.

William Hinton, an Inland Revenue Officer, of Halesowen, Staffordshire, was awarded the **Albert Medal of the Second Class (Land).** Nothing else is known of Mr. Hinton and the whereabouts of his medal are unknown.

The *London Gazette* of January 16, 1883, announced that **Henry Kemp**, Superintendent of Police in the Worcestershire Constabulary was also to be awarded the **Albert Medal of the Second Class (Land)** for gallantry displayed during the above incident. Kemp was born circa 1841 in Leicester and joined the Worcestershire Constabulary on February 1, 1868, aged 27, having previously been a warehouseman. He was married but it is not known if he had any children. He served in Balsall Heath, Ombersley, Bromsgrove, Redditch, Broadwas, Halesowen and Pershore, being promoted Superintendent on October 15, 1872. He was dismissed for misconduct and untruthfulness on November 19, 1892. In September, 1892, it was alleged he had an affair with a local baker's wife in Pershore. The Chief Constable held an enquiry and dismissed him. He brought an action for slander at Birmingham Assizes, the hearing being held on March 16, 1894. The jury found in his favour and awarded him £500 damages but the Chief Constable refused to reinstate him, much to the dismay of his local supporters and he lost his pension which had been due six weeks from his dismissal. He died on July 16, 1895 at Little Comberton. The whereabouts of his Albert Medal are unknown.

Henceforth, until the end of Queen Victoria's reign, to quote from "Gallantry", interest in the award of the Albert Medal appears to have been 'at a low ebb' and detailed citations in the *London Gazette* are the exception rather than the rule, although there were several of some length. The first of what might be termed the abbreviated citations appeared in 1883.

REUBEN SMALLMAN, ARTHUR HENRY STOKES, CHARLES DAY, CHARLES CHETWYND, SAMUEL SPRUCE, FREDERICK SAMUEL MARSH, THOMAS HARRY MOTTRAM, WILLIAM MORRIS, WILLIAM PICKERING, JOSEPH CHETWYND

Date of Deed: October 18, 1881
Date of Gazette: February 10, 1882

THE Queen has been graciously pleased to confer "The Albert Medal" on the following persons, for conspicuous gallantry displayed on the occasion of the Fire and Explosion at the Baddesley Colliery in May last:

"The Albert Medal of the First Class (Land)"
Mr. Reuben Smallman, Mining Engineer.
Mr. Arthur Henry Stokes, Inspector of Mines.
Charles Day, Collier.
Charles Chetwynd, Collier.

"The Albert Medal of the Second Class (Land)"
Mr. Samuel Spruce, Mining Engineer.
Mr. Frederick Samuel Marsh, Certified Colliery Manager.
Mr. Thomas Harry Mottram, Certified Colliery Manager.
William Morris, Collier.

William Pickering, Collier.
Joseph Chetwynd, Collier.

Baddesley Colliery was located near Atherstone, Warwickshire. Mottram's Albert Medal is in a private collection and Smallman's is in Nuneaton Museum. Mottram subsequently had a distinguished career. He was born in 1859, the second son of Henry Mottram, a Civil Engineer of Tamworth, Warwickshire. He was educated at Tamworth Collegiate School and Mason's College, Birmingham. He was married with one son and one daughter. Elected Vice-President of the Institute of Mining Engineers in 1909-10, he became a Chief Inspector of Mines in 1921. He was appointed CBE in the January, 1918, Honours List for special war services and was knighted in 1924. He published several papers on mining subjects and retired to Bessacar, near Doncaster, where he died on March 24, 1937, the last survivor of the Baddesley colliery explosion. Reuben Smallman was born in 1836. He married Rhoda Elizabeth Harris in 1861 and they had two sons and three daughters. In 1871 he was a founder director of the Stockingford Colliery Company and was also General Manager of Oakthorpe, Church Gresley and Reservoir collieries. In 1889 he was one of the first Aldermen of Warwickshire County Council. He died in 1900. Arthur Stokes was born in 1844 at Wednesbury, Staffordshire. He was appointed Inspector of Mines for the Midlands district in 1887, retiring in 1909. He died in 1910. Charles Day was born in 1829. In 1850 he married Eliza Sanders and they had ten children. His three elder sons all died in the explosion at Baddesley. He died in 1899. Charles Chetwynd was born in 1855. He married Lydia Sandall in 1873 and they had nine children. He was killed on December 8, 1913, after a roof fall at Baddesley colliery. Samuel Spruce was born in 1823 and started his working life as a collier but rose through the ranks to become a colliery manager and eventually a consulting mining engineer. Married three times, he had eight daughters and one son. He died on February 6, 1900. Frederick Marsh was born circa 1859. He was twice married, having a son by his second wife. He died, aged only 35, on July 25, 1892. William Pickering was born in 1852. He married Sarah Chetwynd on April 19, 1877 and they had six children. He died on January 17, 1921. Joseph Chetwynd was born in Winecote in 1831, a distant cousin of Charles Chetwynd. He married Patience, another distant cousin, in 1857 and they had eight children. He committed suicide in 1904. William Morris was born in 1853 in Baxterley. He married Lottie Handford in 1892 and they had one daughter. He died on February 14, 1922. Mottram's and Spruce's AMs are in private collections but the whereabouts of the other Albert Medals are unknown.

Image: Unknown

Arthur Henry Stokes

Image: Unknown

Charles Day

JAMES DEE

Date of Deed: January 20, 1883
Date of Gazette: February 20, 1883

*THE Queen has been graciously pleased to confer **"The Albert Medal of the Second Class (Land)"**, upon James Dee, a Constable of the Swansea Police Force, for conspicuous gallantry displayed in endeavouring to save life at a fire, which occurred at Swansea on the morning of Sunday, the 20th January last.*

And that is all we have. However, the late Don Henderson is of assistance here with a few other details from his excellent work "Heroic Endeavour". In his research notes, he tells us that after a fire had broken out in a general dealer and oilman's shop in New Oxford Street, Swansea, Glamorgan, Dee brought out a young boy, sustaining serious burns himself in so doing. It is, perhaps, of interest that the Queen rarely, if ever, presented the Albert Medal in person. It was usually left to the Lord Lieutenant or even the local Mayor to do the honours. It is not known who presented the medal in this case but presumably it would have been some local worthy. James Dee was born in Newcastle Emlyn, Carmarthenshire, in 1852, the son of William and Elizabeth Dee. He joined the County Borough of Swansea Police Force sometime between 1859 and 1883. At that time, the police force country wide was also responsible for the fire service. He married his wife, Margaret, in 1883 and they had four children: three sons and a daughter. After the fire, in which he so distinguished himself, James Dee was dismissed from the police force for frequenting a public house whilst on duty. He moved around the United Kingdom after that, finally becoming an Inspector in the RSPCA. He died, aged 73, in 1925 at Northampton. The whereabouts of Dee's AM are unknown.

The next Albert Medal to be awarded is once more the subject of a less than informative citation. However, in this case, as he was a lifeboatman, we are able to find an account of his deed in that indispensable work "Lifeboat Gallantry" by Barry Cox. This will be used in preference to that in the *London Gazette* of May 18, 1883, since it is much more detailed.

HENRY HOOD

Date of Deed: March 11, 1883
Date of Gazette: May 18, 1883

On the 11th March, 1883, the Drammen schooner Atlas was driven on to the Long Scar Rocks off Seaton Carew, Co Durham, in a violent north-easterly gale accompanied by snow showers and a very heavy sea. The Seaton Carew lifeboat Job Hindley *launched at once, but could find no signs of a wreck. Therefore Coxswain Hood and John Franklin landed on the reef, but darkness made a search extremely difficult. In spite of seas washing over them and, at one point, Mr. Hood*

Image: RNLI

Henry Hood

being washed off, they found the wreck, then, joined by Matthew Franklin, managed to get a line on board her at the stern. The Coxswain rushed into the surf and rescued the schooner's Mate, and four others were brought off the wreck by line. All eight men regained the lifeboat and it was pulled back to shore.

Henry Hood was awarded the **Albert Medal of the Second Class (Sea),** one of only two such awards to lifeboatmen. He was also awarded the Silver Medal of the Royal National Lifeboat Institution for this rescue and a bar when he retired from the lifeboat service in July, 1898. He had been born on October 6, 1833 and was appointed coxswain in September 1867. John and Matthew Franklin were each awarded the Silver Medal of the RNLI for the Atlas rescue. The whereabouts of Hood's Albert Medal are unknown.

WILLIAM McGREGOR

Date of Deed: May 11, 1884
Date of Gazette: October 17, 1884

Image: Unknown

William McGregor

The "Syria" bound from Calcutta to the Fiji Islands, with 494 Coolie emigrants, stranded on the evening of Sunday, 11th May last, upon the Nasalai Reef, some 25 miles to the eastward of Suva, Fiji. This reef is exposed to the full force of the south-east trade winds, which, at the time of the wreck, were blowing with great force; also to the long roll of the sea from the vast expanse of the South Pacific.

Owing to the peculiar set of the tides over the reef, the shipwrecked emigrants who committed themselves to the water in the hopes of swimming ashore were irresistibly carried in an opposite direction, and swept out into the surf, which was breaking 30 feet high over the edge of the reef.

The Captain did not leave the wreck until he believed that all the people were out of it, he then started from the after part of the ship, bringing an Indian woman, who was half drunk, along with him, and was conducting her across a piece of broken mast which lay at a slight incline across the gap that existed between the two portions of the hull, when both were knocked over and over towards the perpendicular edge of the reef, the woman grasping the Captain by the neck like a vice.

An official who was at hand, at the risk of his own life, dashed into the breakers to the rescue, but no sooner had he reached the drowning couple, than he too was thrown down, and all three were being rolled along to destruction, when Dr. MACGREGOR, who was at the time standing by the wreck of the fallen mainmast, leading and directing the removal of the struggling Indians, instantly seized a line forming part of the ship's running rigging, that was floating by, and taking two or three turns with it round his wrist plunged into the surf at the imminent risk of his own life, grasped the struggling bodies of the drifting people, and by main strength dragged them back into shallow water from the destruction which appeared to be inevitable.

It is also stated that but for the energetic, able, and cool way in which Dr. MACGREGOR led the relieving party, the loss of life, which was great, 59 in all, must have been appalling.

William MacGregor was awarded the **Albert Medal of the Second Class (Sea).** Dr. MacGregor had a long and distinguished record in the Colonial Service. Born in

Aberdeenshire in 1847, he was the son of a farmer. Educated in Aberdeen and Glasgow, he graduated MB in 1872 with an MD following in 1874 at Aberdeen. He was also LRCP (Edinburgh) and LFPS (Glasgow) in 1872. Assistant Government Medical Officer in the Seychelles in 1873. In 1874, he was posted to Mauritius as Surgeon to the Civilian Hospital at Port Louis and in 1875 went as Chief Medical Officer to Fiji, where he gained the Albert Medal as described above. In 1888 he was posted to British New Guinea and in 1895 was promoted to Lieutenant-Governor of that colony. By 1899, he was Governor of Lagos in West Africa. In 1904, he transferred to Newfoundland and by 1909 was Governor of Queensland, Australia. He represented the West African colonies at the Coronation of King Edward VII. He retired in 1914 and died in Aberdeen on July 3, 1919. He was appointed KCMG in 1897, CB in 1897, GCMG in 1907 and PC in 1914. He was also a Knight of Grace of the Order of St John of Jerusalem. His Albert Medal and Clarke Gold Medal are in the Marischal Museum of the University of Aberdeen.

WILLIAM COLE

Date of Deed: January 24, 1885
Date of Gazette: February 3, 1885

William Cole

Image: Strand Magazine

THE Queen has been graciously pleased to confer ***"The Albert Medal of the First Class (Land)"*** *upon William Cole, Police Constable in the A Division of the Metropolitan Police Force, for conspicuous gallantry displayed at an Explosion in Westminster Hall, on the 24th January, 1885.*

We are fortunate that the contemporary Strand Magazine contains a comprehensive account of Sergeant Cole's bravery but to encapsulate it, on January 24, 1885, Cole's attention was drawn by two visitors to a small fire on a mat at the bottom of a staircase in the House of Commons crypt. The officer immediately identified the mat as a pad of oily felt with sixteen pockets, each containing a cake of dynamite. Shouting to the few onlookers to get out of the area, he attempted to extract the fuse so, picking up the pad he ran into Westminster Hall. The fuse having burnt low set fire to other parts of the pad which began to melt causing some of the oily, pitchy matter to run on to the officer's hands. He dropped the pad, which exploded as soon as it hit the floor, blowing a hole in the floor of Westminster Hall and precipitating an unconscious Cole fourteen feet into the basement. All Cole's clothing was blown off him and he had to be dug out of the masonry which had fallen on him. He sustained a fractured skull, four broken ribs and severe internal injuries, suffering from the effects of these for the rest of his life.

This award, be it noted, had the shortest time between the date of the act and the award of the medal during the entire currency of the Albert Medal. William Cole was born in Chippenham, Wiltshire, on July 1, 1840. He joined the Metropolitan Police on October 8, 1860, aged 20, being given warrant number 39501. His height was given as 5'8". He served on 'A' (Whitehall) Division as PC 340, PC 278 and after promotion to Sergeant on February 2, 1885, PS53. He resigned on April 21, 1886, due to nervous shock from the explosion and was awarded a pension of £78 per annum. Cole was presented with his Albert Medal by the Home Secretary, Sir William Harcourt. A man called Burton was responsible for the explosion and he was subsequently sentenced to penal servitude for life. William Cole died on November 21, 1900, aged 65. Cole's Albert Medal is in the House of Commons medal collection.

EDWARD CHARLES THOMPSON

Date of Deed: April 4, 1885
Date of Gazette: August 18, 1885

Image: Unknown

Edward Charles Thompson

THE Queen has been graciously pleased to confer "The **Albert Medal of the Second Class (Land)**" *upon Edward Charles Thompson, Esq., M.B. University Dublin, L.R.C.S.I, and Surgeon of the Tyrone County Infirmary, for conspicuous heroism displayed in endeavouring, on the 4th April, 1885, to save the life of a child, named Herbert Mitchell, suffering from diphtheria.*

Edward Charles Thompson was born on April 1, 1851, the son of Henry Thompson, MD of Omagh, Co. Tyrone. He was educated at the Raphoe Royal School and Dublin University, graduating MB in 1871 and serving for a short time in the Royal Navy. Maintaining his Service connection, he served as a Surgeon-Major in the Royal Army Medical Corps Reserve and the North Irish Horse. He became an FRCSI in 1885 and was appointed Surgeon to the Co. Tyrone Hospital in 1875, remaining there for over 50 years. He represented Co. Monaghan in the House of Commons from 1899 to 1906. During WWI, he was the Commandant of the Belgian Field Hospital in Flanders in 1915-16. He was appointed Deputy Lieutenant for Co. Tyrone in 1929, having been High Sherriff for that county in 1925. He was a Past President of the Northern Ireland branch of the British Medical Association. He married twice and had a son and three daughters. He died at East Sheen, Surrey, on January 20, 1933, aged 82 and curiously, there is no mention of his Albert Medal in the British Medical Journal obituary of that time, nor in the contemporary "Sprig of Shillelagh", his regimental journal, although many of his other distinctions are listed. He also held the St John's Life Saving Medal. The whereabouts of his Albert Medal are unknown but it is probably still with his family.

THOMAS WORRALL, JOHN CROOK, CHARLES PARKINSON, GEORGE HIGSON, AARON MANLEY, GEORGE HINDLEY,

Date of Deed: June 18, 1885
Date of Gazette: October 9, 1885

THE Queen has been graciously pleased to confer "The Albert Medal" on the following persons, for conspicuous gallantry displayed on the occasion of the explosion at the Clifton Hall Colliery in June last:-

"The Albert Medal of the First Class (Land)"
Thomas Worrall, *Underlooker.* **John Crook**, *Manager, Agecroft Colliery.*

"The Albert Medal of the Second Class (Land)"

Charles Parkinson, *Fireman,* **George Higson,** *Fireman.* **Aaron Manley,** *Pit Carpenter.* **George Hindley,** *Blacksmith.*

Once more, we are assisted by the late Don Henderson in his book "Heroic Endeavour", where, at page 10, he gives an excellent account of the incident. Clifton Hall Colliery was near Pendlebury in Lancashire. Agecroft pit was nearby and their assistance was enlisted to effect the escape of survivors. John Crook organised this and managed to extricate 116 men, despite having to negotiate three or four hundred yards of road under two feet of water. George Higson was responsible for maintaining signals between the bottom of the pit and the surface, remaining on duty all day, from 4 o'clock a.m. All the men were prominent among the rescuers. Higson's AM is in a private collection but the whereabouts of the others are unknown. John Crook was born in 1832 and died in 1898.

JOHN HENRY WOOD

Date of Deed: October 24, 1885
Date of Gazette: May 21, 1886

*HER Majesty the Queen has been graciously pleased to confer the decoration of the "**Albert Medal of the Second Class (Sea)**" upon MR. JOHN HENRY WOOD, a Member of the South Shields Volunteer Life Brigade, for his gallantry, at the imminent risk of his own life, in rescuing a boy washed off the pier at South Shields during a gale on the 24th October, 1885.*

It seems that two boys were washed off the North Pier. Wood, together with two other men named Dickson and Swainton, jumped in fully clothed and wearing sea boots. There was a heavy sea, with heavy spray over the pier and tons of water coming over the parapet. One boy, Robert Robson, was rescued. Wood failed to reach one boy but assisted Dickson in the successful rescue, although nearly strangled by a rope. All were very exhausted. The Albert Medal, the whereabouts of which are unknown, was presented to Wood by the Inspecting Commander of Coast Guards at Sunderland Life Boat House in June, 1886. The other two men received Letters of Thanks from the RNLI.

EDWARD SCULLION

Date of Deed: August 9, 1886
Date of Gazette: October 15, 1886

*THE Queen has been graciously pleased to confer the "**Albert Medal of the Second Class (Land)**" upon Edward Scullion, a Chemical Labourer, in recognition of the conspicuous gallantry displayed by him on the 9th of August last, in attempting to rescue two men and a boy who had been overcome by sulphur in the air-shaft of an unused sulphureted hydrogen sewer connected with the works of the Newcastle and Gateshead Chemical Company.*

Image: Strand Magazine

Edward Scullion

Edward Scullion was presented with his Albert Medal by the Mayor of Gateshead at Gateshead Town Hall on October 23, 1886. He had previously saved life from drowning on three occasions. The whereabouts of his Albert Medal are unknown.

WILLIAM E. YALDWYN

Date of Deed: July 26, 1886
Date of Gazette: February 11, 1887

THE Queen has been graciously pleased to confer the "Albert Medal of the Second Class (Land)" upon Mr. William E. Yaldwyn. Accountant of the Queensland National Bank at Charleville, in the Colony of Queensland, in recognition of the conspicuous gallantry displayed by him in rescuing six persons from a flood at Charleville on the 26th July, 1886.

William Edward Yaldwyn was twice decorated for bravery in rescuing people from floods in Queensland. At Dalby on August 28, 1879, he saved a Mrs Lese from drowning and was awarded the Royal Humane Society's medal. He died at Waga, New Guinea, on December 4, 1902. The whereabouts of Yaldwyn's Albert Medal are unknown.

Image: Unknown

William E. Yaldwyn

***

Our next award was unique in the history of the Albert Medal. No bars were ever awarded and no provision had been made for them in any of the Royal Warrants. However, in the next case, a way round this dilemma was found, as will be seen.

***

THOMAS AVERETT WHISTLER AND HARRY SALISBURY POCHIN

Date of Deed: December 17, 1885 and December 13, 1886
Date of Gazette: July 29, 1887

HER Majesty the Queen has been graciously pleased to confer the decoration of the "Albert Medal of the First Class (Sea)" upon –

THOMAS AVERETT WHISTLER, First Mate of the ship "Ennerdale" of Liverpool, instead of the "Albert Medal of the Second Class", the grant of which to Mr. WHISTLER Her Majesty had already approved.

The following is an account of the services in respect of which the decoration has been conferred:-

Image: Strand Magazine

Thomas Averett Whistler

On the 17th of December, 1885, soon after 5.30 A.M., as the "Ennerdale" was rounding Cape Horn, an apprentice, named Duncan McCallum, fell from aloft into the sea, striking the rigging in his fall. Immediately, H.S. Pochin, an A.B., leapt overboard after McCallum, but the latter sank before Pochin could reach him. Pochin, afraid of being seized with cramp before a boat could come to his assistance, hailed the ship, asking for a lifebuoy to be thrown to him, and at the same moment, the Master called all hands to man a boat. The First Mate, Mr. THOMAS AVERETT WHISTLER, 24 years old, who had been asleep in his berth, ran on deck and heard Pochin's hail. Calling to the boatswain to heave him a lifebuoy, he at once sprang overboard, secured the lifebuoy which was thrown to him, and succeeded in reaching Pochin. The latter was already on the point of sinking, but, with the help of the lifebuoy, WHISTLER was able to keep him up. The water was bitterly cold, and a huge albatross hovered round the two men preparing to attack them.

Meanwhile, considerable delay had occurred in the despatch of the boat, her lashings had been secured extra firmly for the passage round Cape Horn, and when at last launched, so many men crowded into her that she capsized. When righted and re-launched she finally succeeded in reaching and rescuing WHISTLER and Pochin, who were now entirely exhausted after an exposure of some 40 minutes in the water. The albatross had to be driven off with a boat hook.

Directly they were lifted into the boat both men became insensible, and WHISTLER was delirious for some time afterwards."

About a year later Mr WHISTLER again attempted to save life under the following circumstances:-

On the 13th December, 1886, while the "Ennerdale" was in Sydney Harbour, an apprentice named James F. Beattie was taking the Captain's gig from the starboard to the port side of the vessel, when the boat sheered off, and he was thrown into the water.

Mr. WHISTLER immediately dived, fully dressed, from the poop, but reached the water too close to the boy, who caught him from behind, put his arms around his waist, and locked his legs in his. They both sank, and whilst under water, Mr. WHISTLER cleared himself from Beattie's grasp, caught him by the shoulder and struck out for a lifebuoy which had been thrown overboard. Before it could be reached, both sank a second time, and WHISTLER, who was by this time thoroughly exhausted, was obliged to let go his hold of the boy, who never rose alive again to the surface, and whose body was afterwards found floating in another part of the harbour.

Harry Salisbury Pochin received the **Albert Medal of the Second Class (Sea)** for the first rescue described above, which was announced in the *London Gazette* of July 9, 1889, in similar but shorter terms than those relating to Mr. Whistler. Pochin's exploits were featured in the *Hornet* comic, No. 162 of October 15, 1966. He was also awarded the Silver Medal of the Liverpool Shipwreck and Humane Society. The delay in the announcement of Pochin's award is due to awaiting a satisfactory explanation for his deserting ship on February 25, 1886. Whistler's AM was presented to him by the Mayor of Liverpool on March 8, 1889 and Pochin's by the Mayor of Nottingham on a date unknown. Pochin lost his medal overboard and applied for a duplicate but this was refused. Whistler held a commission in the Royal Naval Reserve, being appointed Sub-Lieutenant on June 30, 1889 and promoted Lieutenant on June 5, 1893. He later served as Chief Officer on the *Coptic*. His Albert Medal and Liverpool Shipwreck Society's medal are in a private collection.

ROBERT GRAY

Date of Deed: April 28, 1888
Date of Gazette: February 22, 1889

On the 28th April, 1888, about 10 P.M., the "Eclipse" was in latitude 70° 8' N., longitude 6° 12' W., when a seaman, named George Pressley, fell overboard. A life-buoy and lines were immediately thrown to him, and the ship's boat was cleared as soon as possible. Pressley got hold of a line, and was being dragged along under the water, when another seaman, named ROBERT GRAY, jumped into the sea with a line round his arm, got hold of Pressley, and kept him up as well as he could until both of them were rescued by the ship's boat.

The sea was intensely cold and covered with ice, and the high waves caused the vessel, which was making considerable headway, to raise the men out of the water, and then dip them under for some time, and both were very much exhausted when picked up.

Robert Gray, a Seaman, was awarded the **Albert Medal of the Second Class (Sea),** which is now in a private collection. Gray was the son of Captain David Gray and he was presented with his medal in a private ceremony by the Provost of Peterhead on April 11, 1889.

JOHN DINNEEN

Date of Deed: November 5, 1888
Date of Gazette: July 26, 1889

On the 4th November, 1888, the schooner "Isabella Hall", of Barrow, stranded on the Tongue Sand, and the crew, having lost their boat in a heavy sea, were obliged to take to the rigging and wait for assistance.

Next morning two boats were despatched from two different steamers to their relief, but could not get near the wreck, owing to the heaviness of the sea, and the shipwrecked crew were in danger of losing their lives, when the steamship "Albatross", of London, which was passing up channel, despatched a boat, manned by the Chief Mate, JOHN DINNEEN, and four seamen, who, notwithstanding strong warnings from the other boats of the danger of the attempt, rowed close to the wreck, and after nearly an hour's struggle, threw a line on board and rescued one of the crew.

He was scarcely got into the boat when a heavy sea nearly swamped her, and washed DINNEEN and three seamen out of her. They, however, managed to regain the boat, and, baling her out, proceeded with their task, and finally succeeded in rescuing the remainder of the shipwrecked men.

The service throughout was attended with very great risk and difficulty, and owed its success chiefly to the energy and determination of DINNEEN, and his constant encouragement of his men.

John Dinneen was awarded the **Albert Medal of the Second Class (Sea),** the whereabouts of which are unknown and the Silver Life Saving Medal of the Shipwrecked Mariners Society. The four seamen who accompanied him during this incident were all awarded the Sea Gallantry Medal.

THOMAS CHAPMAN

Date of Deed: February 5, 1889
Date of Gazette: August 9, 1889

The next award received one of the briefer citations in the *London Gazette*. It said: *THE Queen has been graciously pleased to confer the "Albert Medal of the Second Class (Land)" upon Mr. Thomas Chapman, Pitman of the Drakewalls Mine, Calstock, Cornwall, for gallantry in saving life on the occasion of an accident at that mine on the 5th February last.*

In fact, from Don Henderson's notes, we are told that he saved two men from a landslip. It is quite astonishing and sad how little we know of these heroes of long ago. Most rose from total obscurity and vanished back into it, like Thomas Chapman. The whereabouts of his Albert Medal are unknown.

JOHN SMITH

Date of Deed: May 18, 1889
Date of Gazette: August 13, 1889

*THE Queen has been graciously pleased to confer the **"Albert Medal of the Second Class (Land)"** upon John Smith, for gallantry in endeavouring to save the life of Benjamin Stanley, at the Norfolk Works, Sheffield, on the 18th May last.*

Mr. Smith was severely burned when he saved the life of a fellow worker who had fallen into a pit containing a red-hot steel ingot. He was also awarded the Order of St John's Silver Medal for Lifesaving for this rescue. The whereabouts of his Albert Medal are unknown.

WILLIAM CARTER

Date of Deed: March 31 / April 1, 1889
Date of Gazette: August 27, 1889

The "Gettysburg" was lost by striking on the Morant Cays on the night between 31st March and 1st April, 1889, whilst on a voyage from Monte Video to Pensacola, seven of the crew being drowned.

The sea during the night washed over the ship and over the remaining nine of the crew, who, however, managed to hang on to the wreck until daylight, when WILLIAM CARTER and seven men managed to reach a rock which was seen above water at the distance of about 500 yards.

The Master of the vessel tried to follow, but was injured and exhausted, and the sea was so strong that he was knocked down, and would have been drowned had not CARTER returned and carried him to the rock.

CARTER afterwards swam out and secured part of the topmast and yard, lashed them together, and with assistance brought them ashore, where they were formed into a raft.

The nine men left, got on the raft, and with small pieces of wood commenced to paddle to the nearest Island, distant one and a half miles, CARTER and another seaman at times swimming alongside and directing the raft, which was frequently turned off its course and sometimes upset owing to the heavy sea which was running at the time.

CARTER and six others subsequently swam to a larger island a quarter of a mile distant, the former returning the next day, and assisting the Master and a seaman, who were seriously injured to reach it.

The survivors of the shipwrecked crew remained on the larger Island till the 21st April last, when CARTER and others manufactured a larger raft, on which two of the crew sailed to Jamaica, a distance of 32 miles, in two days, whereby the rescue of all the men was ultimately effected.

William Carter, A.B., was awarded the **Albert Medal of the Second Class (Sea)** the whereabouts of which are unknown.

RONALD MACLEAN

Date of Deed: 1872-1883
Date of Gazette: June 20, 1890

In 1872, a man, while suffering from delirium tremens, jumped off the pierhead at East London, and there being a strong sea and ebbing tide, was rapidly carried out to sea. MACLEAN, who was passing, plunged into the sea, swam out, and reached the drowning man, and brought him close to the bank, when both were assisted ashore.

On the 25th September, 1872, the brig "Wild Rose" stranded near Buffalo River, in a strong gale. The crew were rescued by MACLEAN and five other men in a whale boat. Two days later, a man working on board the wreck of the vessel fell overboard, and would have been drowned had not MACLEAN, who was on board at the time, jumped in after him, and rescued him.

On the 27th November, 1872, the barque "Crixea" stranded on the coast in a heavy gale. MACLEAN rendered most valuable assistance in going far into the surf and assisting out of the breeches buoy the crew who were being saved by the rocket apparatus. A day or two later a man employed on board the wreck of the vessel, jumped into the sea while partly drunk, MACLEAN swam out from land through a heavy surf, and at very great personal risk brought him safely ashore.

On the 28th October, 1873, the brig "Lord of the Isles" went ashore on the East Bank. It was seen that the vessel could not hold together till the arrival of the rocket apparatus, and MACLEAN volunteered to swim out to the vessel for a rope. The sea was extremely high, and he was several times thrown back bruised and bleeding on the rocks. Persevering, however, he at last succeeded in reaching the vessel, and returned with a rope, by means of which the crew were safely rescued. While landing, one of the crew fell out of the breeches buoy, MACLEAN, injured as he was, plunged into the surf and reached him; the man, who could not swim, caught MACLEAN by the throat, and both would have been drowned, had not assistance been rendered from shore. MACLEAN's injuries were so serious that he was for two months confined to his house, and his life was for some time despaired of.

At midnight on the 1st November, 1876, the "Elise" stranded in a heavy gale and high sea. The rocket apparatus being engaged at the wreck of another vessel, MACLEAN volunteered to swim out to the "Elise" for a rope. He succeeded in reaching her, but was unable to make his presence known to the crew, and returned ashore. He renewed the attempt, and after some time a rope was thrown to him, which he carried ashore, and by means of which the crew were saved.

On the 11th November, 1882, two lighters were capsized in a heavy sea in the river. MACLEAN, seeing the accident, rushed down to the jetty, flung himself into the breakers, and succeeded in rescuing three of the crew.

On various occasions during the years 1874-83, MACLEAN rendered most valuable assistance in working the rocket apparatus at wrecks, and helping the crews ashore, and was in consequence selected to take charge of the local Volunteer Rocket Brigade.

Ronald Maclean was awarded the **Albert Medal of the First Class (Sea)**, which is now in the East London Museum, Republic of South Africa. He was born in Cape Colony in 1850 and died in South Africa on May 5, 1910. Maclean was tried for the murder of a man called John Barone with whom Maclean's daughter was intending to elope in 1910. The jury acquitted him of the charge. During the later years of the Albert Medal, the policy seems to have been that rescues launched from the shore were rewarded with the medal for land service; this is clearly not the case here. However, there was much confusion where acts of gallantry were performed in docks and harbours (see awards to Bowman and Mather below). John Howard Davies (q.v.) received the AM for land service, although his rescue was at sea, launched from the shore. Conversely, Frank Hopkins' (q.v.) rescue was from a dock at Newport, South Wales, and he received the medal for sea service! There were many such anomalies during the life of the Albert Medal.

WILLIAM SEED

Date of Deed: March 17, 1891
Date of Gazette: June 26, 1891

On the occasion of the sinking of the British steam ship "Utopia", through collision, off Gibraltar, on the 17th March, 1891, when 551 lives were lost, a number of boats were put out by the vessels of the Channel Squadron to the assistance of the shipwrecked persons.

The launch of Her Majesty's ship "Immortalité", while engaged in the work of rescue, fouled her screw, became uncontrollable, and was beaten on to the shore near the breakwater, where she eventually became a total wreck. Two of her crew were drowned, two others swam safely ashore, and the remainder, with eight emigrants from the "Utopia", were rescued in an exhausted condition by officers and men of the Port Department and of the King's Royal Rifles.

Among the rescuers, WILLIAM SEED, Chief of Police, and Corporal WILLIAM McQUE, of the Rifles, particularly distinguished themselves.

Although the night was intensely dark, with a strong gale blowing and a strong current and heavy sea dashing on the breakwater (which is a low line of jagged rocks, giving no foothold outside the wall of the fortifications), they plunged into the waves with ropes, and although washed back on the rocks, renewed their attempt until they succeeded in reaching the launch, which was eighty yards off shore, when the rescue was effected.

William Seed and William McQue were each awarded the **Albert Medal of the Second Class (Sea)** and the RHS Silver Medal for this rescue. Despite strenuous efforts, it has not proved possible to discover anything about William Seed, other than that he was Chief of Police in Gibraltar from 1883 to 1895. The whereabouts of Seed's Albert Medal are unknown.

JAMES WOOD SMITH

Date of Deed: March 1-2, 1891
Date of Gazette: July 10, 1891

The fishing-smack "Lady Matheson", manned by three men, SMITH (Master), Morrison, and McKay, stranded about midnight on the 1st March, 1891, in a north-west gale and snowstorm, among rocks in 20 feet of water, and about 100 yards from an exposed and dangerous part of the coast at Scarsferry, Scotland.

SMITH swam ashore, but finding that the others were unable to follow him, he swam back to the boat for a line, which he fastened round his waist, and again returned ashore. Morrison, while preparing to make use of the line, was washed off the boat by the waves, and was only saved from drowning by SMITH, who, hearing his cries, rushed into the surf, and pulled him out. SMITH then called to McKay, but the latter replying that he had lost hold of the line, SMITH again swam out to the boat with the line round his waist, and, finding McKay was unable to use it, fastened him on to himself, and both were hauled ashore by Morrison.

As a result of his exertions on the occasion, SMITH has since been under medical treatment, and unable to pursue his calling.

James Wood Smith was awarded the **Albert Medal of the Second Class (Sea)** the whereabouts of which are unknown.

***

The next incident which resulted in two awards of the Albert Medal was brought to official attention by Mr. Frank Wardell, H.M. Inspector of Mines for the Rotherham District. He told the Home Secretary that in his experience the two men's act of bravery had never been surpassed, adding that Clarke had previously saved six or seven other lives. The official *London Gazette* citation of September 1, 1891 is one of the shorter ones but we can elaborate on it from the contemporary *Strand Magazine*

***

AMBROSE CLARKE AND ROBERT DRABBLE

Image: Strand Magazine

Ambrose Clarke

Image: Strand Magazine

Robert Drabble

Date of Deed: July 7, 1891
Date of Gazette: September 1, 1891

An accident occurred in the sinking shaft of the Rotherham Main Colliery in Yorkshire. It resulted in the deaths of four men and the escape of four others, all of them injured to a greater or lesser extent. The shaft in question was some 300 feet deep and in it was some scaffolding, suspended on four chains, which were attached to the shaft by means of four staples. The scaffolding was just over 200 feet down. One of the staples securing the scaffolding broke, causing the scaffolding to tilt, throwing all the men off. One of the men managed to get hold of the bucket into which the shafting boards were being loaded and was pulled to the surface. There were pipes in the shaft, which were connected to a donkey engine. These were filled with scalding steam and when the scaffold tilted, one of them was broken. On hearing of the calamity, Clarke immediately rushed back to his post in time to see the man in the bucket emerging on to the surface. Clarke then descended into the inferno to render what assistance he could. He found Drabble still holding on to the scaffolding upside down but with the hook of the grappling chain embedded in his leg. Clarke went to free him but Drabble told him to rescue the other men who had fallen 90 feet to the bottom of the shaft and were now in water there. Clarke started to descend further down the shaft but returned when he heard Drabble call out that he was slipping. Clarke returned and managed to extricate the hook from Drabble's leg and placed him in the bucket. He then went down to see if there were any other survivors and found one other man with both legs broken, who he helped into the bucket. The bucket was then hauled to the surface.

Ambrose Clarke and Robert Drabble were each awarded the **Albert Medal of the Second Class (Land)** and both men were presented with their medals by the Duke of Norfolk. Both medals are now in private collections, that of Drabble in the Sheesh Mahal Museum, Patiala, Punjab, India.

ALFRED JOHN COOPER

Date of Deed: April 8, 1891
Date of Gazette: September 11, 1891

Image: Unknown

Alfred John Cooper

On the 8th April, 1890, at 10.56 A.M., when the "Massilia" was some 500 miles from Aden, in the Indian Ocean, and going at the rate of 13 knots an hour, a native Indian seaman fell from the rigging into the water. On an alarm being raised, COOPER, who at the time the man fell overboard was in the saloon writing, at once ran up on deck, jumped overboard, swam to the man, and kept him afloat until they were picked up by the ship's boat at 11.7 A.M.

Several sharks were seen hovering round the ship at the moment the boat came alongside. COOPER was encumbered with his clothes and boots and the Lascar at first gave some trouble by clinging to him.

Alfred John Cooper, Fourth Officer of the Steamship "Massilia", was awarded the **Albert Medal of the Second Class (Sea),** which was presented to him on October 1, 1891. He was also awarded the Silver Medal of the Royal Humane Society and later the Stanhope Gold Medal for 1890. The medals are now in a private collection. He was drowned in the Indian Ocean on January 20, 1895.

GEORGE HOAR

Date of Deed: October 13, 1891
Date of Gazette: January 15, 1892

On the occasion of the wreck of the schooner "Peggy", during a severe gale with a very heavy sea on the night of the 13th October, 1891, after four men had been rescued from the wreck by means of the rocket apparatus, the Captain of the "Peggy" informed the Chief Officer of the Coast Guard that there was another man still on board the wreck in a disabled state, he having fallen out of the rigging on to the deck of the vessel in attempting to get into the breeches buoy.

GEORGE HOAR immediately volunteered to go off to the wreck and bring the man on shore, and was hauled off to the wreck, a distance of 150 yards, through the heavy sea, in the face of a tremendous gale from the south-east.

He found, on arriving at the vessel, that he could not reach the man, owing to the hawser having been secured fourteen feet above the deck (where the man lay helpless and in an unconscious state).

He then signalled to be hauled on shore again to confer with the Chief Officer; shortly afterwards he was again hauled off and on reaching the wreck the hawser was eased, so as to allow him (in the breeches buoy) to reach the man on the deck.

As the man was perfectly helpless, GEORGE HOAR with his legs, seized the man round the body, and held him with both hands by his coat-collar; and in this manner the two men were safely hauled on shore, the sea at times washing completely over them.

George Hoar awarded the **Albert Medal of the Second Class (Sea)** the whereabouts of which are unknown.

LAWRENCE HENNESSEY

Date of Deed: November 11, 1891
Date of Gazette: February 12, 1892

On the morning of the 11th of November, 1891, at 4.45 A.M., when the French schooner "Eider" was wrecked on the Sea-wall at Seabrook, LAWRENCE HENNESSEY was on watch, a heavy gale was blowing and tremendous seas were sweeping the Sea-wall. He obtained a heaving line and cane, and unaided, at the risk of his life, saved the lives of four sailors belonging to the French schooner, which broke up as she struck, and was totally wrecked.

The French Ambassador has represented the courageous conduct of HENNESSEY in saving the lives of the four French sailors on this occasion, at the peril of his own.

Image: Unknown

Lawrence Hennessey

At 8 A.M. on the same day, LAWRENCE HENNESSEY, as Coxswain of the Lifeboat, attempted to go afloat from Sandgate, but the boat was thrown on to the beach.

Again at noon, a whole gale blowing at the time, with a very heavy sea breaking on the beach, LAWRENCE HENNESSEY went out in the lifeboat from Hythe; just as the breakers were cleared the lifeboat capsized, HENNESSEY (with the rest of the crew) being washed ashore in an exhausted condition, one man being drowned.

HENNESSEY, though bruised and exhausted, directly he recovered his feet, ran into the surf and assisted in rescuing his comrades, who were still struggling in the breakers.

On the evening of the same day, at 9 P.M., LAWRENCE HENNESSEY went out from Seabrook as Coxswain of the Lifeboat, and succeeded in reaching the wreck of the "Benvenue" and rescuing the twenty-seven survivors, subsequently taking the lifeboat safely to Folkestone.

Lawrence Hennessey, Boatman of Hythe Coast Guard Station, was awarded the **Albert Medal of the Second Class (Sea),** which is now in the Sheesh Mahal Museum in Patiala, Punjab, India. He was also awarded the Silver Medal of the Royal National Lifeboat Institution for the first rescue and a bar for the second. However, that for the second rescue was granted on November 25, 1891 and that for the first rescue on December 10, 1891. He was also awarded the Folkestone, Hythe and Sandgate Medal.

✶✶✶

The first award of the Albert Medal in Australia was awarded to a member of the Submarine Mining Corps of Sydney, New South Wales.

✶✶✶

WILLIAM BORLAND

Date of Deed: April 3, 1891
Date of Gazette: November 18, 1892

On the 3rd April, 1891, a boat, containing twelve men and two officers, was engaged in submarine mining operations, about half a mile from the shore at Middle Head, Sydney, N.S.W. By the accidental explosion of a 100 lb. gun-cotton mine, the after part of the boat was blown to pieces, and the two officers and two of the men were instantly killed, while the others were all more or less severely injured.

SAPPER WILLIAM BORLAND, finding the boat sinking, jumped overboard in order to lighten her, and, whilst holding on to the gunwale, supported Sapper Brentnall, who was semi-conscious. Another of the crew, named Adams, in the excitement of the moment, jumped overboard, but when some yards away, called out for help, as he was unable to swim. BORLAND at once swam to his assistance, and supported him until a boat arrived from the shore some considerable time after.

BORLAND was nearest to the explosion of any of the crew, and received severe wounds on the face, arms, abdomen, and legs, besides injuries to both ears. He was in hospital several weeks, and could not follow his ordinary work for some months.

William Borland was awarded the **Albert Medal of the Second Class (Sea),** which is now in a private collection along with his other medals. In addition to the Albert Medal he was also awarded the Bronze Medal of the Royal Humane Society. Borland served in WWI, earning the 1914-15 Star, British War and Victory Medals. He also received the

Colonial Auxiliary Forces Long Service Medal. He ended the war as a Warrant Officer in the Army Service Corps (Australian Imperial Force). He was born on December 8, 1866 and died on February 27, 1941.

WILLIAM DODD

Image: Strand Magazine

William Dodd

Date of Deed: January 14, 1895
Date of Gazette: March 12, 1895

*THE Queen has been graciously pleased to confer **"The Albert Medal of the First Class (Land)"** upon Mr. William Dodd, Under Manager of the Diglake Pit, for great heroism in saving many lives at the flooding of the Audley Colliery, Staffordshire, on January 14th last.*

It is difficult to understand why such a rare and prestigious award received so brief an announcement in the *London Gazette* but here, again, we are indebted to the contemporary *Strand Magazine* News for providing us with a fuller account of Mr Dodd's gallantry.

"About 240 men were at work down the pit, when it was suddenly flooded with water from the old workings of an adjacent mine. At the time of the incident, Mr Dodd was in his office at the bottom of No. 2 shaft. The first thing he did was to direct many of the miners to a place of safety. Then he went up the main dip, down which was pouring a tremendous volume of water with terrific force. On his way, Mr Dodd had to creep through an air-crossing about two feet wide and having passed through this, he heard several boys screaming. He saw four lads about six yards away. There was a deep pool of water lying between him and them and he instructed them to jump in to the water and he would catch them as they floated by on the current. This he did successfully with all four. At this time, the water was within twelve inches of the roof in this part of the mine. Having directed the boys to a place of safety, Mr Dodd was then himself in considerable danger and to prevent himself being swept away by the current, he took hold of the signal wires which were attached to the walls in order to assist him along. One of the staples holding the lines in place came away and Mr Dodd lost his hold on the wire. He was washed away some twenty or thirty yards but managed to grab a piece of timber and saved himself. However, he was now in dire peril from large baulks of timber which had been loosened by the water and were being swept along in the current. It was, of course, pitch dark. He carried on down the workings, directing men to a place of safety wherever he found them. He eventually got to a ladder to climb to the surface but even then, he was nearly swept away by the fierce current. When he did finally reach the surface, as soon as he had recovered from his ordeal, he descended again into the pit, accompanied by two volunteers to carry on the work of rescue. For more than six hours he had struggled against ice-cold torrents and as a result of his splendid gallantry was instrumental in saving more than thirty lives."

William Dodd was born on May 16, 1852 in Bickerton, near Malpas, Cheshire. He married Ann (née Johnson) in 1873. She died in 1876 and he married again, Elizabeth (née Emberton) in 1882. Both William's children by his first wife died in childhood. He never worked again after his experience and died, aged 54, on January 19, 1907. He is buried, with his second wife, in Audley Churchyard. He was also awarded the Silver Medal of the Royal Humane Society for the incident described above. The whereabouts of his Albert Medal are unknown.

CHARLES WOOD ROBINSON

Date of Deed: April 17, 1895
Date of Gazette: June 25, 1895

While the "Teutonic" was steaming at the rate of about 21 knots an hour in St. George's Channel on the 17th April, 1895, at 6.30 A.M., when few people were about the deck, Mr. ROBINSON noticed a Passenger climbing on to the rail of the ship with the evident intention of jumping overboard. He made an ineffectual attempt to prevent him and then without divesting himself of any of his clothing immediately dived after the man from a height of 25 feet above the water, and only about 30 feet forward of the propellers of the vessel.

Mr. ROBINSON reached the man and did his utmost to rescue him, but his efforts were met with violent resistance, and in the end the man succeeded in drowning himself.

Mr. ROBINSON ran great risk of being drawn under the propellers, and when picked up was in a very exhausted condition.

Sub-Lieutenant Charles Wood Robinson, R.N.R., Third Officer of the R.M.S. "Teutonic" of Liverpool, was awarded the **Albert Medal of the Second Class (Sea).** He was also awarded the Gold Medal of the Liverpool Shipwreck and Humane Society, the Silver Medal of the Mercantile Marine Service Association, the Silver Cross of the Merchant Service Guild and the Conway Boys Silver Medal, 1887, all of which are now in a private collection. He was an Old Boy of the Training Ship "Conway". His medal was presented to him by the Lord Mayor of Liverpool on July 23, 1895.

HEREWARD HEWISON

Date of Deed: November 28, 1894
Date of Gazette: July 12, 1895

Image: Unknown

While a number of men were bathing on the sea beach at Newcastle, New South Wales, on the morning of the 28th November, 1894, the cry of "Shark!" was suddenly raised; every one at once made for the shore, with the exception of Mr. HORACE HEWISON, who cried out that the shark had seized him, and immediately afterwards disappeared under the water.

Mr. HEREWARD HEWISON, realizing the dangerous position of his elder brother, promptly turned, and swimming to the spot, found that the shark had seized his brother's right arm.

Hereward Hewison

He at once grasped his brother round the body, and the two fought the shark as well as they were able until the complete severance of the arm, just below the elbow joint, released Mr. HORACE HEWISON, and afforded them an opportunity to escape without further accident.

Mr. HEREWARD HEWISON assisted his injured brother by keeping behind him and pushing him forward.

Hereward Hewison, of Newcastle, New South Wales, was awarded the **Albert Medal of the Second Class (Sea)**, which was presented to him by the Governor of New South Wales on December 17, 1895. Its whereabouts are unknown. He was also awarded the Australian Royal Humane Society's Silver Medal. He was born circa 1877. He married Elizabeth Phillips in Newcastle, N.S.W. when he was 21 and they had three children; two daughters and a son. He died at Mosinan, New South Wales, on December 16, 1944, aged 67.

WILLIAM JOHN NUTMAN

Date of Deed: January 19, 1896
Date of Gazette: April 14, 1896

William John Nutman

Image: Strand Magazine

At 2 A.M., on the 19th January, 1896, while the S.S. "Staffordshire", of Liverpool, was on a voyage from Marseilles to Port Said, signals of distress were observed to be proceeding from the S.S. "Aidar", also of Liverpool, and the "Staffordshire" immediately proceeded to her assistance. As the "Aidar" was found to be sinking fast, three of the "Staffordshire's" lifeboats were at once launched, and with great difficulty, owing to the darkness and the heavy sea, succeeded in rescuing her passengers and crew, 29 in number.

At 6.10 A.M. the only persons left on the "Aidar" were Mr. NUTMAN (the Master), and an injured and helpless fireman, whom he was endeavouring to save, and whom he absolutely refused to abandon.

The steamer was now rapidly settling down, and as it was no longer safe to remain near her, the Officer in charge of the rescuing boat asked Mr. NUTMAN for a final answer. He still persisted in remaining with the injured man, choosing rather to face almost certain death than to leave him to his fate.

The men in the boat were obliged to pull away and immediately afterwards, at 6.17 A.M., the "Aidar" gave one or two lurches and foundered.

After she disappeared, Mr. NUTMAN was seen on the bottom of an upturned boat, still holding the fireman. Half an hour elapsed before the rescuing boat could approach, but eventually Mr. NUTMAN and the fireman were picked up and taken on board the "Staffordshire, where the injured man was with difficulty restored by the Ship's Surgeon.

William John Nutman, was awarded the **Albert Medal of the First Class (Sea)**. He was also awarded the Gold Medal of the Liverpool Shipwreck and Humane Society, the Silver Medal of the Royal Humane Society, the Silver Medal of the Mercantile Marine Service Association, the Gold Medal of the Shipwrecked Fishermen's and Mariners' Royal Benevolent Society and the Lloyd's Large Silver Medal for Saving Life at Sea for this rescue, all of which are now in a private collection.

FREDERICK MILLER TIMME

Date of Deed: 24 September 1899
Date of Gazette: 18 December 1900

THE Queen has been graciously pleased to confer the "Albert Medal of the Second Class" upon Mr. Frederick Miller Timme, in recognition of his gallantry in saving life during a cyclone at Darjeeling, Northern India, on the night of the 24th September, 1899.

Once again, Don Henderson comes to our assistance with his research notes from the Home Office files. Timme saved three lives from houses on the east side of Observatory Hill. After doing all he could, he climbed straight up the bank for a hundred feet or more on to The Mall and checked around. He went alone and without a lamp through the slips. He eventually slid down the bank to the Diocesan School with the idea of helping them. He was the only man to do this from several parties.

Timme's Albert Medal was presented to him by the Lieutenant-Governor of Bengal on May 6, 1901. He was born on April 5, 1863, in Camberwell, London, one of three children of William and Clare (née Dixon). After service in the Australian Merchant Navy, he became a tea planter with his cousin at Darjeeling. He died at Darjeeling on June 1, 1921, aged 58. The whereabouts of his Albert Medal are unknown.

✳✳✳

The first awards of the reign of King Edward VII went to two citizens of Malta. It is the last of the much abbreviated citations to appear in the Gazette.

✳✳✳

GIOVANNI BILOCCA AND GUISEPPE ZAMMIT

Date of Deed: August 27, 1901
Date of Gazette: February 18, 1902

*THE KING has been graciously pleased to confer the **Albert Medal of the Second Class (Land)** upon Giovanni Bilocca and Guiseppe Zammit, Dockyard Labourers, in recognition of their gallantry in saving the lives of fellow labourers who were overcome by poisonous fumes in a shaft at the Extension Works at His Majesty's Dockyard at Malta, on the 27th August last.*

Little is known of these two men, although thanks to research undertaken by the late Major Albert Abela for his book "Malta's George Cross and War Gallantry Awards", a chink of light is shed upon them.

In the early hours of the morning of August 27, 1901, two labourers in the Superintending Civil Engineer's Department, Carmelo Mifsud and Angelo Spiteri had returned to their work at the bottom of a 50-foot shaft, where blasting had taken place some time earlier. The work involved diversion of the sewers in connection with the extension of the dockyard and the air was vitiated. When they had reached 40 feet below the surface, Spiteri managed to return to the surface but Mifsud proceeded to the bottom of the shaft. Those at the top of the shaft could get no answer from Mifsud; a number of flares were lowered but each one went out. Giovanni Bilocca now volunteered to attempt Mifsud's rescue. He descended the shaft and found Mifsud, who was in a state of collapse. Bilocca then secured Mifsud to his own rope and had him hauled to the surface. He was then overcome by the fumes. Zammit then volunteered to go down to rescue Bilocca, taking an extra rope with him. He managed to secure Bilocca and they were then both hauled to the surface, although both appeared dead and it took some time to revive them.

Both men were presented with their awards on the Palace Square by Lieutenant-General Sir Francis (later Field Marshal Lord) Grenfell, Governor of Malta, on March 9, 1902. Zammit was a part-time soldier with 2nd Battalion, The Royal Malta Regiment. Bilocca came from Zabbar. He died on January 8, 1953, aged 78 and his AM is still proudly held by his family. These were the last awards of the Albert Medal to civilians to bear the original narrow ribbons. Each man also received a medal from the Royal Humane Society. From this time, the Royal Mint took over from Phillips as manufacturers of the Albert Medal. The whereabouts of Zammit's Albert Medals are unknown but it is likely that it is still with the family.

ALBERT VICTOR HARDWICK

Date of Deed: December 21, 1904
Date of Gazette: February 14, 1905

On the evening of the 21st December, 1904, No. 4 Platform at Finsbury Park Station was crowded with people (estimated at over a thousand) awaiting down trains. A dense fog prevailed at the time.

An elderly lady fell from the platform just as an incoming train loomed out of the fog at a distance of a few yards. If her rescue was to be effected nothing but great promptitude, resourcefulness, and bravery could avail, seeing that but a few seconds remained for action, and the lady had injured her ankle and could not save herself.

Mr. Hardwick leapt on the line, and just succeeded in placing the lady and himself at full length on the ground between the rail and the wall supporting the platform when the train overtook them.

The engine and four coaches had passed the spot where they were lying before the train was brought to a standstill. The Railway Officials, having satisfied themselves that both the lady and Mr. Hardwick had escaped injury, directed the train to be moved forward slowly, and rescued and rescuer, to the great relief of the onlookers, were assisted to the platform in safety.

Albert Victor Hardwick was awarded the **Albert Medal of the First Class (Land).** His home address was noted as Arkell, Muswell Road, Muswell Hill, London and he was presented with his award by the King at Buckingham Palace on February 10, 1905. There is a note on his Home Office file that he was killed in action in 1915, but the writer has a note that he died in Ontario, Canada on April 24, 1961. He does not appear to feature in the Commonwealth War Graves Commission records. The whereabouts of his Albert Medal are unknown.

✳✳✳

Five awards in 1905 are worthy of note as being the greatest number of awards for one incident of saving life at sea. The circumstances, too, were rather unusual.

✳✳✳

WILLIAM SMITH, ARTHUR REA, CHARLES BEER, HARRY SMIRK and EDWIN COSTELLO

Date of Deed: October 21-22, 1904
Date of Gazette: May 16, 1905

The steam trawler "Crane" was so badly damaged by the gun fire of the Russian Baltic Fleet in the North Sea on the night of the 22nd October last, that she began to sink. The skipper and the third hand of the vessel had been killed, and, with one exception, the surviving members of the crew were all wounded.

The mate, William Smith, was severely wounded while on his way to assist the injured boatswain, and when he found that the skipper was killed, took charge of the sinking vessel. He subsequently signalled for assistance, and when the boat from the steam trawler "Gull" arrived he assisted in getting the wounded and the bodies of the dead into the boat, and was the last to leave the "Crane" just before she sank.

As the Chief Engineer had been wounded and rendered insensible soon after the firing began, the Second Engineer, Arthur Rea (22 years of age), took charge of the engines, and, although the lights had been extinguished, he went into the stokehold to discover the cause of a loud report and an escape of steam. He was knocked down by a shot on his way but went on, and finding the stokehold more than a foot deep in water and steam blowing from the engine side, looked at the gauge glass and pumping additional cold water into the boiler partially drew the fires with the object of averting an explosion. He also set the pumps of the vessel working, and, after reporting that the vessel was sinking, went a second time into the darkened engine room and stopped the engines. Although wounded he did not stop working till he left the ship.

In answer to signals of distress from the "Crane", Charles Beer, Mate, Harry Smirk, Chief Engineer, and Edwin Costello, Boatswain, of the steam trawler "Gull", after the firing, which had been heavy and sustained, went in a boat to the "Crane", and succeeded with great difficulty in rescuing the wounded from the rapidly sinking vessel, and in bringing away the dead bodies of those who had been killed.

William Smith and Arthur Rea were both awarded the **Albert Medal of the First Class (Sea),** while Charles Beer, Harry Smirk and Edwin Costello each received the **Albert Medal of the Second Class (Sea).** These were the first awards to civilians to carry the new wide ribbon for the Second Class medals. All except Costello, who was unable to attend, were presented with their medals by the King at Buckingham Palace on May 13, 1905. Costello's was sent to him. Smith's and Rea's medals are now in private collections and Costello's is in Hull City Museum. The whereabouts of the others are unknown. The Russian Fleet, on its way to Vladivostok from the Baltic during the Russo-Japanese War, had apparently mistaken the fishing boats for a hostile Japanese force in the North Sea! William Smith died in 1908.

EDWARD NICHOLLS

Date of Deed: April 18, 1905
Date of Gazette: December 8, 1905

Edward Nicholls

Image: Unknown

On the 18th April, 1905, Nicholls (with two other miners, Bentley and King) was working in a "stope" on the 1,200 feet level of the Lake View Consols Mine, at Kalgoorlie. He and his comrades had charged a round of holes with dynamite, had lit the fuses, and were in the act of retiring to the level below for safety. Bentley had not retreated more than ten feet when one of the charges exploded. Nicholls was six or eight feet further away down the "stope", and, consequently, partially sheltered from the force of the explosion. All lights were put out by the explosion and the mine was in complete darkness. Nicholls called to ascertain if any one was hurt, and hearing the groans of his comrade Bentley, groped his way back to the top of the rill (which is the name of the pyramid forming the floor of the "stope"), in this case about 40 feet high. On the top of the rill he found Bentley, on whose body a big stone was resting. He had to roll this stone away before he could move him, but he succeeded, at the peril of his own life, in getting his comrade down the rill. While they were at the foot of the rill the other holes exploded. Bentley subsequently died of the injuries he had sustained.

When Nicholls returned to aid his comrade, the lighted fuses of four other charged holes were burning, and other explosions were momentarily to be expected. The fuses averaged 6 feet in length, and the rate of burning was about 90 seconds per yard, that is to say, the explosions were timed to take place within 3 minutes of lighting the fuse.

Edward Nicholls was awarded the **Albert Medal of the Second Class (Land)** the whereabouts of which are unknown. He was also awarded the Silver Medal of the Royal Humane Society and the Life-Saving Medal of the Order of St. John of Jerusalem. In later life he became an attendant at the Claremont Mental Hospital and died in June, 1935.

JOHN WARDROP THOMSON

Date of Deed: October 21, 1905
Date of Gazette: January 12, 1906

John Wardrop Thomson

Image: Stirling Observer / Family

On the night of Saturday, the 21st October, 1905, while Thomson was on duty at the Stirling Railway Station, his attention was called, by an outcry, to the fact that a man was lying on the metals of the down main line.

An engine was approaching rapidly, and was not more than 30 yards distant, when Thomson, without hesitation, sprang to the man's assistance, and both men disappeared from view as the engine passed by. The railway officials and passengers on the platform who witnessed the occurrence thought that both men had been run over, especially as another engine passed by, almost at the same moment, on the next line of rails. Thomson had, however, managed to drag the man on to the six foot way. The rescued man was of heavy build and was quite unable to help himself, being in a state of intoxication; he was unhurt, while Thomson only received cuts about the face.

John Wardrop Thomson was awarded the **Albert Medal of the Second Class (Land),** which was presented to him by the King at Buckingham Palace on January 9, 1906. He was also presented with a gratuity by the District Traffic Superintendent in the Postmaster's Room at Stirling on November 14, 1905. John Wardrop Thomson was born circa 1883 at Stirling. After education he joined the Post Office as a Boy Messenger, subsequently working his way up the ladder of promotion to postman, head postman and assistant inspector. He was a man of wide interests, serving as Secretary and Treasurer of the Civil Service Benevolent Society for twenty years and holding appointments in the sports association, which included golf, bowling and soccer. He was a keen member of Stirling Amateur Boating and Swimming Club, Riverside Bowling Club and Victoria Golf Club. His wife was Margaret (née Stevenson). He became a member of the Territorial Army in 1908 and served throughout WWI as a Staff Sergeant in the Army Service Corps with 51 (Highland) Division, later moving to the 47 (London) Division as a Warrant Officer Class 2. He retired from the TA in 1929, having been awarded the 1914-15 Star, British War, Victory and Territorial Efficiency Medals (the latter in 1922). In addition to all this, Mr Thomson was a keen Freemason, being a Past Master of Lodge Stirling Royal Arch No. 76, a life member of the Provincial Grand Lodge of Stirlingshire, a member of Stirling Rock Arch Chapter No. 2 and of the Preceptory of Greyfriars. He died at Stirling on September 22, 1962, aged 79, his address at that time being 14 Shiphaugh Place. The whereabouts of his Albert Medal are unknown.

JOHN LESLIE URQUHART.

Date of Deed: January 8-10, 1905
Date of Gazette: March 27, 1906

*The KING has been graciously pleased to award the **Albert Medal of the First Class (Land)** to Mr. John Leslie Urquhart, a British Vice-Consul at Baku, for conspicuous gallantry in saving the lives of four British workmen who, in September last, during the outbreak which occasioned serious losses to the Petroleum Industry at Baku, were surrounded by the insurgents in an isolated position at Balachani Zabrat and were in imminent danger of losing their lives, a fate which shortly after their rescue befell all the persons remaining in the buildings where they had been shut up. The four Englishmen had already been isolated for some time when news of their perilous position reached the British Embassy at St. Petersburg, and Mr. Urquhart, accompanied by two Cossacks and several Tartars from the village of Mushtagee, started to relieve the beleaguered men. The district was full of armed Tartars, and in such a state of unrest that when Mr. Urquhart started upon his expedition it was not expected by the remainder of the British Colony in Baku that he would live to return.*

On the night of his departure Mr. Urquhart proceeded to a farm which he possesses in the neighbourhood, where he hoped to be able to get help from his own farm hands, who were Tartars, and also to collect supplies, and notwithstanding that the party was stopped and fired on from time to time the supplies were collected and a start was made early the next morning for Balachani.

Mr. Urquhart's courageous and spontaneous action was rewarded with success. He got through and found the four Englishmen in a dreadful condition, especially on account of want of water, and after feeding them he persuaded them to go with him in carts which he had brought, with as many Armenians as they could bring with them. Immediately afterwards the whole of the buildings were carried by storm and everyone found therein put to death.

Mr. Urquhart was presented with his Albert Medal by the King at Buckingham Palace on November 1, 1906. John Leslie Urquhart was born in 1874 and was a Scottish mining engineer and entrepreneur in Tsarist Russia and at Mount Isa in Australia. He was appointed Vice-Consul at Baku on December 20, 1902 but this was suspended pending recognition by the Russian Government. He was re-appointed on September 8, 1905 and resigned on April 6, 1907. He died in London on March 13, 1933. His exploit was featured in *Hornet* comic No. 147 dated July 2, 1966. The whereabouts of his Albert Medal are unknown.

PATRICK CULLINAN

Date of Deed: November 16, 1905
Date of Gazette: March 27, 1906

Image: Unknown

Patrick Cullinan

On the evening of the 16th November, 1905, between 6 and 7 o'clock, while a special cattle train was running through Ennis Station from Limerick, a woman fell between the rails in front of, and about 15 yards from, the approaching train. Inspector Cullinan, who was on the platform at the time, immediately jumped on the track, and just succeeded in dragging the woman into the six-foot way, though not before the guard of the engine had come in contact with her clothing. So little time remained for action that but for Inspector Cullinan's promptitude and great personal strength the woman's life would have been lost.

Patrick Cullinan was born on July 17, 1868 at Ardsollas, not far from Ennis, in County Clare. Nothing is known of his early life but in 1882, he was appointed to a post with the Waterford & Limerick Railway. By 1900, Mr Cullinan had risen to the rank of Traffic Inspector, Limerick Coaching on the Great Southern & Western Railway, as the W & L had become. By July 1, 1904, he was earning thirty shillings (£1.50) a week and was based at Ennis, the county town of Clare.

Patrick Cullinan was awarded the **Albert Medal of the Second Class (Land).** He was presented with his medal by the Lord Lieutenant of Ireland in the Throne Room of Dublin Castle on March 14, 1906. Patrick Cullinan married Ellen Torpey in 1919 and they had three children, the last of whom died only in 2002. All are buried in the family grave in St. Finian's Churchyard, Quin, Co. Clare. The family originally came from Cashel in Co. Tipperary and Pat's father worked at Ardsollas. By 1922, Mr Cullinan was a Supervisor and he retired on pension on May 20, 1929, aged 60. He died on December 4, 1933 and family tradition has it that his AM was buried with him.

ROBERT MUNRO

Image: The Northern Scot

Robert Munro

Date of Deed: April 28, 1906
Date of Gazette: October 2, 1906

On the 28th April last, Munro and a road foreman named Alexander Ross, and William Morris, the labourer who lost his life, having ceased work for the day on the Earlsmill-road, at Darnaway, were crossing the railway bridge over the Brodie Burn on the Highland Railway on their way home, when they were overtaken by a train travelling on the line of rails next the south parapet of the bridge by which they were walking.

Morris was walking between the rails, and Munro, who was in advance of Morris, but beside the parapet of the bridge and clear of the rails, made a brave endeavour to drag his comrade from the railway track. He had grasped Morris's shoulder, when he was caught by the engine and thrown into the space about five feet wide between the near rail and the parapet of the bridge. Unhappily his brave act has resulted in his being maimed for life.

Robert Munro was awarded the **Albert Medal of the Second Class (Land).** He was 28 at the time of this incident, having been born circa 1877 and hailed from Muirton of Davey, near Forres, Elgin. William Morris, the man who lost his life, was aged 78. They were dragged for fifty to sixty yards and Munro had his foot cut off, while sustaining a broken right arm. His medal was presented to him by the King at Aberdeen, when His Majesty was attending the opening of the University. Munro is thought to have been a farm worker in his early years and after the accident he set up a business as a hairdresser in Burghead, being known as "Bob the Barber". He was married with two daughters and a son. He died on March 28, 1949 and is buried in Burghead. His medal is still in the possession of the family.

***

On July 13, 1907, a Royal Warrant instituted the Edward Medal, to be awarded in two classes (like the Albert Medal), Silver and Bronze, to those who had displayed courage in saving life in mines and quarries. This was followed, on December 1, 1909, by a further Royal Warrant extending the scope of the medal to courage in saving life in industry generally. The second medal, of course, had a very much wider scope and was awarded, for instance, to farm workers, among others, as well as more conventional industrial situations. For some years after the institution of the EM, however, the two awards (Albert and Edward Medals) were used, as it were, in parallel, as will be apparent from the accounts that follow. In later years, it was generally accepted that a Silver Edward was the equivalent to an Albert Medal of the Second Class.

***

1907 – 1914

WILLIAM HENRY PEARCE

Date of Deed: December 4, 1905
Date of Gazette: September 10, 1907

Image: Sydney Mail

William Henry Pearce

On the morning of the day mentioned (4th December, 1905), while the passenger train running between Maitland and Sydney was approaching Thornton Railway Station, at the rate of 45 miles an hour, a boiler plate of the engine collapsed, and through the opening, about 12 inches square, steam and boiling water were ejected with great force. Both the driver of the engine, James Pead, who has since succumbed to his injuries, and the fireman, Pearce, were severely scalded. Pead was quite incapacitated, and was still exposed to the full force of the escaping steam when Pearce, at great personal risk, lifted him to a place of safety behind the bunker tank.

Pearce having endeavoured, without success, to close the throttle valve, climbed over the cab of the engine, along the boiler, to the front of the engine, exposing himself again to the escaping water and steam, and having reached the footplate of the engine, and placed one foot in the draw hook for support, he reached under the buffer plank for a distance of about 18 inches, and opened the cock of the air pipe, thus applying the automatic brake and bringing the train to a standstill.

William Henry Pearce, of Islington, near Newcastle, New South Wales, was awarded the **Albert Medal of the First Class (Land),** which was presented to him by the Governor-General of Australia at Government House, Sydney, on July 16, 1907. In addition to the Albert Medal, Pearce was awarded the Clarke Gold Medal of the Royal Humane Society of Australia, the Gold Medal of The National Shipwreck Relief and Humane Society of New South Wales and £50 from His Majesty's Commissioners for Railways. His AM is now in a private collection.

CECIL ALBERT FRANCIS HERBERT HUGHES

Date of Deed: March 19, 1907
Date of Gazette: September 17, 1907

Image: Unknown

Cecil Albert Francis Herbert Hughes

On the 19th March, 1907, an exceedingly heavy and sudden downpour of rain in the Bonnievale District caused a flood, and the inundation of the Westralia and East Extension Mine from the lower level (1,354 feet from the surface) to the No. 9 (990 feet) level.

With the exception of an Italian named Modesto Varischetti all the miners effected their escape. He was working by himself in a rise 28 feet above the No. 10 (1,000 feet) level, and was cut off by the flood waters and imprisoned, as in a diving bell, the air in the rise unable to escape keeping the water at a lower level than in the main shaft, and in the stopes above the No. 10 level, where the surface of the water was 50 feet above the point where Varischetti was imprisoned.

It was at first thought that the entombed miner must have lost his life, but efforts were made to communicate with him by knocking on the rock, and after a time his signals were heard in response. It was at once decided to attempt his rescue by the aid of divers, seeing that by making use of all the available means of draining the Mine at least ten days would have elapsed before the water could have been lowered to the No. 10 level.

Diving dresses were telegraphed for to Perth, and through the energetic assistance of the Chief Harbourmaster at Fremantle were obtained without delay, so that in less than eight hours from the time of the despatch of the telegraphic message a special train was on its way to the Goldfields with two divers, Messrs. Curtis and Hearne, with their assistants and diving outfits. Meantime two other divers, Messrs. F. Hughes and Fox, of Kalgoorlie, who had lately followed the occupation of miners, and were familiar with the local mining practices, had volunteered their services and had gone to the flooded mine.

The first-mentioned divers arrived early on the morning of the 22nd March, and it was considered advisable that Hughes and Fox, on account of their mining experience, should make the first attempt at rescue. They would have to descend through an ore-pass from the No. 9 to the No. 10 level, a distance of 100 feet, then turn at right angles along the latter level, and go along it 250 feet to reach the foot of the rise where the man was imprisoned. Both divers would have to go down the ore-pass, and one would then remain at the bottom of it to pass his comrade's air-pipe and lines round the angle so as to prevent them from fouling. The work was of a difficult and dangerous nature, having to be performed without knowledge of the shape of the cavities to be passed through, and often in very cramped space, and subject to the continual danger that the flooding might have displaced timbers or so loosened the "filling" in the worked out ground as to make it liable to run into the pass or the level and overwhelm the rescuers.

Hughes led the way and after some difficulty reached the bottom of the pass, where he found the shoot into the level choked with about half a ton of ore; he cleared this out, took the door off the shoot, and got down into the level, but then had to return twice to No. 9 as the other diver did not come down to him. It proved that Fox had been unable to get down, and on making his second attempt he sustained an injury to his leg which caused him to retire from further participation in the work. Diver Hearne then took his place, and Hughes and he went down to the No. 10 level, but both had to return to arrange certain matters. They then descended again, and Hughes struggled along the level, knee deep in sludge, to the rise, where he was able to find the air hosepipe leading to Varischetti's rock-drill, and after shaking it several times obtained a signal in reply from the imprisoned man. Hughes was then so exhausted that he had to return after fixing a guide-line for future use.

After a rest of 3½ hours Hughes and Hearne again descended, the descent being the fifth that Hughes had made that day. He succeeded in reaching Varischetti, shook hands with him, and supplied him with an electric lamp, food and other necessities. Next day he again made a visit, Hearne as before staying at the angle at the foot of the ore-pass; and daily visits were repeated until the 28th March, when the water had been lowered sufficiently to make it just possible for a man to wade along the No. 10 level from the ore-pass with his head out of the water. Diver Hughes then went in twice without his diving dress and talked to Varischetti, and then made a third trip and brought him out, carrying him (a) portion of the way, the entombed man's strength having failed him.

Cecil Albert Francis Herbert Hughes was awarded the **Albert Medal of the Second Class (Land)**. He was born on November 11, 1861, in Wrexham, North Wales and was educated at Ruabon Grammar School. By 1886, he was in Australia and on October 22, 1887, he married Martha Cobble at Manse Methodist Church, North Street, Maryborough, Queensland. They had six children, three sons and three daughters between 1889 and 1899. He died in Brisbane on June 1, 1919, his wife dying in 1941. The whereabouts of his AM are unknown.

ARTHUR HARDIMENT

Date of Deed: August 30, 1907
Date of Gazette: November 15, 1907

Arthur Hardiment

Image: Illustrated London News

The KING was pleased, this day, at Windsor Castle, to present to Mr. Arthur Hardiment, an artisan of Tivetshall, in the county of Norfolk, the **Albert Medal of the Second Class (Land)**, conferred upon him, by His Majesty's command, for gallantry in endangering his own life in order to save the life of a child at Tivetshall Railway Crossing as detailed below:-

On the 30th August last, at the hour of 2.30 P.M., while the Cromer Express Train on its way from Norwich to London was approaching the level crossing at Tivetshall at the rate of 50 miles an hour, Hardiment and Horace Bloomfield, the crossing-keeper, were standing near one of the gates about 29 feet from the railway track when Bloomfield's little boy, aged 18 months, was seen to be making for the line from the opposite side of the track to join his father.

The cries of the men did not avail to stop the child, and Hardiment thereupon dashed across the line towards the child, knowing that the father, who had lost a leg and an arm, was incapacitated from attempting the rescue.

Notwithstanding that Hardiment was but a few paces from the railway track the risk to life was very great seeing that the train was only some 130 feet distant at the moment. Before he *was clear of the track, the footplate of the engine had struck his left forearm fracturing both the bones and hurling him into a hedge nine feet away. Just before he was caught by the engine he had the satisfaction of knowing that the child had turned away from the approaching train and had escaped unhurt.*

Arthur Hardiment now disappears from the pages of history and back into obscurity. He spent six weeks in the Norfolk and Norwich Hospital as a result of the injuries he received in this incident. We do know that he served in the Metropolitan Police at Gypsy Hill Police Station (P Division) between August 17, 1896 and July 18, 1898, so there should be a Metropolitan Police Diamond Jubilee Medal at large somewhere. He was discharged due to insanity and spent some time in Lambeth Workhouse as a lunatic. The Eastern Daily Press raised £22 for him. His Albert Medal is now in a private collection.

ALFRED HUNT

Date of Deed: August 7, 1908
Date of Gazette: December 18, 1908

Image: Family

Alfred Hunt

On the day in question (7th August, 1908), two brothers, Robert and Alfred Hunt, were employed at Messrs. Johnson Brothers' Pottery at Tunstall in cleaning out a tank, nine feet three inches deep and nine feet wide, under the engine house floor, containing hot water and oil, when Robert Hunt, who was bending over the opening of the tank, fell in.

Alfred Hunt, who was working close by at the time, hearing his brother cry out as he fell, immediately jumped into the tank after him, although he knew that the water must be very hot, and succeeded in pulling him out. Robert Hunt was so badly scalded that he succumbed to his injuries.

Alfred Hunt was born on April 1, 1881 at Burslem, Stoke-on-Trent, to Robert and Esther Hunt. His father was a collier and although nothing is known of his early life or education, he seems to have been employed variously as a railway driver (presumably of road vehicles) or bricklayer. According to family folklore, he was also employed at Alexandria Pottery in Tunstall, Staffordshire. He was involved in a dispute with his employers over underpayment of earnings and left to volunteer for the army. Around February, 1898, he enlisted into the North Staffs Militia as number 4509 and it is thought that he lied about his age to do so. On May 6, 1898, he transferred to the Cheshire Regiment (Militia) as number 6952. He is believed to have served with 2nd Battalion, the Cheshire Regiment in the South African War 1899-1902, for which he received the Queen's South Africa Medal *(Cape Colony, Orange Free State, Transvaal)* and King's South Africa Medal *(South Africa 1901, South Africa 1902)*. He re-engaged with 1st Battalion The Cheshire Regiment on April 12, 1904 to complete nine years with the colours. He later saw service with the Royal Field Artillery, where his number was 36437. On January 28, 1907, he transferred to the Army Reserve and it is not known what he did after this date but it was during the period between then and his mobilisation in 1914 that he was awarded the Albert Medal.

Alfred Hunt was awarded the **Albert Medal of the Second Class (Land)**, which was presented to him by the King at Buckingham Palace on December 14, 1908. He was also awarded the Bronze Medal for Saving Life by the Order of St. John of Jerusalem, according to entry number 211 in the roll of medals of that Order. He was presented with this at Marlborough House on July 9, 1909, by HRH the Prince of Wales (afterwards King George V), who was Grand Prior of the Order. The account in this roll is at variance with that in the *London Gazette,* in that it describes the depth of the tank as *nineteen* feet.

Hunt re-engaged for the reserve on June 21, 1910 and was mobilized on August 4, 1914 as a driver and joined 32 Battery, 33 Brigade, Royal Field Artillery. Having completed his time, he was discharged on November 5, 1915. He re-enlisted into the RFA as number 112028 on March 1, 1916 at Newcastle-upon-Tyne and was posted first to India and then Mesopotamia. He went to Egypt in 1918 and eventually returned to France, where he was discharged to the Class Z Reserve on April 8, 1919.

He had married on November 2, 1909, a widow, Rose Emily Bailey, at Kidsgrove, Staffs. She already had two children and they later had three more. It is not known what Alfred Hunt did subsequent to his discharge from the army. He may have returned to his old job in the potteries. He may have served in Civil Defence or the Home Guard in WWII. He died in 1956, at the age of 75.

His family has his St. John's Medal and a replacement Albert Medal, although his two South African War Medals and his 1914 Star trio are all missing. They are still being sought by the family. This is one of the cases which might have been considered for the Edward Medal (Industry) but this award had not been instituted at the time of the incident or the gazetting.

ARTHUR ECCLESHALL

Date of Deed: October 2, 1908
Date of Gazette: July 23, 1909

Arthur Eccleshall

Image: Family

On the 2nd October, 1908, between 1 and 2 P.M., three children were making their way over the level crossing at Bushbury Railway Station, where Eccleshall was employed as a porter. A light engine was approaching at the time, travelling at about 10 miles an hour, and seeing that the children's lives were endangered Eccleshall shouted to them, when two of the children ran forward and got clear of the rails on which the engine was travelling, while the third, a little boy, tried to escape by running between the platform and the rails; the engine was almost upon him when Eccleshall jumped from the platform in front of the engine and lifted the child clear of the railway track. In so doing he was struck by the engine and thrown into the four-foot way, being rendered unconscious.

Arthur Eccleshall was awarded the **Albert Medal of the Second Class (Land).** He was born at Lichfield, Staffs, on January 16, 1889, the third eldest of a family of eleven. In 1903, aged 14, he joined the staff of the London & North Western Railway and by 1908 was a porter at Bushbury. He served the LNWR, LMS and BR for 47 years, retiring in 1950 as Chief Clerk at Dudley Passenger Station. He was a keen sportsman, supporting Wolverhampton Wanderers FC and County Cricket. He was a member of Tabernacle Baptist Church in Dunstall Road, Wolverhampton and acted as their Treasurer for 25 years. He enlisted with 2/6 South Staffordshire Regiment for WWI and was a POW in Minden. He received the British War and Victory Medals for his service. He married Edith Emily Banks on September 1, 1915 and they had two daughters. She died in 1977. Arthur Eccleshall died at Wolverhampton on August 30, 1958 and his medal is now in a private collection.

GEORGE HENRY SMITH

Date of Deed: October 24, 1908
Date of Gazette: July 23, 1909

Image: Local Newspaper

George Henry Smith

On the 24th October, 1908, a workman at the Woburn Sands Brickworks, named Charles Griffin, was precipitated to the bottom of one of the kilns owing to the roof collapsing, and was imprisoned by hot ballast and bricks, the upper part of his body alone being free. His comrade Smith on hearing of the accident at once went to his rescue, but to effect an entry proved to be a work of some difficulty as the wicket through which the bricks were taken into and removed from the kiln was almost completely blocked. He succeeded, however, in reaching his comrade and in removing the bricks and ballast imprisoning the fallen man, who was eventually drawn up to the top of the kiln by means of a rope fastened under his armpits. Griffin subsequently died of the injuries he sustained.

George Henry Smith was awarded the **Albert Medal of the Second Class (Land).** He was also awarded the Silver Medal of the Royal Humane Society for this rescue and subsequently the Stanhope Gold Medal for the bravest rescue of 1908. Nothing at all is known of Smith, although his medals are now in a private collection.

JAMES KENNEDY CHAPMAN and ARCHIBALD WILSON

Date of Deed: November 27, 1908
Date of Gazette: July 23, 1909

On the 27th November, 1908, workmen were engaged painting the inside of an iron tank in the stokehold of a steamer lying in dry dock at Jarrow.

Owing to the fact that very strong fumes were given off by the anti-corrosive paint or solution used the men were working in relays, each squad of three men being relieved after 10 or 15 minutes had elapsed.

A workman named Graham was overcome by the fumes, and the chargeman, Archibald Wilson, sacrificed his life in endeavouring to save Graham.

Thomas McCormack, who had already been affected by the fumes while at work in the tank, went to Wilson's assistance, but was himself rendered insensible and was rescued by James Kennedy Chapman, Works Manager at the Dock, who, having pulled McCormack out, re-entered the tank and endeavoured to save Graham, but was himself overcome by the fumes.

The rescue of Chapman and Graham was eventually effected from the top of the tank.

James Kennedy Chapman and Thomas McCormack were each awarded the **Albert Medal of the Second Class (Land).** Archibald Wilson was awarded a posthumous **Albert Medal of the Second Class (Land)** for this incident, the first posthumous award of the Albert Medal, which was presented to his widow, Mrs Isabella Wilson, by the Deputy Mayor of South Shields on August 18, 1909. He was born on October 15, 1867 in Sunderland, County Durham. He married Isabella Graham on December 25, 1895 at St Jude's Church, South Shields and they had six sons and two daughters. The whereabouts of his AM are unknown. James Chapman's AM is now in a private collection.

This case is noteworthy in that Thomas McCormack was the senior Albert Medallist to exchange his original award for the George Cross in 1971. His Albert Medal was donated to the Bede Gallery, Springwell Park, Jarrow-upon-Tyne. He died in 1973, aged 87.

JAMES VIVIAN REED and HENRY SMITH

Date of Deed: December 28, 1908
Date of Gazette: July 23, 1909

On the occasion of the earthquake at Messina on the 28th December 1908, the steamship Afonwen, *of Cardiff, was lying at her moorings, having arrived at Messina on the 24th December.*

The first intimation the Master of the ship (Captain William Owen) had of the disaster was on being awakened in the early morning of the 28th December by the noise of the upheaval and the commotion caused by the tidal wave, but owing to the darkness and the dense clouds of dust the full extent of the disaster could not be realised for some time. The danger to shipping claimed the first attention of the Captain, but having satisfied himself as to the safety of his vessel he proceeded ashore with his crew, as the dawn broke, to render assistance.

The particular act of gallantry in respect of which the Albert Medal has been awarded was performed when a building of five storeys was reached, where children were noticed at a great height from the ground crying for help. The interior of the building had for the most part collapsed, and one of the walls had disappeared; the structure was therefore in a very dangerous condition.

The Captain having given the word, Henry Smith, Able Seaman, and, shortly after, James Vivian Reed, Second Mate, swarmed up a rope to the rescue of the children, who had lowered string by means of which the rope was hauled up and made fast. The rescue of the children having been effected, three persons were lowered down from a storey above.

James Vivian Reed and Henry Smith were each awarded the **Albert Medal of the Second Class (Sea).** Reed was presented with his award by HM the King at Buckingham Palace on June 22, 1909, while Smith received his from the King at St James's Palace on June 21, 1910.

While we know nothing of Henry Smith, nor the present whereabouts of his medal, that of James Vivian Reed was in the collection of the National Maritime Museum at Greenwich. However, it is now in the Mansion House at Cardiff. Reed was also awarded the Messina Medal, 1908, the British War Medal, Mercantile Marine War Medal, Victory Medal and the Order of the Crown of Italy (Knight).

THOMAS LEWIS

Date of Deed: July 2, 1909
Date of Gazette: December 21, 1909

Thomas Lewis

Image: Unknown

Soon after 5 P.M. on Friday, the 2nd July, 1909, a terrible accident occurred at the Alexandra Dock Extension Works, Newport, a heavily timbered trench, 238 feet long and about 50 feet deep and 35 feet wide having suddenly, and without warning, collapsed. The sides fell in and killed between 30 and 40 of the workmen who were engaged in excavating the trench, and seriously injured others.

Praiseworthy and determined efforts were immediately made by the workmen and others who happened to be close at hand to rescue the survivors, and these efforts were continued throughout the night.

At about 2 o'clock in the morning a man was discovered alive, his left arm having been caught between the elbow and the wrist, and he could only be reached by means of a small hole between two struts, too small for an ordinary man to go through. The boy Lewis volunteered to try and effect his rescue. He succeeded in getting underneath the man, and worked there for about one and a half to two hours, being eventually successful in releasing the man's arm. It then became possible to cut away the timber round about the man, and some time later he was extricated alive. There is no doubt that, but for the work which Lewis performed, the man could not have been rescued from his perilous position.

While Lewis was among the timbers, from 10 to 12 feet below the surface, he was in imminent peril of losing his life, for the ground was slipping and settling and the debris moving. It appeared as if any moment he might have been crushed by a further subsidence.

Thomas Lewis was awarded the **Albert Medal of the Second Class (Land)**, which was presented to him by the King at Buckingham Palace on December 13, 1909. Tom 'Toya' Lewis was born circa 1893. It appears he was something of a character, being a familiar figure in the local courts. After the incident, he was sent to Rosyth Dockyard for an apprenticeship but he does not seem to have stayed the course there. He joined the Special Reserve with a view later to joining the army. However, he changed his mind about this as he was then in good employment. He joined the Royal Welch Fusiliers with number 4439 on the outbreak of war and went to France on November 2, 1914. He was awarded the 1914 Star (without bar), British War and Victory Medals for his war service. He died in April, 1969. His medals are thought to be still with the family.

PAOLO BONNICI and ANTONIO DINGLI

Image: Grandson

Paolo Bonnici

Image: Unknown

Antonio Dingli

Date of Deed: May 31, 1909
Date of Gazette: March 1, 1910

On the night of the 31st May, 1909, and the early morning of the following day, men were engaged in emptying the cess pit of certain premises at Zabbar, Malta. The foul air in the pit rendered any lengthened period of work impracticable, and resulted in one of the men losing his life.

Antonio Dingli was the first man to descend, but he was compelled in a short time to return to the surface, for another to take up the task.

The next man to descend had almost regained the surface after a short absence, when he collapsed and fell back into the pit. Dingli descended at once, and succeeded in getting him to the pit opening when he himself lost consciousness, and both fell back into the pit.

Bonnici then tied a rope round his waist and descended to the rescue of his comrades. As he was unable to lift Dingli, a rope with a hook attached was lowered, and the rope having been made secure, Dingli was hauled up to the pit head in an apparently lifeless condition.

Bonnici was rescued by means of the rope.

The third man succumbed before he was brought to the surface.

Both men were awarded the **Albert Medal of the Second Class (Land)**, which was presented to them at a ceremonial parade on the Palace Square, Valletta, by the Governor of Malta, General Sir Leslie Rundle, on February 20, 1910. Antonio Dingli was born in Zabbar, Malta on December 16, 1861 and died there on March 3, 1942. Paolo Bonnici was born in Zabbar on December 24, 1882 and died there on April 4, 1959. Bonnici's AM is still with the family and it is probable that Dingli's is also.

THOMAS REYNOLDS

Date of Deed: January 21, 1910
Date of Gazette: April 26, 1910

The ill-fated express train left Sudbury, Ontario, for Minneapolis, at noon on the day in question in charge of Conductor Thomas Reynolds. It consisted of the engine, a mail and baggage car, an express-package car, a second class coach, a colonist car, a first class coach, a dining car, and a Pullman sleeping car and, as it approached the bridge crossing the Spanish River at a point where the stream is 250 feet wide and 30 feet deep, Conductor Reynolds and several passengers were seated at dinner in the dining car. On reaching the bridge a part of the train left the track and plunged down the embankment.

Two of the vehicles, a first class car and the dining car, crashed through the ice, which is said to have been 18 inches thick, and sank to the river bed. The first class car falling into some 15 feet of water, it is not likely that any of the occupants escaped. The dining car was almost completely submerged, and but for the resourcefulness and heroic conduct of the conductor the disaster would have resulted in a much heavier death toll.

The fore part of the car rapidly filled with water and the occupants hurled to the end of the car, were in danger of drowning in 10 feet of water, their situation being made more perilous by the accumulation of debris. Reynolds, on coming to the surface, found daylight entering from the top of a window some 6 inches above the level of the water, and, grasping a hat rack, he smashed with his feet the heavy plate glass windows. He then turned his attention to the imprisoned passengers, rescuing those in danger of drowning, and urging all to make use of the only means of support, namely, hat racks, lamps, &c. The passengers having been assisted in this way, he turned to effect an exit, only to find that the car had settled down, and that the opening made was submerged. After swimming about and locating the broken window with his feet, he dived and cautiously pushed himself through the window frame, in order that his body might not be swept away by the strong current.

With great difficulty he brought his body between the broken ice and the submerged car and succeeded in gaining a foothold on the top of the car. He at once commenced wrenching the fan lights from the roof and succeeded in rescuing a lad and still another passenger through the small opening thus made. When, shortly after, an axe was brought to him, in response to his cries for help, he enlarged the opening sufficiently to allow of the rescue of the other imprisoned passengers.

Thomas Reynolds was awarded the **Albert Medal of the First Class (Land),** which was presented to him by the Governor-General of Canada at Montreal on March 16, 1910. Thomas Arthur Reynolds was born in Ireland on August 13, 1862. He emigrated to Canada in 1875. He married Maude (née Downer) in 1892 and they had four children, a son and three daughters. He died at North Bay, Ontario, on March 6, 1928 and is buried there. The whereabouts of his Albert Medal are unknown.

✳✳✳

The following two awards were rather unusual, in that they were awarded more than ten years after the acts of gallantry described and it was at the instigation of Winston Churchill, who had been involved in the incident, that they were so recognised.

✳✳✳

CHARLES WAGNER and ALEXANDER JAMES STEWART

Date of Deed: November 15, 1899
Date of Gazette: June 14, 1910

On the 15th November, 1899, near Chieveley Station, in Natal, an armoured train which had been sent out on patrol was intercepted by the Boers and three carriages were thrown off the line. These vehicles lay between the rest of the train and the track over which it must travel on its homeward journey, and until they were removed the train, the engine and its escort – about 150 men – were exposed to a severe converging fire of rifles and artillery from the surrounding hills.

The sole means by which the line could be cleared was the engine, which moving to and fro butted the wreckage until after about 50 minutes' work it was heaved and pushed off the track. The part played by the driver of the engine, Charles Wagner, and by the fireman, Alexander James Stewart, was therefore indispensable to the rescue of the wounded with whom the engine and tender became crowded. The working of the engine itself was a difficult matter, because at each collision with the wreckage at which it was butting it might easily have been derailed.

The danger was exceptional. The heavy fire of shells and bullets inflicted many casualties, and more than one quarter of all in the train were killed or wounded. The shells repeatedly struck the engine and at any moment might have exploded the boiler. The driver, a civilian, under no military code, was wounded severely in the scalp by a shell-splinter almost immediately. Although in great pain he did not fail during the whole of this affair to manage his engine skilfully, and by clearing the line saved from death and wounds a proportion at least of the 50 or 60 persons who effected their escape upon the engine and its tender.

Both the driver and his fireman are still in the service of the Natal Government Railways.

Charles Wagner was awarded the **Albert Medal of the First Class (Land)** and Alexander James Stewart the **Albert Medal of the Second Class (Land)**, which was presented to them by the Acting General Manager of South African Railways at Johannesburg on August 16, 1910. Wagner's medal is now in the Durban Museum, Republic of South Africa. The whereabouts of Stewart's medal are unknown.

***

Almost thirty years had elapsed since the last award of the Albert Medal to a woman, although the event took place five years before the citation appeared.

***

CAROLINE HUGHES

Date of Deed: October 14, 1905
Date of Gazette: June 24, 1910

Caroline Hughes

Image: Unknown

On the 14th October, 1905, a fire occurred on the premises, 129, Clarendon-road, Hove, where two children named Austen, aged 11 and 4 years respectively, had been left at home by their mother who was out working. Mrs. Hughes, whose house was in the same street, and who was informed of the outbreak by her daughter, ran to the house and on entering found a paraffin lamp in flames on the table, and the two children crouching in the far corner, too frightened to move. She led them out one at a time, and in shielding them from the flames her dress caught fire.

Mrs. Hughes afterwards carried out the blazing lamp, and while doing so sustained serious injuries to her face, chest and arms, which eventually led to the amputation of her left arm two years later.

Caroline Hughes was awarded the **Albert Medal of the Second Class (Land)**, which was presented to her by the King at St James's Palace on June 21, 1910. Her arm having been amputated at the elbow, a fund was raised to purchase an artificial limb for her. The whereabouts of her Albert Medal are unknown.

ROBERT RALPH WILLIAMS

Date of Deed: March 11, 1910
Date of Gazette: December 30, 1910

Robert Ralph Williams

Image: D. Carpenter

On the 11th March, 1910, Mr. Williams noticed a large volume of water running down towards his school – a dam having burst on the mountain side – and realising that the girls' and infants' departments of the school were in great danger, he at once gave instructions for the boys to be dismissed, and rushed to give warning to the other departments, but not before the approach to the front of these schools was entirely cut off by an immense volume of water. His only route was through a doorway between the playground of the two departments. He unlocked this door and shouted to the children playing in the yard to make their escape to the boys' school yard, and one class escaped in this way. Mr. Williams afterwards opened the back doors of the girls' department, which all opened inwards, and closed the front door.

Mr. Williams then went to the infants' department, having to wade through a current up to his armpits. He satisfied himself that there was no imminent danger provided the walls of the girls' school could withstand the force of the water, and decided to take the girls to a slope near the back entrance of their school; but he found that the volume of water had greatly increased, and had burst in the front door and broken the lower parts of the windows. He succeeded, however, in entering the school and finally got all the children out safely, although the water inside the building was now fully four feet six inches in depth. While the last of the children were being rescued, a wall, eighteen yards long, ten feet high, and two feet three inches thick, which had formed a partial breakwater, was swept away, and the increased rush of water carried Mr. Williams out of the building, down a flight of steep steps, where he was severely bruised and narrowly escaped drowning. At the bottom of the steps he found about twenty girls struggling in six feet of water, and these he assisted to safety in the infants' school yard.

In the meantime, Mrs. Colville, an assistant teacher, and her class were caught in another corner of the yard, bounded by a high wall, which met the full force of the flood. She and the children were being whirled round by the torrent, but all were rescued by Mr. Williams, who, with a child in his arms, caught Mrs. Colville as she was sinking and being carried away.

Valuable assistance was rendered by Mr. Matthew Lewis and other members of the school staff.

Robert Ralph Williams was born on October 16, 1870, at Graigfach, Llanon, a small village on the Welsh coast between Aberystwyth and Cardigan. He was educated at University College, Cardiff, graduating in July 1894. His first appointment, in 1894, was as a teacher at Ferndale Infants' School but he resigned in December, 1895, to become Headmaster of Cwmclydach Boys' School in January, 1896.

Robert Ralph Williams was awarded the **Albert Medal of the Second Class (Land).** He subsequently had a distinguished career in education, being appointed an Assistant Inspector of Schools in 1913 and Inspector in 1914. In 1915, he was appointed Deputy Director of Education for the Rhondda and in March 1928, was appointed Director of Education for the Rhondda. Regretfully, he had to retire from this post due to ill-health and moved back to the family home at Llanon. In June, 1932, he was appointed OBE for services to education. The same year, he had an honorary MA conferred upon him for his contribution not only to education but also his interest in Welsh cultural interests throughout Wales. In October, 1942, he was appointed JP for the District of Carmarthen, a duty which he performed right up to his death, aged 77, in July, 1948. He was buried at Llwynteg Congregational Chapel, Llanon and his Albert Medal is now on display at the National Museum of Wales. Robert Williams was married about 1896 to Esther John and they had a son and two daughters. Their son, Vivian, a Captain in the army, was killed in action in France in May, 1917. Mr. Williams married again after the death of his first wife, to Miss Rachel Ann Jones, who had been his secretary. She died in 1970.

FRANK DIAMOND

Date of Deed: June 17, 1910
Date of Gazette: February 24, 1911

Image: Glendining Catalogue

Frank Diamond

On the 17th of June, 1910, Diamond saw one of the patients climbing a stack pipe at the (Claybury) Asylum, and, realising the man's danger, immediately followed him up the pipe. The man got on to the roof, at a height of about 37 feet, where Diamond reached him, and succeeded in supporting him until a rope and ladder were brought, and the patient was rescued unhurt.

Frank Diamond was awarded the **Albert Medal of the Second Class (Land),** which was presented to him by the King at St. James's Palace on February 23, 1911. He was aged 27 at the time of the incident and lived at Woodford Bridge in Essex, being employed at the Claybury Asylum. He served in World War One in the Norfolk Regiment with number 26285 being killed in action on May 19, 1917, aged 33 and buried in Mont Huon Military Cemetery, Le Treport, grave III.E.7A. He was the husband of M. Diamond, of 5 Canfield Road, Woodford Bridge. He was also awarded the British War and Victory Medals and his AM and other medals are now in a private collection.

FRANCES MAUDE WRIGHT

Date of Deed: December 26, 1910
Date of Gazette: February 24, 1911

On the 26th December, 1910, at about 1 a.m., Mrs. Wright had left her house to go to friends, when she saw a man running in her direction pursued by Police Constable Haytread. The man deliberately turned round – pausing to take aim – and fired at the constable; he then ran on, and again turned and fired a second shot. The constable was then close to his man, who fired a third time, before he was seized and a struggle ensued. Haytread called to Mrs. Wright to help and asked her to blow his whistle; she came up without hesitation, well aware of the risk, and got hold of the man's collar and struck him in the face with her fist. She then broke the police whistle off its chain and blew it. A severe struggle now ensued between the officer and the burglar, through which Mrs. Wright still retained her hold on the latter. He, however, got his arm free and again fired; locked with the constable he then fell to the ground and pressed the revolver against Haytread's head and pulled the trigger, but the weapon providentially missed fire. Mrs. Wright had in the meantime struck the man in the face and in so doing injured her left hand; her cries for assistance were probably responsible for bringing Seaman Barber to the spot. The burglar still held the revolver, but with further assistance he was overpowered.

Mrs. Wright is the wife of a newsagent's carman and has six children. But for her fearless action, the consequences might have been serious, and a most dangerous criminal (for he had previously attempted to shoot a constable) would not improbably have escaped.

Mrs. Frances Maude Wright was awarded the **Albert Medal of the Second Class (Land)**, which was presented to her by the King at St. James's Palace on February 23, 1911. The gunman in this case was one Charles Arthur, aged 31, who had been attempting to break into the Virginia Point public house in Great Dover Street. The brave PC Haytread was awarded the King's Police Medal for Gallantry for his actions. Mrs. Wright received a reward of £25 from the Police Fund. Her Albert Medal is believed to be still with her family.

AMY MADELINE JACQUES

Date of Deed: March 26, 1911
Date of Gazette: May 26, 1911

On the 26th March last her brother, Mr. Francis Jacques, was suddenly attacked by a bull, knocking him on the ground. A cowman who was with him at the time shouted for help, and Mr. Jacques, sen., aged 74, came to the yard and struck the bull on the head with his stick. The animal turned and tossed the old man, and again attacked the son. Mr. Jacques, sen., fortunately not seriously hurt, was dragged out of the yard by the cowman, and Miss Jacques, who had been attracted to the scene by the shouting, went to the house for a gun. She was afraid, however, of using the gun, as the bull had pinned her brother against a wall. With great presence of mind she got hold of the bull by its horns and pulled the head away, but was unable to release her brother. She ran to the house, and, bringing back the cowman, who was helping her father indoors, she again held the bull's horns, while the cowman dragged Mr. Francis Jacques, who was insensible and severely injured, into safety. Happily Miss Jacques escaped without injury, though narrowly, for the doorway through which she rushed on releasing her hold of the bull, was immediately charged by the infuriated animal.

Miss Jacques, who was forty years old at the time of this incident, was awarded the **Albert Medal of the Second Class (Land)**, which was presented to her by the King at Buckingham Palace on May 23, 1911. Its present whereabouts are unknown. The farm where the attack took place was Otterwood Farm at Beaulieu in Hampshire and it still exists today. There were at least three awards of the Edward Medal (Industry) for similar incidents to the above and one wonders why the AM was awarded in Miss Jacques' case.

PERCY HOPE MELLON

Date of Deed: February 24, 1911
Date of Gazette: May 26, 1911

Mr. Mellon is the lock-keeper at Iffley Lock, on the Thames, near Oxford, and the Albert Medal was awarded to him for bravery in saving the life of a woman who had fallen into the river. On the night of the 24th February the lock-keeper was called from his house and informed that a woman was in the river. He hastened to the spot, but owing to the darkness was unable to find any trace of the woman. Returning towards the lock he observed in the water a dark object which was rapidly carried by the strong stream and high wind towards the partly opened weir. Swimming towards it he discovered that it was a woman floating on her side apparently lifeless, and was able to bring her safely to land, aided by his son, who had pluckily swum out to his father's assistance. The woman was taken from the river unconscious, but she soon recovered, and was able to go home.

Percy Hope Mellon was awarded the **Albert Medal of the Second Class (Land)**, which was presented to him by the King at Buckingham Palace on May 23, 1911. The woman he rescued was a Mrs. Leslie, a cook at Court Place, Iffley, Oxford. The Royal Humane Society awarded Percy Mellon its Bronze Medal for his gallant rescue, while his son was awarded a Testimonial on Vellum for his part in the rescue. Percy Mellon was born in India in 1866, where he father was swerving with the 15th Hussars. He served in the Royal Navy for ten years, transferring to the Coastguard Service after he left the navy. He was married to Mary Cooper and they had four sons. After he left the Coastguard, he worked for the Thames Conservancy, with whom he was employed when he was awarded the AM. He retired in 1924 and died on March 2, 1935, aged 69. His Albert Medal and other memorabilia relating to him are now held by the River and Rowing Museum at Henley-on-Thames.

ALBERT SWAINSTON

Date of Deed: February 28, 1911
Date of Gazette: July 11, 1911

Albert Swainston

Image: Unknown

On the 28th of February a boy, aged thirteen, went for a walk along the bank of the river Tees, with some companions, and, while playing with a piece of wood in the water, overbalanced and fell into the river, which was running very high and almost 12 ft. deep. Albert Swainston, an apprentice plumber, being called to the spot by the cries of the boy's companions, immediately jumped into the river, fully dressed, and swam towards the boy, who was then about 22 yards from the bank. He got hold of the boy, and struck out for the bankside, but, owing to a strong current of water, he lost his grip.

He soon recovered the boy again, and, after considerable difficulty, brought him to the side of the bank, where he managed to get hold of a wall which projects from the bankside, but, owing to his exhausted condition and the boy's continued struggles, he was unable to pull the boy up, and the current of water carried him away. The lad went under the water, and this time did not rise to the surface, and Swainston was too exhausted to attempt again to rescue him.

Albert Swainston was awarded the **Albert Medal of the Second Class (Land)**, which was presented to him by the King at Buckingham Palace on July 6, 1911. He was also awarded the Royal Humane Society's Bronze Medal. Swainston was born circa December, 1892 at Blackwell, Co. Durham. He served in World War One with 160 (Wearside) Brigade, Royal Artillery, enlisting on March 17, 1915 (Army No. L/11521) at Darlington, giving his home address as 36, Beaconsfield Street, Darlington, where he followed his trade as a plumber. He served in France and Germany for a total of 5 years and 15 days, being demobilised on May 17, 1919 and then residing at 14, Bartlett Street, Greenbank, Darlington. He was awarded the British War and Victory Medals for his war service. The whereabouts of his Albert Medal are unknown.

ROBERT DUNN DOW

Date of Deed: August 30, 1906
Date of Gazette: September 26, 1911

Image: Family

Robert Dunn Dow

On the 30th August, 1906, a fire broke out in one of the Magazines of the Ferozepore Arsenal comprising 5 cells, in which were stored cordite, small arms' ammunition and gunpowder. At an early stage the ends of one of the outer cells (No. 10) were blown out by an explosion of cordite, while from cell No. 9, where small arms' ammunition was stored, smoke was seen to be issuing.

Major-General Anderson, who directed the subsequent operations from a roof at the edge of the Magazine Compound, at a distance of some 20 yards, having ordered all persons to be cleared out of the fort, and placed a cordon round it at 1,000 yards distance, a steam fire engine was got to work, and the fire party which had been organized commenced their highly dangerous task of clearing cell No. 8, in which was stored some 19,000 lbs. of gunpowder; they eventually succeeded in so doing, thereby cutting off the fire by the intervention of the empty cell. Had the powder in this cell exploded, the explosion must have been communicated to cells in an adjoining magazine, where 300,000 lbs. of gunpowder were stored.

Captain Donovan volunteered to clear cell No. 8, and led the fire party, and all concerned acted with the greatest coolness in circumstances calling for a high degree of courage. The door of the cell was opened and the fire hose turned on. Major Campbell joined the party by the cell, and returned in a short while and reported to General Anderson that though the cell was full of smoke, and the barrels hot, there was no actual fire in the cell. As, however, the explosions in the ruined cell No. 10 were becoming more violent, General Anderson, fearing that the barrels of powder which were being removed from cell No. 8 would be ignited, ordered the discontinuance of efforts to clear the cell; the pumping engine was, however, kept at work by Mr. Dow and some native assistants.

A series of heavy explosions of cordite now took place, and on the occurrence of a lull, Captain Clarke went to reconnoitre, and reported that cell No. 9 was still apparently intact. Major Campbell and Mr. Pargiter subsequently went into the enclosure to investigate, and on their report being received a party including 50 lascars was organized, and the removal of the powder barrels in cell No. 8 was recommenced under cover of the fire hose. During their removal the last important explosion of cordite took place some 12 yards away. Eventually all the barrels were removed without accident.

Robert Dunn Dow was awarded the **Albert Medal of the Second Class (Land).** It is not known when he was presented with his award or by whom. One Albert Medal of the First Class and eight Albert Medals of the Second Class were awarded for this incident, the others being Charles Creagh Donovan (First Class), Charles Alexander Anderson, Malcolm Sydenham Clarke Campbell, Hugh Clarke, Frederick Handley, Henry Pargiter, Arthur James Robinson and George Smith, all of whom were servicemen. Mr Dow was married twice and had five sons, three of whom served in WWI. He died on October 31, 1932. His family still has his Albert Medal.

ALGERNON EDWARD MANN

Image: Family

Algernon Edward Mann

Date of Deed: February 25, 1911
Date of Gazette: September 26, 1911

On the afternoon of Saturday, the 25th February, 1911, when the Steamship "Leicestershire", of the Bibby Line, was being brought alongside the Sule Pagoda Wharf, Rangoon, a Cingalese servant, who was leaning against a loose railing, fell overboard between the vessel and the Wharf, striking his head against the edge of the Wharf in falling, and was in imminent danger of being drowned or crushed between the incoming steamer and the Wharf.

Mr. Mann was awaiting the arrival of the vessel, and at great risk to his own life, for the moving vessel was only a few feet away at the time, immediately started to clamber down the stanchions of the Wharf. He slipped and fell into the river, but was able to reach the drowning man, and swim with him to one of the stanchions, where he supported him until ropes were lowered, and both were rescued.

Algernon Edward Mann was awarded the **Albert Medal of the Second Class (Sea),** which was presented to him by the Lieutenant-Governor of Burma at Rangoon on February 27, 1912. Mr Mann was born in Wexford, Ireland, on September 22, 1887. Educated at Brighton House School, Redland, Bristol and Dean Close School, Cheltenham, he trained as a civil engineer. In August, 1899, aged 11, he saved two people from drowning at Fishguard, South Wales, earning for himself the Bronze Medal of the Royal Humane Society. After qualifying, he was appointed Assistant Engineer of the Rangoon Municipality and on January 24, 1911, was commissioned into the Rangoon Volunteer Rifles. He served throughout WWI in Gallipoli and Mesopotamia, being twice Mentioned in Despatches. By the end of the war, he had attained the rank of Lieutenant-Colonel in the Royal Engineers and was appointed OBE in the *London Gazette* of June 3, 1918. After the war, he returned to his civilian occupation and also to the Rangoon Volunteer Rifles, where he was awarded the Volunteer Decoration (India) in about 1923. He married Sylvia Spankie after the war and they had two sons. He was awarded the Silver Jubilee Medal in 1935 and the Defence and War Medals for his war service with the Royal Engineers in the United Kingdom. He retired to Hom Lodge, Ross-on-Wye, Herefordshire and died at Cheltenham on June 6, 1949. There is a memorial to him in Iken Church, Suffolk. His medals are still proudly held by his family.

JAMES MOULDER

Image: Unknown

Date of Deed: July 12, 1911
Date of Gazette: October 13, 1911

On the 12th July last, Mr. Petty, aged 72, a manufacturer of fireworks, was at work in one of the sheds of his factory at Barton Moor, near Manchester, charging bombs, when an explosion occurred, followed a few moments later by a second and more violent explosion. As a result of the explosions the shed was partially wrecked and set on fire, while Mr. Petty was hurled to the ground and pinned down among the burning debris. His son, who was approaching the shed at the time, was caught and knocked down by the second explosion. Mr. James Moulder, a farmer, was working in a field about one hundred and fifty yards away, and, on hearing the first explosion, ran towards the shed. He had covered about forty yards when the second explosion occurred, and he saw Mr. Petty's son knocked down, but, regardless of the risk of further explosions, he ran on, and, entering the burning shed, brought Mr. Petty out from amongst the mass of burning wreckage and exploding fireworks to a place of safety.

James Moulder was awarded the **Albert Medal of the Second Class (Land)**, which was presented to him by the King at Buckingham Palace on May 23, 1911. He was born in 1876, the son of James Moulder, Senior, in Willenhall, Staffordshire and had two brothers. James, Junior, had five children; three daughters and two sons. He died in June, 1956, aged 80. The family still has his Albert Medal.

JACK HEWITT

Image: Roger Drury

Date of Deed: May 11, 1911
Date of Gazette: October 13, 1911

On the evening of May 11th last a boy friend of Hewitt's, named Drury, aged nine, was playing on the quay by the side of the River Ouse at Goole, when he overbalanced and fell into ten feet of water. As the river at that point is as broad as the Thames at London Bridge, and a strong tide was flowing, Drury, who could not swim, was in immediate danger of being swept away and drowned. Hewitt, a lad but one year older than his companion, without a moment's hesitation, jumped into the river to his rescue, fully dressed, and, though both were carried out some yards by the tide, succeeded in seizing Drury, and after skilfully controlling his struggles and turning him over on his back, brought him in to the bank, where both were helped out.

Jack Hewitt was awarded the **Albert Medal of the Second Class (Land),** one of two ten-year-old boys to receive it, which was presented to him by the King at Buckingham Palace on October 10, 1911. He was also awarded their Bronze Medal by the Royal Humane Society and a silver watch by the Carnegie Hero Fund Trust. He later qualified BSc and worked for the local electricity company. In 1928, he was enquiring whether he was entitled to the use of post-nominal initials "AM", since the original authorisation of 1916 only applied to service personnel. He was born on July 21, 1900 and died at Houghton-le-Spring, Co Durham, on September 28, 1971, missing by only one month the exchanges of the Albert Medal for the George Cross. The whereabouts of his Albert Medal are unknown but it is probably still with the family.

ARTHUR JAMES DYE

Date of Deed: September 30, 1911
Date of Gazette: December 12, 1911

Arthur James Dye

Image: D. Durrant

The Steam Drifter "Marie", when about 65 miles N.E. by N. of Haisborough Lightship, North Sea, at 10 p.m. on the 30th September, 1911, shipped a heavy sea, which broke the skylight, flooded the cabin, and extinguished the cabin light. The mate, who was in his berth asleep, was awakened by the sudden inrush of water, and, finding the cabin in darkness, lit a match. Immediately the gas from a tin of carbide of calcium exploded, and the cabin was set on fire.

The Skipper, Arthur James Dye, hurried below from the wheelhouse, seized the burning tin in his hands, and threw it into the galley, from which it was rolled on to the deck. Dye seized it again and tried to push it overboard. It rolled inboard at the first attempt, but he again took hold of it, and ultimately managed to throw it overboard.

In rendering these services Dye's left hand and his face were badly burnt, and on arrival in port he had to receive treatment at the hospital. A gale was blowing at the time, with a heavy sea.

Arthur James Dye was awarded the **Albert Medal of the Second Class (Sea)**, which was approved by the Councillors of State on November 11, 1911, owing to the absence of the King at the Delhi Durbar. Dye was presented with his award by the King at Buckingham Palace on March 6, 1912. He was born in Corton, Suffolk, on January 24, 1872, the son of Charles and May Dye. After the incident described above, he had to leave his occupation of fisherman and in later life became a Trinity House pilot at Great Yarmouth. He died around December 1948 at Gorleston and is buried in Gorleston churchyard. His AM is believed to be still with his family.

EDWARD BELL

Date of Deed: July 11, 1911
Date of Gazette: April 5, 1912

Image: Unknown

Edward Bell

On the 11th July, 1911, a disastrous fire broke out in the neighbourhood of South Porcupine, Ontario, destroying the town and a mining camp, and the perilous situation of the inhabitants was aggravated by a sudden tornado.

A party, including the manager of the Mines and his family and two employees of the mining company, managed with great difficulty to pass through the smoke and flames to some water barrels, but then collapsed from exhaustion, and were unable to use the water so as to keep their clothes from catching fire from the showers of sparks.

Bell, notwithstanding the dense smoke, which had incapacitated the party, went to their rescue, and stood by them for nearly two hours, damping their clothes, and by this and other means preventing further injury by fire. By his courageous action he was instrumental in saving the lives of seven persons.

Edward Bell was awarded the **Albert Medal of the Second Class (Land)**. He was also awarded the Silver Medal of the Society for the Protection of Life from Fire. Both medals are now in a private collection.

NEIGHBOUR

Date of Deed: February 1, 1911
Date of Gazette: May 7, 1912

Neighbour

Image: National Museum of Australia

On the 1st February, 1911, Neighbour, who had been placed under arrest, was being conveyed to the Roper River Police Station by William F. Johns, a trooper of the Police Force of the Northern Territory. On the morning of the day in question the Wilton River – which was found to be in full flood – had to be crossed, and Johns, who was on horseback, and was holding in his hand the neck chain by which Neighbour was secured, set the prisoner to swim in front of him whilst he followed. The horse got into difficulties in mid-stream, and before the trooper could clear himself he was kicked in the face by the animal and carried off by the current. Neighbour, instead of using the opportunity of making his escape, went to Johns' assistance and brought him ashore with great difficulty and at the risk of his own life.

Neighbour, an Aboriginal and the first of his race to receive an official gallantry award, was awarded the **Albert Medal of the Second Class (Land)**, which was presented to him by the Administrator of the Northern Territories on December 16, 1912. It was to be retained by the Aborigine Department and worn on special occasions. Trooper Johns subsequently became a Commissioner of Police and always regarded Neighbour's action as one of exceptional gallantry. Johns himself weighed over 12 stone and Neighbour a mere 10 stone. Moreover, when the Wilton River was in flood, it was literally alive with crocodiles. Neighbour died in June, 1954, at Nutwood Downs Station, where he had worked for some years. His exploit was featured in an edition of the *Eagle* comic. Neighbour's AM is now in the National Library of Australia, Canberra.

ALFRED BARLOW and WILLIAM D. MCKAY

Date of Deed: January 26, 1912
Date of Gazette: September 12, 1912

While James Edward Morgan was bathing at Lane Cove, Sydney, New South Wales, on the 26th of January, 1912, he was attacked by a shark when some distance from the shore.

In response to his cries for help, Alfred Barlow and William D. McKay, who were in the water, went to his assistance, and succeeded in bringing him to land. While they were actually engaged in doing so, the shark made a second attack on Morgan, and inflicted injuries to which he succumbed.

The rescuers were fully aware of the danger, and incurred very considerable risk in rendering their services.

Alfred Barlow and William D. McKay were each awarded the **Albert Medal of the Second Class (Sea)**. The whereabouts of their Albert Medals are unknown.

ARTHUR HANSON

Date of Deed: November 13, 1911
Date of Gazette: November 19, 1912

On the day in question (13th November, 1911) a number of houseboats containing foreign refugees from Szechuan were proceeding down the Yangtze River, and in one of the gorges encountered a strong wind blowing against the current, with a result that several boats were caught in a dangerous whirlpool. With one exception the boats were brought out of the whirlpool by the strenuous efforts of those on board, but the remaining boat, which contained several women and children, was left drifting in the whirlpool in a perilous position, her rudder having been broken off. At great personal risk Mr. Hanson, who was on shore some considerable distance away, swam out with a rope tied round him, and succeeded in attaching this to the boat, which by this means was safely pulled to land.

Arthur Hanson, an employee of Burroughs Wellcome and Company, was awarded the **Albert Medal of the Second Class (Land)** the whereabouts of which are presently unknown. He was presented with his award by the Consul-General at Shanghai on March 27, 1913.

ELIZABETH HOLLEY

Date of Deed: November 22, 1912
Date of Gazette: January 31, 1913

The KING has been pleased to approve of the **Albert Medal of the Second Class (Land)** *being awarded to Miss Elizabeth Holley, a nurse at Kingsdown House, Box, in the county of Wilts, in recognition of her gallantry in endeavouring, at great risk to her own life, to save the life of a lady patient who, while in her charge, was killed by an express train at Box Station, on the Great Western Railway, on the 22nd November last.*

Elizabeth Holley was presented with her award by the King at Buckingham Palace on February 6, 1913. This is a very bald citation. It would appear that Miss Holley was in charge of a Lucy Geraldine Deykin, aged 36, an inmate of Kingsdown House, when she broke away from the nurse and leapt on to the line, flinging herself in front of the express, which was travelling at 60 mph, and was cut to pieces. Nurse Holley made a brave attempt to save her and was almost herself pulled under the train, which tore the cuff off her dress, but she saved herself by half a second. Despite determined efforts, it has not been possible to discover anything at all about this heroic woman nor the whereabouts of her medal.

GEORGE EDWARD BENNETT

Date of Deed: December 28, 1911
Date of Gazette: August 26, 1912

George Edward Bennett

Image: Unknown

On the 28th December last while an exhibition was being given at the Empire Cinema Palace, Slough, some cinematograph film, which a boy, aged 13 years, was rewinding, caught fire. In response to the boy's shouts an operator from the adjoining operating chamber tried to put out the fire with a wet blanket, but the flames were too fierce for his efforts to prove successful. Mr. Bennett, the proprietor, was in the hall, and on learning that the boy was in the rewinding room, he at once climbed the vertical iron ladder leading to the trap-door of the room, from which volumes of flame and smoke were issuing. On entering the room he found the boy lying on the floor, and succeeded in dragging him to the trap-door and down the ladder into the hall, and thus saved the boy's life. Some 5,000 feet of film were destroyed. Mr. Bennett was badly burned, and ran very serious risk to his own life.

Mr. Bennett was awarded the **Albert Medal of the Second Class (Land)**, which was presented to him by the King at Buckingham Palace on August 12, 1913. He was also awarded the Silver Medal of the Society for the Protection of Life from Fire. The boy whose life he saved was Gerald Whitaker, who had dropped a lighted fragment of a cigarette on to some film. Two ironies of all this was that the film showing at the time was entitled "A Fire at Sea" and Mr. Bennett was a member of the Windsor Volunteer

Fire Brigade. He was in the King Edward Hospital, Slough, for three weeks with serious burns to his face and ears. The whereabouts of his Albert Medal are unknown.

GEORGE FREDERICK IRISH

Image: Redditch Advertiser

George Frederick Irish

Date of Deed: April 27, 1913
Date of Gazette: August 26, 1913

On the 27th April, 1913, while young children were playing at Redditch, Worcestershire, on a piece of ground through which a sewer was being carried, a boy, one of their number, fell into the sewer and disappeared. Attracted by the children's cries, Irish ran to the spot, where the sewer was open for some 30 or 40 yards. The boy was not to be seen, but the place where he had fallen in having been pointed out, Irish jumped into the sewer, which was 2½ feet wide and 14 feet deep with perpendicular sides, and with some difficulty succeeded in finding the child in the water at the bottom. He lifted him out and found him to be insensible. The water was level with the rescuer's head, and owing to the narrowness of the sewer and the steepness of the sides he was unable to climb out, so he had to support the boy until assistance arrived. The child was apparently dead, but by the aid of artificial respiration he was brought round and recovered.

George Irish was awarded the **Albert Medal of the Second Class (Land),** which was presented to him by the King at Buckingham Palace on August 12, 1913. Irish was unable to work for three days, suffering from exposure and shock. In addition to his Albert Medal, the Carnegie Hero Fund Trust presented him with a silver watch and £5. George Irish was born in 1892 at Redditch in Worcestershire. Before WWI, he worked for his uncle who was a coal merchant. He enlisted in the 14th Battalion the Gloucestershire Regiment (a Bantam unit) with the number 27465 and was killed in action on August 22, 1916, aged 23. He has no known grave but is commemorated on the Thièpval Memorial on the Somme, pier and face 5A and 5B. His name is also recorded on the Redditch War Memorial. He was awarded the British War and Victory Medals for his war service and his medals are still proudly held by his family.

HERBERT FREDERICK EWINGTON

Date of Deed: July 1, 1913
Date of Gazette: December 19, 1913

Image: Unknown

Herbert Fredrick Ewington

On the 1st of July last a fitter in the employment of the Metropolitan Railway, while crossing the permanent way at Aldersgate Street Station, slipped and fell across a live electric rail. Whilst a porter was fetching the insulating rubber gloves – without which it is considered very dangerous to touch anyone who is in contact with a live rail – a train was seen entering the Station on the same line. At that moment Ewington jumped on to the line and managed to pull the man's leg clear of the rail, though he received several shocks in doing so; and he succeeded in getting the injured man into safety between the two sets of rails before the train was pulled up a few feet away. The danger was increased by the fact that another train was approaching in the opposite direction. Had it not been for Ewington's exceptional bravery, there is little doubt that the fitter, who was unable to release himself, and whose leg was badly burned, would have lost his life.

Herbert Frederick Ewington was awarded the **Albert Medal of the First Class (Land),** which was presented to him by the King at Buckingham Palace on December 16, 1913. Ewington was a waiter at Spiers and Pond Restaurant in London. He was aged 29 at the time of the incident, having been born in 1884. He was married to Florrie Trent at St Mark's, Dalston, on August 15, 1909. He had previously saved a man from drowning at Brighton, for which he was given a gold watch and chain. He went on to serve in World War One as a Corporal with the Army Ordnance Corps (number 034470), for which he received the British War and Victory Medals. His medals are now in a private collection.

JOHN JONES

Date of Deed: May 13, 1913
Date of Gazette: February 24, 1914

Image: Family

John Jones

As a passenger train, travelling about seven miles an hour, was entering Pontypool Road Railway Station, on the 13th May, 1913, a boy of fifteen fell from the platform on to the rails, when the train was only twenty yards away. Jones, who was waiting on the platform, at once jumped down, and, as there was not time to lift the boy on to the platform, lay down between the rails and the platform and held the boy on his breast until the train had passed. Neither was injured, but it is evident that the boy owes his life to the courage and presence of mind displayed by Jones.

John Cynon Jones was awarded the **Albert Medal of the Second Class (Land)**, which was presented to him by the King at Buckingham Palace on February 12, 1914. He was also awarded a silver watch by the Carnegie Hero Fund Trust. Aged 28 at the time of the incident, John Jones was born in January, 1885 at Mynydd Islwyn, Monmouthshire. He was a collier at Blackwood at the time of the rescue. He was married with one daughter. He served during World War One with 2/1 Glamorgan Yeomanry, going to France on May 31, 1916. He was invalided out on September 20, 1918 and received the British War and Victory Medals for his service. He is believed to have died at Weston-super-Mare, Somerset, some time in the early 1960s. His medals and the watch are now in a private collection.

HUGH ADAMSON

Date of Deed: December 3, 1913
Date of Gazette: July 3, 1914

Image: The Irish Independent

Hugh Adamson

On the afternoon of the 3rd December last the manager of the Banbridge Gasworks, County Down, was engaged in examining a gas exhauster which had become choked, when a loud explosion occurred, blowing out the window of the engine-house. Hugh Adamson, who is a labourer employed at the Gasworks, had just left the engine-house on a message for the manager, and was thrown down by the force of the explosion. On getting up he saw the exhauster house in flames, and, hearing the manager's call for help, burst open the door, which had jammed. He found the manager enveloped in flames, but managed to drag him outside and then collapsed. On recovering Adamson succeeded in turning the gas into another gasometer, thereby saving the premises from being blown up, though the engine-house was actually destroyed. Adamson was severely burned, and the manager succumbed to his injuries a few days later.

Hugh Adamson was awarded the **Albert Medal of the Second Class (Land)**, which was presented to him by the King at St James's Palace on June 29, 1914. The Carnegie Hero Fund Trust also presented him with £10. He was born on January 17, 1855, in Banbridge, Co Down, the son of Joseph Adamson and Martha (née Williams). Nothing is known of his early life. His trade was painter and decorator. He married Margaret Robinson on April 2, 1877, in Scapatrick Parish, Banbridge. They had one son. Hugh died on July 31, 1920, and is buried in Forrestdale Cemetery. His wife died on February 24, 1923, and is buried with him. His Albert Medal is believed to be still with his family.

JAMES JULIAN CARTER

Date of Deed: May 10, 1914
Date of Gazette: March 19, 1915

On the day in question (10th May, 1914) Carter was on the engine of a train running between Havelock and Smith's Falls in the province of Ontario. The train was rounding a curve near Tweed at a speed of about 18 miles an hour, when Carter, who was on the inside of the curve, saw the child trying to cross the line 200 feet ahead. He shouted to the driver to stop, and immediately made his way along the footboard to the "pilot" on the front of the engine. Realising that the train, the speed of which had been reduced to about 8 miles an hour, could not be pulled up in time, he jumped from the engine and, rushing forward, just succeeded in rescuing the child, falling with her into the ditch at the side of the line. The train was stopped when the engine and 8 coaches had passed the spot where the child was rescued.

James Julian Carter was awarded the **Albert Medal of the Second Class (Land)**, which was presented to him in Ottawa by HRH the Duke of Connaught, the Governor-General of Canada. The little girl whose life was saved was Violet Freeman, aged 3, of Tweed, Ontario. Carter was born in 1884 at Havelock, Ontario and was married to Jennie Loucks on October 4, 1905. They had two daughters, one of whom worked for the Secretary of State at Ottawa. Having joined the CPR at Havelock in 1903, he retired from the CPR at the beginning of 1946 to his home in Renfrew, north Ontario, having served for 43 years. The whereabouts of his Albert Medal are unknown. Violet became Mrs Robertson and died on January 20, 2010, aged 97.

WALTER RUSSELL BROWN

Date of Deed: September 13, 1913
Date of Gazette: July 16, 1915

This was the last Albert Medal to a civilian to be earned for an act of gallantry prior to the outbreak of the First World War.

Walter Russell Brown

Image: John Tamplin

On the 21st September, 1913, when fierce street fighting was raging in the City of Chungking, Mr. Brown, assisted by his French colleague, Monsieur Bodard, in response to a message from the Chamber of Commerce, acted as an intermediary between the two forces, and succeeded in bringing about a suspension of the hostilities. Both the officers ran great risk, as they were frequently exposed to the firing of the troops, and but for their prompt intervention it is probable that the fighting would have resulted in one body of troops being exterminated and the City, which contains a population of between 300,000 and 400,000 inhabitants, many of them British subjects, being pillaged and burnt to the ground.

Walter Russell Brown was awarded the **Albert Medal of the Second Class (Land)**, which was presented to him by the King at Buckingham Palace on July 12, 1915. He was born on May 12, 1879, the son of Walter Edward Brown. He had a distinguished career in the Consular Service in China, where he spent his entire career, commencing as a student interpreter in 1901. He retired as a Consul–General in 1932. He was gazetted CBE (Civil) in the *London Gazette* of January 1, 1931. In 1908, he married Helen Maud Armstrong. He was a JP for Devonshire from 1943 to 1948 and he died on February 27, 1966. The whereabouts of his Albert Medal are unknown.

1915 – 1919

Looking at the roll of Albert Medallists for this period, it is clear that by far the majority of recipients of the AM were service personnel and members of the mercantile marine. There were very few awards indeed to civilians, other than Merchant Navy, as will become apparent.

JOSEPH CONNOLLY

Date of Deed: October 1, 1916
Date of Gazette: January 30, 1917

On the 1st October, 1916, the steamship "Vanellus", of Cork, struck a mine in Havre Roads, and the vessel, which was laden with petrol, immediately burst into flames.

Owing to the rapidity with which the flames spread it was impossible to clear away the boats, and most of the crew jumped overboard. Three lives were lost by the casualty (sic).

Although the engine-room telegraph was broken by the explosion Mr. Connolly remained at his post in the engine-room until everyone else had left the ship. He kept the engines working astern, and thus made it possible for a lifeboat to be lowered on the port side, and by this means a number of lives were saved.

Before finally leaving the ship he again went below and stopped the engines. Mr. Connolly was badly burnt in rendering the services.

Joseph Connolly, Third Engineer, S.S. "*Vanellus*", was awarded the **Albert Medal of the Second Class (Sea)**, which was presented to him by the King at Buckingham Palace on February 24, 1917. He was born in Belfast circa 1873. Eight months after the presentation of the AM, he was again at sea, this time as Second Engineer of the S.S. "*Aylevarroo*", sailing out of Limerick. On October 7, 1917, this ship was torpedoed by U-57 off Ballycotton Island, County Cork and was lost with all hands. Joseph Connolly, who was aged 44 at the time of his death, was the son of Martin and Mary Connolly of 20, Berkley Street, Liverpool and he is commemorated on the Tower Hill Memorial, London. He was also entitled to the Mercantile Marine War Medal, this now being in the collection of the author.

ROBERT JOHN FORBES

Date of Deed: August 21, 1916
Date of Gazette: March 27, 1917

On the 21st of August, 1916, at 2.30 p.m., a fire broke out at the works of the Low Moor Munition Company Limited. Three motor fire engines answered the alarm, one of which in the charge of the Chief Officer, drove into the yard of the premises, where a violent explosion had already taken place, while the other two remained outside. Another explosion took place almost immediately, injuring the Chief Officer and his chauffeur, and stunning Superintendent Forbes. On recovery Forbes went to the assistance of the Chief Officer and chauffeur, when a still more violent explosion occurred, killing seven firemen and seriously injuring twelve others, including Forbes. Forbes nevertheless brought the Chief Officer to a place of safety and returned and rescued two other injured firemen, who would otherwise have lost their lives. After driving the engines away from the yard, and thus saving them from danger, he collapsed. His injuries incapacitated him from duty for five weeks."

Robert John Forbes was awarded the **Albert Medal of the Second Class (Land)**. He was originally refused the Albert Medal and the award of the King's Police Medal was suggested (Fire Brigades at that time came under the control of the local constabulary) but apparently the Town Clerk of Bradford disagreed. Some discussion about the matter ensued and it was eventually decided that the appropriate award would be the Albert Medal, which was presented to Forbes by the King at Buckingham Palace on March 21, 1917. The whereabouts of his Albert Medal are unknown.

PETER THOMSON

Date of Deed: November 14, 1916
Date of Gazette: March 27, 1917

On the 14th November, 1916, the steamship "Polpedn", of London, was torpedoed in the English Channel, and rapidly began to sink.

The crew had just time to get into the starboard lifeboat and cut the painter, the steamer's bridge-deck then level with the water line, when the lifeline was found to be fastly coiled round Mr. Thomson's leg.

Realising the danger of the boat being capsized, Mr. Thomson at once jumped overboard, thus freeing the boat, and allowing her to be pushed away as the vessel foundered.

While under water, Mr. Thomson managed to free his leg from the lifeline, and he was afterwards picked up by those in the boat. Mr. Thomson ran the greatest possible risk of losing his life, and by his self-sacrifice undoubtedly prevented serious loss of life.

Peter Thomson, Second Officer, was awarded the **Albert Medal of the First Class (Sea)**, which was presented to him by the King at Buckingham Palace on April 13, 1918. His medals, which include the AM, British War, Mercantile Marine War and Victory Medals, are all now in the Castle Museum, Edinburgh.

JAMES CAMPBELL HURRY

Date of Deed: November 8, 1916
Date of Gazette: September 7, 1917

On the 8th November, 1916, while the steamship "Earl of Forfar", of Glasgow, was lying at Archangel, a fire broke out on a Russian steamship and spread to the "Earl of Forfar", which was lying immediately ahead. Captain Hurry, who was on shore, attempted to return to his vessel, but was unable to do so. He proceeded, however, to render assistance to other vessels which were in danger of being burnt. While doing so, he heard voices coming from his own ship, which was burning and exploding furiously. Calling for volunteers, he led them on board his steamer, and seven injured men were rescued, some of whom he personally carried to a tug. While thus engaged considerable risk was incurred by Captain Hurry, who had to lift several live shells from the deck of the vessel in order to get at the wounded.

Within ten minutes of the last man being rescued the deck blew up.

Captain James Campbell Hurry was awarded the **Albert Medal (Sea),** which was presented to him by the King at Buckingham Palace on November 14, 1917. He was born in Aberdeen on September 1, 1867, being 49 at the time of the incident and his home at the time was in Penarth, South Wales. However, when he was issued with his British War and Mercantile Marine War Medals in 1921, he was resident in Dyce, near Aberdeen. He held the rank of Lieutenant in the Royal Naval Reserve. On August 28, 1917, a Royal Warrant was issued which decreed that henceforth the Albert Medal of the First Class would be known as the Albert Medal in Gold and the Albert Medal of the Second Class would be known as the Albert Medal. Thus, Captain Hurry's award was the first civilian one to be described under the new nomenclature and its whereabouts are presently unknown.

EDGAR TWIDLE, WILLIAM FRANCIS GORDON MARTIN AND ROBERT MACBRYDE

Date of Deed: January 26, 1917
Date of Gazette: September 7, 1917

Image: TNA MN Records

Edgar Twidle

On the 26th January, 1917, a series of fires and explosions occurred at Economia, port of Archangel. When Captain Twidle arrived on the scene his ship was burning fiercely.
On being informed that the Chief Engineer was alive, Captain Twidle climbed on board but found that he was dead.

He then examined the other rooms and found a Chinese sailor in a dazed condition.
With the assistance of Mr. Martin and Mr. MacBryde this man was got over the ship's side across the ice and eventually to the Red Cross station.
About four minutes after the seaman had been removed the vessel blew up.

Edgar Twidle, William Francis Gordon Martin and Robert MacBryde were each awarded the **Albert Medal (Sea),** which was presented to them by the King at Buckingham Palace on March 23, 1918. Edgar Twidle was born at Blackheath, Kent, on February 10, 1880. He was also awarded the British War and Mercantile Marine War Medals. William Martin was born at Whithorn on November 24, 1887. He served in both wars in the merchant service and is thought to have died around 1950. Martin's AM is now in a private collection but the whereabouts of the others are presently unknown. Robert MacBryde died in Glasgow on July 6, 1918 and is buried in Craigton Cemetery.

JOHN DAVID BULMER

Date of Deed: January 31, 1917
Date of Gazette: September 7, 1917

On the 31st January, 1917, while the steamship "Rhydwen", of Cardiff, was lying at Genoa, a fire broke out in the ship's magazine.

A fire signal was immediately hoisted, but before assistance arrived Bulmer and Brown went below, unlocked the door of the magazine and got the hose at the seat of the fire.

Water was then played on the magazine and the ammunition was taken out on deck, and, owing to the prompt action of the ship's crew, the fire was extinguished. Considerable risk was incurred by Bulmer and Brown in rendering the service.

John David Bulmer and Private John Edward Brown R.M.L.I. (who appears in the first volume) were each awarded the **Albert Medal (Sea)**. Bulmer was the Boatswain of the "Rhydwen". He was born in Selby, Yorkshire in 1881 and was awarded the British War and Mercantile Marine War Medals for his WWI service. According to his papers, he died on July 24, 1928 while serving on board the *"Athelmonarch"*. The whereabouts of Bulmer's Albert Medal are unknown.

ALEXANDER MCINTYRE SPENCE

Date of Deed: July 3, 1917
Date of Gazette: October 30, 1917

On the 3rd July, 1917, while the steamship "Shuna" was anchored in the River Seine, a fire broke out among some cases of grenades which formed part of the deck cargo.

Captain Spence immediately hurried to the scene of the fire, but by the time he reached the spot, the cases were well alight. With a few buckets of water he succeeded in extinguishing the fire before the first hose could be started, and he then removed the charred cases. Later on some others caught alight, but the fire was got under by means of the hose.

Considerable risk was incurred by Captain Spence in rendering the service, and his prompt action undoubtedly averted an explosion and thus saved a great many lives.

Captain Alexander McIntyre Spence was awarded the **Albert Medal (Sea)**, which was presented to him by the King at Buckingham Palace on July 31, 1918. Captain Spence was born in Moray in 1866. He had been at sea since 1890 and served throughout the war. He was still at sea in 1933. The whereabouts of Spence's Albert Medal are unknown. There do not appear to be any papers in TNA, though he was probably entitled to the British War and Mercantile Marine War Medals.

ROBERT LEIPER LINDSAY AND JAMES STILL

Date of Deed: July 9, 1917
Date of Gazette: November 23, 1917

On the 9th July, 1917, one of the oil pipe valves at the Tembi Pumping Station of the Anglo-Persian Oil Company burst. The pressure at this point was 700 lbs. to the square inch, so that a great fountain of oil was thrown in all directions to a great height. The burst occurred within thirty yards of the open and glowing furnaces of the boilers, and it was obvious that a disastrous fire, involving the whole station and compound, which was populated by nearly three hundred natives, was a question of seconds.

The only means of averting a disaster was to turn off the oil fuel supply to the furnaces, thus extinguishing them, and to stop the pumps, thus cutting off the shower of oil.

Mr. Lindsay was near the furnaces; but to reach them it was necessary to pass through the oil shower, and thus arrive at the furnace doors soaked and dripping with oil. To do so meant almost certainly a terrible death, but Mr. Lindsay did not hesitate. Shouting to his assistant, Mr. Still, to turn off the pumps, he dashed through the oil, and had succeeded in turning off the first oil-cock, when the whole atmosphere burst into flame. He staggered away, but died from his injuries some hours later.

Meanwhile Mr. Still had succeeded in turning off most of the pumps when the fire burst out. He was cut off from all doors, but managed to escape by a window, stupefied by heat and smoke. He then sought for and found Mr. Lindsay, and having removed him returned to do what he could to limit the damage. Thanks largely to his efforts a new pumping-house, which had just been established, was saved.

Robert Leiper Lindsay was awarded the **Albert Medal in Gold (Land)**, which was presented to his father, Mr. John Lindsay of Moorfield House, Kilmarnock by the King at Buckingham Palace on February 9, 1918 and James Still the **Albert Medal (Land),** which was presented to him by the GOC Karun Frontier at Ahwaz on October 21, 1918. The whereabouts of both Albert Medals are unknown.

CHARLES JOHN CARNE

Image: Mrs L. M. Wale

Charles John Carne

Date of Deed: September 22, 1917
Date of Gazette: December 18, 1917

On the day in question a train loaded with ammunition was running to the coast when, on reaching a point near a town, a truck loaded with fuses was seen to be on fire. The train was stopped and the burning truck was detached, but in the meantime two other trucks containing large loaded shells became ignited. Carne, who had been summoned to the spot when the trucks had been burning for a considerable time, and had been warned of the great danger of an explosion, mounted one of the trucks and then took steps to put out the fire with the help of the engine-driver, fireman and guard. In spite of difficulties in getting water the fire was ultimately extinguished. Had it not been for the courage and resourcefulness of Inspector Carne a destructive explosion would probably have occurred, with loss of life and valuable material.

Charles John Carne was awarded the **Albert Medal (Land),** which was presented to him by the King on January 16, 1918. Charles Carne was born in Wales on February 13, 1869, one of three brothers. He commenced employment with the London Brighton and South Coast Railway in 1882, aged 13. In 1888, he was appointed porter at Thornton Heath and after passing through various grades, he was appointed Head Goods Guard in 1906. He was working at the company's head office at London Bridge when the above incident occurred. He married Lily May Rawson on September 14, 1891 and they had six children. Transferring to the Southern Railway at the grouping in 1923, Mr. Carne eventually became Stationmaster at Wimbledon Park, from where he retired in 1929. He died in October, 1952, aged 83. His Albert Medal is still with the family.

ANTHONY FARRER

Date of Deed: September 23, 1917
Date of Gazette: December 21, 1917

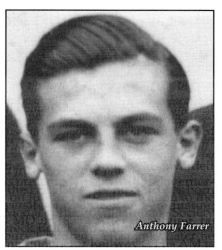

Image: Brentwood College

Anthony Farrer

On the 23rd September, 1916, the two children left their homes at Cowichan Lake for the purpose of catching their ponies and, when about half a mile from home, they were attacked by a cougar. They were almost upon the animal before they saw it crouching in a path at a corner. The little girl was first attacked; the cougar sprang upon her, and she was knocked down with her face to the ground, the animal being on her back. The boy at once attacked the cougar with his fists and riding bridle, and drove the animal off the girl; it then attacked him, and his companion, getting to her feet, came to his rescue, fighting with her clenched hands and bridle, and even putting her arm into the cougar's mouth, to try to prevent it from biting Anthony. She succeeded in getting it off the boy, and it stood on its hind-quarters and fought with her, but evidently it was disturbed by some sound, for presently it slunk away and ran under a log, where it was afterwards killed. The children, though both badly injured, were able to make their way home. The cougar measured over 7 feet from nose to tip of tail.

Doreen Ashburnham (aged 11) and Anthony Farrer (aged 8) were each awarded the **Albert Medal (Land),** which was presented to them by the Duke of Devonshire, on behalf of the King. Doreen Ashburnham survived to become a George Cross holder in 1971. Anthony Farrer eventually was commissioned into the Princess Patricia's Canadian Light Infantry and was sadly killed in an accident on a shooting range at Camp Hughes on July 9, 1930, aged only 21. In 1975, the Courage Brewery named one of their public houses in Street, Somerset, "The Albert Inn" as a tribute to the two children. The inn sign seems to have been removed in 1985; it is not known whether it has been reinstated. The whereabouts of Anthony Farrer's AM are unknown.

ALFRED WILLIAM FURNEAUX

Alfred William Furneaux

Image: TNA MN Records

Date of Deed: April 28, 1917
Date of Gazette: January 22, 1918

In April, 1917, the steamship in which Furneaux was serving was torpedoed by the enemy, and a Lascar, who was on the spot where certain deck plates had buckled and broken, had his legs so firmly caught between the plates that he would have gone down with the ship. Mr. Furneaux, however, went to the man's assistance and managed to get one leg out, but the other was nearly severed through above the knee. Finding it impossible to pull this leg out, Mr. Furneaux amputated it with an ordinary clasp knife and then carried the man to a boat. When in the boat he dressed the wound as well as possible, and gave the life belt he was wearing to the wounded man. Mr. Furneaux also rendered first aid in the boat to another Lascar who was badly scalded. Mr. Furneaux was in imminent danger of losing his life in rendering the service.

Alfred William Furneaux was awarded the **Albert Medal in Gold (Sea)**, which was presented to him by the King at Buckingham Palace on February 6, 1918. He was born in London on July 10, 1887 and spent most of his life at sea. He served throughout WWI, earning the British War and Mercantile Marine War Medals. He also served during WWII, being discharged as medically unfit on August 31, 1942. Presumably he would have been entitled to some campaign medals for WWII. He was a Chief Steward for much of his career. His Albert Medal is now in a private collection.

FREDERICK WRIGHT

Date of Deed: October 19, 1917
Date of Gazette: May 3, 1918

On the occasion of an enemy air raid which took place on the 19th October, 1917, a bomb fell on two adjoining houses, killing ten persons and imprisoning eighteen under the wreckage. When helpers arrived it was found that some of the persons who were imprisoned in the basement of one of the houses were alive, but the work of rescue was exceedingly dangerous, for escaping gas in the basement became ignited and set fire to the debris above. Inspector Wright, with an axe, made a small opening in the floor over the basement, which was in a slanting and tottering condition, the joists which supported it being broken, and through this opening, though with much difficulty, thirteen persons were rescued. It was then ascertained that two children were left in the basement, and Inspector Wright, with Police Constables Robert Melton and Jesse Christmas, dropped into the basement through the opening and searched for the children under very dangerous conditions. In addition to the fumes from the escaping gas, which were suffocating, and the fire raging above, there was a possibility of a further movement of wreckage, which might have proved fatal to all below. The space was so confined that they were barely able to reach the back of the premises. The children were found to be dead.

Inspector Wright, on reaching the open air, collapsed, overcome by the fumes and by his exertions; but, after medical care, he recovered sufficiently to be sent home. He returned to the scene of the disaster shortly after, and continued his work of rescue throughout the night.

Frederick Wright was awarded the **Albert Medal (Land)**. PCs Melton and Christmas received the King's Police Medal for Gallantry. Frederick Wright was born on March 4, 1868 in Southampton. He joined the Metropolitan Police on February 4, 1889, with warrant number 74225. He was promoted to Sergeant on October 7, 1898, becoming a Station Sergeant in January, 1904. He was promoted to Inspector on September 16, 1909 and transferred to 'L' Division, where he spent the whole of WWI. As a result of his bravery, he was promoted to Chief Inspector, without examination, on April 1, 1918. He resigned from the Metropolitan Police on February 16, 1920, after 31 years' service. In addition to his AM, he held the 1897 Metropolitan Police Jubilee Medal, the 1902 Metropolitan Police Coronation Medal and the 1911 Metropolitan Police Coronation Medal, all of which are now in a private collection.

CHRISTOPHER WATSON

Date of Deed: November 8, 1916
Date of Gazette: July 9, 1918

On the 8th November, 1916, a series of fires and explosions occurred at Bakarista, Port of Archangel, on merchant ships and on the wharves. The S.S. "Baron Driesen" had blown up at 1 p.m. and part of the S.S. "Earl of Forfar" forty minutes later. The latter ship, with a cargo of explosives, was on fire, and might have blown up at any moment, and explosions were continually taking place in the immediate vicinity. The ship was alongside the main fire on shore, and burning embers were constantly showered over her.

Lieutenant Richardson, 2nd Engineer Watson and Able Seamen Henry and Thompson, of the Tug "Sunderland", nevertheless volunteered to board the "Earl of Forfar" and effected the rescue of a considerable number of wounded and helpless men who would otherwise have perished.

They displayed the utmost gallantry and disregard of their own personal safety in saving the lives of others.

Second Engineer Christopher Watson was awarded the **Albert Medal (Sea),** as were the other three mentioned, who appear in volume one. The whereabouts of his Albert Medal are unknown.

REGINALD CURTIS CLAYTON

Date of Deed: March 24, 1918
Date of Gazette: August 27, 1918

In March last the steamship in which Mr. Clayton was serving was in collision, and a serious fire broke out on board. Mr. Clayton was aft, where the accommodation for the crew was situated. It was his fire-station duty to stand by the flood valve of the magazine; and, in spite of the whole of the deck being in flames, he groped his way through the fire, found the valve, and turned it on to "flood". He received such severe injuries that he succumbed in hospital four days later.

Those of the crew who survived no doubt owed their lives to the flooding of the magazine.

Apprentice Reginald Curtis Clayton was awarded a posthumous **Albert Medal (Sea),** which was presented to his father, Mr. C.C. Clayton, by the King. The ships involved were *S.S. O.B. Jennings* (American oil carrier) and *S.S. War Knight* (Clayton's ship), which was carrying naphtha. The collision took place in Freshwater Bay, Isle of Wight. Among ships involved in rescue work was *H.M.S. Garland* and two members of this ship's company received the Sea Gallantry Medal in Silver for their gallantry. They were Lieutenant E.S.F. Fegen RN (later to achieve immortality as the Captain of *H.M.S. Jervis Bay* in which he won a posthumous VC engaging the *Admiral Scheer*, thus allowing his convoy to escape) and C.P.O. Patrick Driscoll RN. Reginald Clayton was born in Sheffield in 1898. He was only 18 at the time of the incident. He was also awarded the British War and Mercantile Marine War Medals for his war service. Apprentice Clayton is not commemorated on any CWGC memorial, as his death was not attributable to enemy action. The whereabouts of his Albert Medal are unknown.

ROBERT COULSON

Date of Deed: April 12, 1918
Date of Gazette: August 27, 1918

The steamship in which Mr. Coulson was serving was struck by a torpedo in the stokehold. The engine-room became full of escaping steam, and Mr. Coulson and the fourth engineer were seriously scalded. Instead of making for safety, however, Mr. Coulson, in spite of his injuries, carried the fourth engineer, who was in a helpless condition, up the engine-room ladders to the top platform, out of immediate danger of steam and the inrush of water, and he then himself became exhausted.

The chief engineer, who had run to the engine-room from the bridge, assisted both the injured men out of the engine-room, and with help managed to get them into a lifeboat. After being landed they were taken to hospital, where both succumbed to their injuries.

Second Engineer Robert Coulson was awarded a posthumous **Albert Medal (Sea),** which was presented to Mrs Florence Coulson of West Hartlepool by the King at Buckingham Palace on October 24, 1918. He was born at West Hartlepool in 1884. He was awarded the British War and Mercantile Marine War Medals for his WWI service. He does not appear to be on the CWGC website. The whereabouts of his Albert Medal are unknown.

CHARLES MCKENZIE

Date of Deed: December 6, 1917
Date of Gazette: August 30, 1918

Image: John O'Malley

Charles McKenzie

A violent explosion, followed by a fire, occurred in one of the holds of the steamship in which Mr. McKenzie was serving, which had a cargo of petroleum and case oil. Four men were in the hold at the time, and received serious injuries.

Mr. McKenzie, who was on duty at the top of the hold, immediately rushed down, regardless of the possibility of further explosions, found the ship's carpenter, and assisted him to a sling, by means of which the man was hauled up on deck. Mr. McKenzie then searched the hold again and rescued a seaman in the same way. Both men, however, subsequently died of their injuries.

Mr McKenzie also found the third man, who was badly burnt and assisted him to mount the ladder. The fourth man managed to escape by his own exertions.

Chief Officer Charles McKenzie was awarded the **Albert Medal (Sea),** which was presented to him by the King at Buckingham Palace on December 11, 1919. He was born in Dundee in either 1872 or 1879 (both dates appear on his papers) and was at sea from at least 1900 until his death on December 24, 1931, by which time he had become a Master. He earned the British War and Mercantile Marine War Medals for his service in WWI. The incident in question took place in Port Melbourne, Australia. The whereabouts of his Albert Medal are unknown.

JOHN ALLAN

Date of Deed: June 12, 1918
Date of Gazette: September 20, 1918

Image: Unknown

John Allan

As the R.F.A. "Mixol" was dropping alongside to fuel one of H.M. Battle Cruisers on the 12th June, 1918, an Able Seaman slipped and fell overboard between "Mixol" and the Cruiser; "Mixol" was only about ten feet clear of the Cruiser, and was closing at the time. Donkeyman John Allan, who was standing on the fore well deck of "Mixol", saw the man fall and that he was struggling in the water. Although it was clear that the man in the water was in imminent danger of being crushed between the two ships, Allan at once jumped overboard in the clothes he was wearing to save him. He assisted the Able Seaman to keep afloat until a rope was thrown, which he gave to him, the Able Seaman being hauled on board before Allan took the rope himself.

The ship was in an open anchorage, and the temperature of the water was 50°.

John Allan was awarded the **Albert Medal (Sea).** He was born in South Shields, Co. Durham. His father, John, was a Master Mariner. He survived the war and left Mixol to go to HMS Eaglet in Liverpool on August 10, 1919. He was married to Selina and they lived at 546 Williamson Street, South Shields. The whereabouts of his Albert Medal are unknown.

MAURICE LISTER

Maurice Lister

Image: Unknown

Date of Deed: May 30, 1918
Date of Gazette: October 15, 1918

The steamship on which Lister was serving was torpedoed and at once began to settle down and finally disappeared twenty minutes after being struck.

Lister and a pantry boy, both of whom were on their first voyage, were below in a cooling chamber when the explosion occurred, and they both received serious injuries.

When Lister regained consciousness he found that both his ankles were helpless. He made his way to the top of the stairs, but found that the door was jammed. There was, however, a hatchway opening overhead, and Lister placed some of the planking, which had been blown up, against this opening in order to clamber up the planking and escape. Hearing cries of distress at this moment, however, he returned and searched the chamber on his hands and knees until he found the other boy with both legs broken, and managed by half dragging and half supporting him to get him up the planking to the steps leading to the deck. Other members of the crew then assisted both boys into boats, which were picked up after several days. The pantry boy, after being taken to hospital succumbed to his injuries.

Maurice Lister, assistant butcher, Mercantile Marine, aged 16, was awarded the **Albert Medal (Sea),** which was presented to him by the King at Buckingham Palace on March 25, 1920. The shipwrecked sailors spent nine days in an open boat before they were rescued. Maurice Lister was born in Haworth, Yorkshire, in 1902. He was only 15 when he signed on for the Merchant Navy on October 2, 1917 at Liverpool. His father was the manager of the butchery department of Haslingden Co-operative Society. Before going to sea, young Lister worked as a weaver at Harle Syke and also at Messrs. Stanworth's joinery works in Burnley Lane. Two of his brothers served in WWI, his elder brother being killed in action with the Royal Field Artillery, aged 21. He went back to sea after his ordeal and was a waiter with Cunard in the mid-1920s. He was also awarded the British War, Mercantile Marine War and Victory Medals for his WWI service and he received the Silver War Badge. His Albert Medal is now in a private collection.

ARTHUR HAMILTON AMBURY

Date of Deed: June 3, 1918
Date of Gazette: January 3, 1919

Arthur Hamilton Ambury

Image: An Unknown Few

On the 3rd June, 1918, Mr. Ambury, with his wife and two friends, were climbing on Mount Egmont, Taranaki, New Zealand, and had reached an altitude of about 5,500 feet when a call for help was heard from above.

Two members of Mr. Ambury's party immediately commenced to climb to render assistance, and Mr. Ambury, after placing his wife in a safe place, went up after them. At a height of about 7,300 feet they found two climbers, one of whom had been hurt. They took charge of the injured man, and his companion, who had an ice axe, proceeded higher up the mountain to assist a third member of the party.

The injured man had been assisted down some 1,000 feet and Mr. Ambury had nearly reached the party who were descending a steep ice slope in which they had to cut steps, when one of the two men in the rear slipped and slid down the slope at a terrific pace.

Mr. Ambury, who was about 60 feet lower down, braced himself and endeavoured to stop the falling man by seizing his alpenstock which was trailing behind him, but the alpenstock was jerked out of his hand and he was precipitated down the slope of the mountain. He was an experienced mountaineer and must have realised how terrible a risk he was running in endeavouring to save the falling man.

Arthur Hamilton Ambury was awarded a posthumous **Albert Medal (Land)**, which was presented to his widow by the Governor-General of New Zealand in Wellington on May 8, 1919. Arthur Ambury was born in Cheltenham, Gloucestershire, on September 27, 1880. His family emigrated to New Zealand in 1893. He attended school at New Plymouth Boys' High School from 1893-97. After school, he established his own gentlemen's outfitters in that city. He married Annie Newbold in 1906 and they had two sons and two daughters. There is a memorial to Arthur Ambury on Mount Egmont today. The whereabouts of his Albert Medal are unknown.

GLADYS LAURA WHITE

Image: Unknown

Gladys Laura White

Date of Deed: October 1, 1918
Date of Gazette: January 31, 1919

Early in the morning of the 1st October, 1918, a serious fire occurred in No. 36 Casualty Clearing Station at Rousbrugge, in Belgium. At the time some of the patients were undergoing serious operations in the abdominal and general operating theatres, the walls of which were composed of wood. The first intimation of danger in the theatres was the extinction of the electric light accompanied by volumes of smoke, and almost immediately the wooden walls burst into flames. The two sisters and the staff nurse assisted in carrying the unconscious patients to safety, and returned to the burning wards to assist in carrying out other patients. During this time ether bottles and nitrous oxide cylinders were continually exploding, filling the air with fumes and flying fragments of steel.

Sister Gladys White was awarded the **Albert Medal (Land)**, as were Sister Gertrude Walters Carlin and Sister Harriet Elizabeth Fraser (later GC), both of the Territorial Force Nursing Service, which was presented to them by the King at Buckingham Palace on April 10, 1919. Gladys White was born in 1883 in Portsmouth. She did her training at Guy's Hospital between 1907 and 1910 and by 1915 was nursing for the British Red Cross Society in France. She was a qualified masseuse (now a physiotherapist) as well as being a midwife. From 1914-15 she was a member of the Millicent Sutherland Ambulance. By the end of the war, in addition to the Albert Medal, she had been awarded the Royal Red Cross, Second Class (ARRC), Mentioned in Despatches and awarded the BRCS Special Service Cross. Her final accolade was the rare Florence Nightingale Medal, which she received in 1920. Returning to nursing in a civilian hospital, she eventually became Assistant Matron and then Matron of the Royal Surrey County Hospital in Guildford, Surrey. She volunteered once again for the BRCS in WWII and served from 1941-46 as Commandant of a local VAD. She retired to The Downs, Portsdown Road, Portsmouth and died, aged 80, on November 1, 1963, a truly distinguished member of her profession. Her AM and other medals are thought to be still with the family.

DAVID FALCONER

Date of Deed: March 24, 1918
Date of Gazette: March 25, 1919

On the 24th March, 1918, the British S.S. "War Knight" was proceeding up Channel in convoy, in company with the United States Oil Carrier "O.B. Jennings". About 2.30 a.m. the "War Knight" struck the other vessel on the starboard side abreast the bridge. Flames and fumes of naphtha appear to have spurted out of the "O.B. Jennings", rushed the whole length of the "War Knight", and set her on fire. The after part of the "O.B. Jennings" also was soon burning furiously and the ships swung together, the "War Knight" being to leeward of the "O.B. Jennings" and consequently completely enveloped in the smoke, fumes and flames from the weather ship.

Immediately after the collision flames swept across the top of the engine-room through the open skylight. Mr. Falconer stood in the flames and shut the skylight down to prevent the fire from entering the engine-room.

Later on, when the third engineer and a fireman, who had remained below, made their way on deck, the former was severely burnt and gassed, and Mr. Falconer dragged both men to a place where there were less flames and fumes, and then put them into the engineers' mess-room with others whom he had collected from their bunks, and by breaking the skylight he assisted them all to get out to the boat deck.

Finally, although he could not swim, he took off his own lifebelt and put it on the third engineer, and did not leave the ship until he was satisfied that there were no others in need of assistance.

Mr. Falconer displayed the greatest gallantry in rendering these services; but he was so injured that he subsequently succumbed in hospital.

Chief Engineer David Falconer was awarded a posthumous **Albert Medal (Sea),** which was presented quietly at the Mercantile Marine Office at Dundee on May 3, 1919 to his widow, who lived at Leuchars in Fife. He died in the Royal Hospital, Portsmouth, on April 6, 1918. This was the same incident for which Reginald Curtis Clayton was awarded the Albert Medal (q.v.). David Falconer is not commemorated on any CWGC memorial as his death was not attributable to enemy action. The whereabouts of his Albert Medal are unknown.

ALICE BATT

Date of Deed: October 1, 1918
Date of Gazette: April 25, 1919

Image: The Diary of Alice

On the 1st October, 1918, a fire broke out at No. 36 Casualty Clearing Station at Rousbrugge, Belgium, and quickly reached the operating theatre, where the surgeon was performing an abdominal operation. The lights went out, and the theatre was quickly filled with smoke and flames, but the operation was continued by the light of an electric torch, Miss Batt continuing her work of handing instruments and threading needles with steadfast calmness, thereby enabling the surgeon to complete the operation. Miss Batt afterwards did splendid work in helping to carry men from the burning wards to places of safety.

Alice Batt was awarded the **Albert Medal (Land),** which was presented to her by the King at Buckingham Palace on April 10, 1919. Alice Maud Batt was born on November 13, 1889 in Witney, Oxfordshire. As did so many members of the VADs, she came from a well-to-do family and was educated at home and later at Wycombe Abbey School, High Wycombe, Buckinghamshire. She joined the Oxford 22 Voluntary Aid Detachment in 1911 and in November, 1914, she reported for duty with the Lady Evelyn Mason Hospital for Officers. In March, 1916, she arrived at No. 9 British Red Cross Hospital, also known as the Millicent Sutherland Ambulance. By a coincidence, this was the same unit that Gladys White (q.v.) had joined on the outbreak of war. Alice spent the war in a number of different hospitals and casualty clearing stations. On September 7, 1915, while on leave, she saved Patty Hickman, aged 11, from drowning at Brigg, on the Cumbrian coast, for which she was awarded the Bronze Medal of the Royal Humane Society. The BRCS awarded her their Special Service Cross in 1917 and she received the British War and Victory Medals for her war service. She never married and died aged 79, in 1969 at Burford, Oxfordshire. Her medals are still held by the family.

HUGH BROWN

Date of Deed: June 25, 1918
Date of Gazette: May 23, 1919

On the 25th June, 1918, the ship (S.S. Orissa) was torpedoed and sunk in the North Atlantic Ocean, six lives being lost.

The explosion took place about twenty feet from the store-room, where some members of the crew, including Brown and his son, who was the Steward's Boy, were receiving their tobacco issue. The store-room was immediately flooded, but the Boatswain and his son were able to fight their way to the stairway leading to the weather deck, the bottom stairs of which were blown away.

The boy managed to reach the weather deck, but Brown then heard the Storekeeper, who was still in the flooded store-room, calling for help. As soon, therefore, as he had been assured of his son's safety, Brown wished the lad farewell, and, though he could probably have saved himself together with his son, turned back in the hope of assisting the Storekeeper. The water was continually rising, and Brown must have been aware that he had very little chance of being able to win his way to the deck a second time.

The ship sank not long after, and neither the Boatswain nor the Storekeeper was seen again.

Boatswain Hugh Brown was awarded a posthumous **Albert Medal (Sea)**, which was presented to his widow, Mrs Mary Ellen Brown, by the King at Buckingham Palace on June 28, 1919. Her address was given as 105 Bentinck Street, Birkenhead. He was awarded the British War and Mercantile Marine War Medals for his WWI service. He was born in 1875. The whereabouts of his Albert Medal are unknown. He does not appear to be on the CWGC website.

THOMAS WILLIAMS

Date of Deed: March 13, 1919
Date of Gazette: July 15, 1919

On the 13th March, as a train was entering Pembroke Station, an elderly gentleman, Canon Bowen, of Pembroke, in stepping aside to avoid a luggage barrow, fell off the platform on to the rails. The train was not more than thirty yards away from him when he fell, and was travelling fast. The Station Master, who was close by, at once jumped down in front of the engine and just succeeded in rolling Canon Bowen off the track, and held him down alongside the rails until it was safe to allow him to get up.

Thomas Williams

Image: G. J. Williams, Esq

Although the brakes were applied it was found impossible to bring the train to a standstill until the engine and two coaches had passed the spot where rescued and rescuer were lying. Had it not been for Mr. Williams' presence of mind and courage Canon Bowen could hardly have escaped instant death.

Thomas Williams was awarded the **Albert Medal (Land)**, which was presented to him by the King at Buckingham Palace on August 2, 1919. He was also awarded a cheque for £10 from the Carnegie Hero Fund Trust. Thomas Williams was born on December 27, 1871 at Tenby. He spent most of his working life on the railway, with the Great Western Railway Company, commencing employment with the Pembroke and Tenby Railway at Penally. He married his wife, Annie, on May 11, 1886 and they had three sons and two daughters. Two of his sons worked for the GWR and one of them, Eric, followed his father as Station Master at Pembroke. Retiring from the railway in 1926, he went to work for Lloyd and Thomas, Auctioneers of Carmarthen. He died at Pembroke on July 5, 1937, aged 75, his wife dying the day after. The Albert Medal is believed to be still held by his family.

DAVID ATKINSON MACMILLAN

Date of Deed: April 9, 1918
Date of Gazette: July 18, 1919

On the 9th April, 1918, a serious fire broke out in the residential quarter of the town of Keonjhar Garh, in the Feudatory State of Keonjhar, India. Nearly all the men were absent at work, and a panic arose among the women and children. Mr. MacMillan at once hastened to the scene of the fire, organised parties for fighting it, and by his personal efforts and direction brought it under control. When his work was nearly finished a burning roof fell in upon four men who were assisting to extinguish the fire. Regardless of his own safety, Mr. MacMillan at once entered the building, which was full of smoke and flame, and rescued all four men, one of whom was severely burned. Mr. MacMillan was seriously injured, and died on the 19th September following.

David Atkinson MacMillan was awarded a posthumous **Albert Medal (Land)**, which was presented to his widow, Mrs Grace MacMillan but it is not known by whom or on what date. The whereabouts of his Albert Medal are not known.

SAMUEL JAMES HAINES

Date of Deed: June 17, 1919
Date of Gazette: December 12, 1919

On the 17th June last a fire occurred on a Russian motor launch in the Harbour of Archangel, and a Russian tug and a picket boat from an American man-of-war proceeded to render assistance, Mr. Haines going in the tug.

Just before the tug reached the launch an explosion took place on board the latter. Immediately the tug got alongside, the crew of the launch abandoned her.

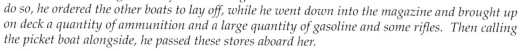

Samuel James Haines

Image: TNA MN Records

Mr. Haines at once went on board the launch and endeavoured to extinguish the fire, but being unable to do so, he ordered the other boats to lay off, while he went down into the magazine and brought up on deck a quantity of ammunition and a large quantity of gasoline and some rifles. Then calling the picket boat alongside, he passed these stores aboard her.

While Mr. Haines was alone on board the launch, the cabin abaft the engine room and before the magazine took fire.

The fire was ultimately got under, but not before the launch had been gutted.

Mr. Haines displayed great gallantry in rendering the service, for had the fire reached the magazine an explosion would undoubtedly have occurred, and he would have had no chance of saving his life.

Samuel James Haines was awarded the **Albert Medal (Sea)**, which was presented to him by the King at Buckingham Palace on February 20, 1920. Samuel Haines was born in London on December 18, 1884. He was a Junior Officer in the Mercantile Marine Reserve at the time of his award. He was also awarded the MBE in 1919 "for valuable services in the Naval Transport Service, North Russia". The Imperial Russian government awarded him the Order of St Stanislaus, Third Class with Swords. He was entitled to the British War, Mercantile Marine and Victory Medals for his war service but apparently never claimed them, although his group now contains erased examples of the BWM and VM. All his medals, including the AM, are now in a private collection. Curiously, the MBE with his group has the military ribbon, whereas he would have been entitled to the civilian version as a merchant seaman.

THOMAS STRATFORD KNILL

Date of Deed: October 14, 1919
Date of Gazette: April 27, 1920

At Novorossisk on the 14th October, 1919, when the steamship "War Pike", laden with stores and several hundred tons of explosives, took fire, Captain Knill, although deserted by most of his crew, and in spite of the intense heat and frequent explosions, remained on board his ship, casting off hawsers from the quay and making fast others to a tug, only abandoning ship by order of the

Captain of His Majesty's Ship "Grafton" as his vessel was being towed out of the entrance of the harbour. He then boarded a tug, stood by his ship after she had grounded; and later, though the bridge, boats and starboard coal bunker were a mass of flames, boarded her and assisted in getting hoses to work, successfully preventing the fire from spreading aft, where there were still large quantities of explosives. The vessel was then towed towards shallow water, where she grounded. By his gallantry and devotion to duty Captain Knill undoubtedly averted an explosion, and thus probably saved many lives.

Captain Thomas Stratford Knill was awarded the **Albert Medal (Sea),** which was presented to him by the King at Buckingham Palace on June 8, 1920. Captain Knill was awarded the British War and Mercantile Marine War Medals for his war service and Lloyds awarded him their Silver Medal for Meritorious Services. He was born in Seaham, Co. Durham in 1867 and was at sea between 1887 and 1933. He died in May, 1949 at Low Fell, Gateshead, Co. Durham. The whereabouts of the Albert Medal are not known.

WILLIAM MATHERS AND JOSEPH BOWMAN

Date of Deed: August 27, 1919
Date of Gazette: May 21, 1920

(Able Seaman) Brewer had descended into the Wet Provision Room of H.M.S. "Tiger", in company with J.H. Anderson, a shipwright, when he was overcome by poisonous gases and collapsed. Anderson, himself feeling the effect of the gases, left the compartment as quickly as possible to obtain assistance, and Mathers and Bowman, who were near to the scene, descended without hesitation to endeavour to rescue Brewer. They did not wait for further assistance or for safety appliances, though they were fully aware of the cause of Brewer's collapse and consequently of the grave risk they were running. They were at once overcome by the noxious gases in the compartment, and when removed were in an unconscious condition.

Every endeavour was made to restore them to consciousness, but without success.

William Mathers and Joseph Bowman were each awarded a posthumous **Albert Medal (Land)**, which was presented by the King at Buckingham Palace to Mrs Catherine Mathers, widow, of 64 Station Street, Barry Dock, Glamorgan and Miss Isabella Bowman, sister of Joseph Bowman, of 38 Lorne Street, Sinclairtown, Kircaldy, respectively. The incident took place in H.M. Dockyard, Rosyth. It is of interest that Mathers' Christian names are given as Matthew Ronald in some sources but the *London Gazette* names him as William, so that is the name used here. His Albert Medal, which is named to him as Matthew Ronald Mathers, is now in a private collection. Two members of the Royal Navy were involved in this incident; yet another occasion where officialdom decided that the RN would get Sea medals and the civilians the Land award. This was probably due to the recommendations emanating from different sources, i.e. the Admiralty and the Board of Trade. The whereabouts of Bowman's Albert Medal is unknown but it is probably still with his family.

GHARIB SHAH

Date of Deed: June 3, 1919
Date of Gazette: July 27, 1920

On the 3rd June, 1919, a large Religious Fair was being held in India at Nariana, on the right bank of the River Beas, and a great many pilgrims were being conveyed across the river by means of a ferry boat. Two boatloads had been taken over successfully, and the boat was crossing a third time when it got out of control. The river was in flood and the rapids very dangerous, and the boat, which was filled to its utmost capacity, entered the rapids and was swamped, all the passengers being precipitated into the rushing water. Gharib Shah, a young waterman, 25 years of age, who was in charge of a timber raft some 30 yards away, managed to get his raft close to the overturned boat, and immediately set to work to save the passengers as they were carried past him. Time after time he plunged into the river, and succeeded in rescuing fifteen drowning persons. Others in the water who had struggled to the raft were pulled on to it by him, and in this manner other lives were saved.

It is estimated that 150 passengers were on board the boat when it started, and of the forty-five saved it is certain that Gharib Shah was responsible for the rescue of at least thirty by his bravery and resourcefulness. The District Magistrate who held an inquiry into the occurrence highly commended Gharib Shah's conduct, and mentioned that this was not the first time that he had saved persons from drowning, for in the year 1914, at the risk of his own life, he had rescued five persons from the same river.

Gharib Shah was awarded the **Albert Medal (Land)** but no details of its presentation or its whereabouts are known.

DAVID FRASER AND AARON EDWARD HIGGINS

Date of Deed: August 27, 1919
Date of Gazette: August 10, 1920

On the 27th August, 1919, when the Steamship "Melville Dollar" was in the North Pacific Ocean, the main steam pipe burst, killing the Second Engineer and five Chinese Fireman.

Attempts were immediately made to get down into the engine-room to rescue the injured and to shut off steam from the boilers. The Chief Engineer, Mr. David Fraser, tried first, but was not able to get beyond the fiddley door, being badly scalded about the arms, throat and face. The Master and Mates then fitted up two tarpaulins as wind-sails, in order to force as much air as possible down the skylights into the engine and boiler-rooms.

Meanwhile, Mr. Aaron Edward Higgins, Third Engineer, having wrapped himself in coverings as a protection against the still escaping steam, made several attempts to get to the valves, but he was driven back each time by the high-pressure steam which filled the engine-room. The Master then descended with him and put a bowline around him as a life line, and Mr. Higgins made another attempt, this time reaching the burst part of the steam pipe, but he became exhausted and found it impossible to get to the valves, and had to be pulled back by the life line.

It was not until an hour and a half after the explosion that the pressure in the boilers fell sufficiently to permit a descent, when the bodies were removed, the fires drawn, and the steam shut off, which was done by Mr. Higgins.

Both officers incurred very considerable risk in rendering the services, as the engine-room was filled with super-heated steam, and Mr. Fraser had to be removed to hospital on account of his injuries.

Chief Engineer David Fraser and Third Engineer Aaron Edward Higgins were each awarded the **Albert Medal (Sea)**. Mr. Fraser was presented with his by the King at Buckingham Palace on December 2, 1920, while Mr. Higgins was presented with his by the Governor-General of Canada at Vancouver, British Columbia, on August 6, 1921. Both men received Lloyd's Silver Medal for Meritorious Service. The whereabouts of these two Albert Medals are unknown.

FLORENCE AMY EMMITT

Date of Deed: December 7, 1919
Date of Gazette: August 17, 1920

Florence Amy Emmitt

Image: Daily Mirror

On December 7th, 1919, Mrs. Emmitt and her children were sitting with her husband, who was in bed with fever. The eldest boy, aged 17, had occasion to go into the sitting-room, and as he entered that room he found an Indian coming in from the garden. On the boy questioning the man as to what he was doing, the intruder immediately attacked him with an axe, breaking the boy's forearm. The boy closed with his assailant, and on his mother coming into the room she found that the man, who had dropped the axe, was stabbing her son with a dagger. She at once rushed to her son's assistance and seized the man, never relaxing her hold in spite of receiving a stab in her side. At this stage her husband came from his sick bed to the rescue; the Indian wrenched himself free from Mrs. Emmitt and stabbed Mr. Emmitt in the thigh. Thereupon Mrs. Emmitt again seized the man by the wrist, and in spite of receiving several more wounds on her hand and arm succeeded in getting hold of the handle of the dagger. Eventually, with the aid of some servants, the assailant was overpowered, and Mrs. Emmitt continued to show the greatest courage by ignoring her own wounds until both her husband and son had been attended to and sent to hospital. All three have now recovered, and their assailant, who proved to be a murderous fanatic, was tried, sentenced, and duly hanged. There can be no doubt that Mrs. Emmitt's bravery saved her son's life and probably her husband's too.

Mrs Florence Amy Emmitt, the wife of the Station Master at Peshawar, North West Frontier Province, was awarded the **Albert Medal (Land),** which was presented to her by the King at Buckingham Palace in March, 1921. Her Albert Medal is now in a private collection.

THOMAS WILLIAM BROWN

Date of Deed: December 23, 1919
Date of Gazette: October 8, 1920

Thomas William Brown

Image: Unknown

On the 23rd December, 1919, at about 4 p.m., a fire, which speedily attained serious proportions, broke out at Cross House, Westgate Road, Newcastle-on-Tyne, in the basement of the building, where cases containing a large quantity of cinematograph films were stored, and flames were quickly shooting up the lift shaft and the staircase.

The work of the Fire Brigade was performed under most difficult and dangerous conditions, owing to the great heat, noxious fumes and explosions caused by the burning films. Flames were already shooting across the street on one side of the building when the Brigade arrived on the scene within a few seconds of the call having been received, and it was from the windows of the upper floors that a large number of the rescues were effected; the actions of Fireman Thomas William Brown in reaching the top of the building by means of a hook ladder being an outstanding feature of the work of rescue.

A 50 ft. fire escape had been pitched on one side of the building, and Brown, having ascended the escape, fastened to a window on the fourth floor a 14 ft. hook ladder which he carried, and by this means enabled thirteen persons to escape. He then threw up the hook ladder to the main cornice above, which projected 2½ feet from the building, and with great coolness and daring ascended to the parapet, where he effected the rescue of three other persons by making fast the hook ladder in another position and attaching it to a 65 ft. escape. There was great risk of the hook slipping while the Fireman was ascending the ladder some 70 feet from the ground, seeing that by reason of the overhang of the cornice the ladder was clear of the wall.

Upwards of 100 persons were in the building when the fire broke out. Twelve deaths resulted, 57 were rescued, while 50 others effected their escape from the windows of the lower floors.

Fireman Thomas William Brown was awarded the **Albert Medal (Land)**, which was presented to him by the King at Buckingham Palace on November 2, 1920. Thomas Brown was born in South Shields, Co. Durham, on March 15, 1889. During WWI he served with the Royal Navy, and was demobilised as a Petty Officer First Class being awarded the 1914-15 Star, British War and Victory Medals for his service. He also held the Royal Fleet Reserve Long Service Medal and Society for the Protection of Life from Fire awarded him its Silver Medal for his heroism. He was subsequently promoted to Leading Fireman for his part in this rescue. Mr Brown was a keen founder member of the Albert Medal Association from 1966 until his death in a traffic accident in London, on October 27, 1969. His medals are now in a private collection.

1920 – 1939

There were fifteen awards of the Albert Medal to civilians who did not survive to exchange their awards for the George Cross during this period, only one of which was in Gold. This is fewer than one per year and may, in part, be due to the institution of the Medal of the Order of the British Empire for Gallantry (otherwise known as the Empire Gallantry Medal (EGM)) in 1922.

CHARLES CHAPMAN

Date of Deed: March 27, 1920
Date of Gazette: February 16, 1923

Charles Chapman

Image: Unknown

In the early hours of March 27th, 1920, great destruction was caused by a severe flood which swept through the Paparoa Valley. An immense volume of water descended from the upper valley, where for miles the course of the torrent was marked by land slides. Houses and huts were washed away and, unhappily, some of the occupants lost their lives.

Chapman, on receiving news of the disaster, put on a bathing costume and at once set out for the Paparoa Township, to find that the River which runs through the Township had become a raging torrent, the water reaching almost to the top rail of the bridge spanning the river. Two men (one of whom could not swim) were clinging to timber in the middle of the river, while a crowd of terror-stricken people looked on helplessly from the bank.

His first act was to rescue these men. This he did – twice swimming out to them – but only after very strenuous efforts. He then heard that a woman and her child were in danger higher up the river, and went to their assistance. He found the woman clinging to a tree and swam out to her; but to effect a rescue he had to return for a plank. A wooden form was available, and this he endeavoured to tow out to the woman and child. The rope broke, but his second effort, when a length of fencing wire had been procured, was successful, and he brought first the child then the mother to the bank.

Charles Chapman of Huarau was awarded the **Albert Medal (Land),** which was presented to him by the Governor-General of New Zealand, Lord Jellicoe, at Government House, Auckland, on June 4, 1923. Mr. Chapman was also awarded its Gold Medal by the Royal Humane Society of New Zealand. The whereabouts of his Albert Medal are unknown but it is probably still with his family. Charles Chapman died in Auckland in 1945.

VICTOR GEORGE HAYWARD *and* ERNEST EDWARD MILLS JOYCE

Image: "South" by Shackleton

Victor George Hayward

Date of Deed: October 9, 1915 – March 20, 1916
Date of Gazette: July 6, 1923

The (Shackleton Trans-Antarctic) Expedition had for its object the crossing of the Antarctic Continent from the Weddell Sea to the Ross Sea, via the South Pole, a distance of about seventeen hundred miles. Sufficient supplies for the journey could not be carried, and it was therefore necessary to establish a chain of depots on the Ross Sea side as far southwards as possible. With this end in view the ship "Aurora" was sent to McMurdo Sound at the southern extremity of the Ross Sea and, as it was intended that the vessel should winter there, a portion only of the stores and equipment was disembarked. McMurdo Sound was reached in January, 1915, but during a blizzard in May, the "Aurora" was blown out to sea and was unable to return, and the nine members of the Expedition who were on shore were left stranded. They recognised that failure to establish the depots would undoubtedly result in the loss of the main body and resolved, in spite of their grave shortage of equipment to carry out the allotted programme.

For this purpose a party under the command of Sub-Lieutenant A.L. Mackintosh, R.N.R., and consisting of the Reverend A.P. Spencer-Smith, Messrs. Joyce, Richards, Hayward and Wild and three other members who assisted for a part of the outward journey left Hut Point, Ross Island, on October 9th. They took with them two sledges and four dogs, and 162 days elapsed before the surviving members of the party were back at Hut Point, the total distance covered being approximately 950 miles.

Mr. Spencer-Smith had to be dragged on a sledge for 42 days, mainly by hand labour, the distance covered being over 350 miles. When more than 100 miles remained to be covered the collapse of Lieutenant Mackintosh imposed an additional burden on the active members of the party who were all suffering from scurvy and snow blindness and were so enfeebled by their labours that at times they were unable to cover more than 2 or 3 miles in 15 hours.

Mr Spencer-Smith died when only 19 miles remained to be covered, but Lieutenant Mackintosh was brought in safely to the base.

Victor George Hayward and Ernest Edward Mills Joyce were each awarded the **Albert Medal (Land)**, as were Richard Walter Richards (later GC) and Petty Officer Harry Ernest Wild R.N. Hayward, born in London in 1889, died on May 7, 1916, so his 76-year-old father accepted his award from the King at Buckingham Palace on February 28, 1924. Joyce, an ex-Petty Officer, R.N., was presented with his award by the King at Buckingham Palace on July 25, 1923. Hayward was also awarded the Polar Medal with clasps *Antarctic 1914-16* and *Antarctic 1917* and his medals are now in a private collection. Joyce was born in Bognor, Sussex, in 1875 and entered the Royal Navy from Greenwich Royal Hospital School in 1891 and served in the South African War 1899-1902 as a Petty Officer First Class, being awarded the Queen's South Africa Medal with bar *Cape Colony* for service in HMS *Sybille*. He was awarded the unique Polar Medal with four clasps: *Antarctic 1902-04*, *Antarctic 1907-09*, *Antarctic 1914-16* and *Antarctic 1917*, together with the Scott Medal, 1904 and Mount Joyce in the Antarctic is named after him. His Polar Medal is now in the Scott Polar Research Institute collection. He died on May 2, 1940. The whereabouts of Hayward's Albert Medal are presently unknown.

VELADI SAMMAI

Date of Deed: November 9, 1924
Date of Gazette: May 12, 1925

On 9th November, 1924, Mr. H.S. George, Deputy Conservator of Forests of the South Chanda Division of the Central Provinces, had just completed his inspection of a piece of forest and was returning to camp along a jungle path accompanied by Veladi Sammai, a Gond villager of the district who was carrying Mr. George's gun and walked in front. Suddenly and without warning a man-eating tiger jumped upon Mr. George's back, seized him by the neck and proceeded to drag him into the jungle. Veladi Sammai behaved with extraordinary gallantry; he rushed at the tiger, placed the muzzle of the gun against it and pulled the trigger but was unable to discharge the weapon owing to the safety catch with which he was not familiar. He then shouted and waved his arms thus driving the tiger off for a short distance. Mr. George was badly bitten in the neck and covered with blood but with the Gond's assistance he managed to stagger slowly along and reached his camp which was about two miles away. The tiger followed them for some distance but was kept off by the shouts and demonstrations of the Gond.

It was known that a man-eating tiger was in the neighbourhood and had killed several villagers but it had never attacked anyone on the path used by the forest officer, and neither Mr. George nor the Gond had any suspicion of the tiger's presence until the attack was made. Veladi Sammai's action was an extremely brave one and he gravely imperilled his own life. He certainly saved Mr. George's as only his prompt and gallant action prevented the tiger dragging the forest officer into the jungle and eating him.

Veladi Sammai was awarded the **Albert Medal (Land),** which was presented to him at Sironcha on April 14, 1926 but it is not known by whom nor are its whereabouts known.

GORDON LEES

Date of Deed: March 12, 1925
Date of Gazette: September 29, 1925

A youth named Jack Canning was attacked by a man-eating shark when bathing from the beach at Newcastle, New South Wales, on the 12th March, 1925.

A rush was made to launch the surf boat but before this could be done Gordon Lees, employed by the City Council to patrol the beach and assist surf bathers in difficulties, put on a belt with a life line attached, and swam out alone to Canning's assistance. Canning had been attacked three times by the shark and was terribly injured, and Lees reached him just as he appeared to abandon all further effort to save himself. The shark was then only a few yards away from rescuer and rescued. Lees lifted Canning up when he was almost submerged and the two were then immediately hauled in to the beach by the life line. The rescued man, unfortunately, died from his injuries shortly afterwards.

Gordon Lees was awarded the **Albert Medal (Sea)**, which was presented to him by the Governor of New South Wales at Newcastle on February 25, 1926. He was born *circa* 1892. He married Grace Westling *circa* 1928 and they had a son, James, born *circa* 1929. He died on March 24, 1934, aged 41 and is buried in the Presbyterian Cemetery, Sandgate, New South Wales. The whereabouts of his Albert Medal are unknown but it is probably still with his family.

GEORGE HENRY WHITE

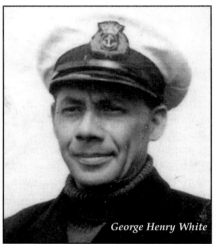

Image: Ron White

George Henry White

Date of Deed: May 4, 1925
Date of Gazette: November 17, 1925

On the 4th May, 1925, the "Paul Beau" was proceeding from Hongkong to Canton when a tube blew out in the starboard boiler projecting a stream of boiling water and steam 35 feet long into the after end of the Boiler Room and Engine Room; the Engine and Boiler Rooms are in one compartment, there being no dividing bulkhead. At the time of the accident, two men, Hau Foong and So Hau were on duty on the boilers, and two others on the engines. Hau Foong was immediately overcome and collapsed and So Hau at once went to his assistance and at the risk of his own life, managed to drag him clear of the scalding water before making his way on deck when he collapsed also. Meanwhile, the other two men sought refuge in the tunnel way.

Observing a thick cloud of steam rising from the Engine and Boiler Rooms to the level of the promenade deck, George Henry White suspected what had happened, and, wrapping his face in wet towelling, he made his way through the steam along the top of the boilers and shut off the valves connecting the boilers to the engines, and the valve connecting the two boilers. The three men in the Engine and Boiler Rooms were reached as soon as the steam had cleared away and were removed in a state of collapse to the upper deck. But for the gallantry of Mr. White they would in all probability have been suffocated by the escaping steam.

Mr. White ran a very grave risk, since he had to grope about in the scalding steam fog, blinded by the covering on his head, in his endeavour to shut the stop valves on the boilers, and he might have encountered the full force of the issuing steam, in which case the result would have been fatal. In spite of being badly scalded, he took charge and having effected the necessary repairs, raised steam again, thus enabling the vessel to be brought safely to the wharf at Canton where the injured men were removed to hospital.

Second Engineer George Henry White was awarded the **Albert Medal (Sea)**, which was presented to him in Hong Kong by HRH Prince George (afterwards Duke of Kent) on March 13, 1926. So Hau was awarded the Sea Gallantry Medal in Bronze in the same citation.

George White was born in Hong Kong on May 8, 1900. He was educated in the Diocesan Boys' School, Hong Kong and on leaving school became an engineering apprentice in the Royal Naval Dockyard, Hong Kong. He served in the Mercantile Marine during WWI and was awarded the British War, Mercantile Marine War and Victory Medals. Most of his time in the Merchant Navy was spent in the Far East. He married his wife, Dorothy, in Hong Kong cathedral in 1940. Eventually becoming a Chief Engineer, he served throughout WWII, earning the 1939-45, Africa and Pacific Stars and the War Medal. He retired to Exmouth, Devon, in 1963 and died in Bristol Hospital of a brain haemorrhage on February 17, 1965. His Albert Medal is still proudly held by his family.

FRANK HOPKINS

Date of Deed: August 18, 1927
Date of Gazette: November 4, 1927

Image: Mrs K. Grimes

Frank Hopkins

On the night of the 18th August, 1927, the s.s. "Cambrian Baroness" was lying ready to sail in South Lock, Newport, Mon., with a space of two or three feet between her side and the quay wall. At the last moment a fireman returning to the ship began to climb the pilot ladder but lost his hold and fell into the lock between the vessel and the wall of the lock. The ladder was lowered to the water and the man caught hold of it, but as the ladder was being hauled up his hold gave way and he fell back into the lock.

Among the bystanders on the quay was an unemployed seaman, Frank Hopkins. Seeing the accident Hopkins went down the ladder to the water level fifteen feet below. By the light of an electric torch from the ship's deck he caught hold of the fireman, who was now unconscious, and began to carry him up the ladder. The fireman was a dead weight and Hopkins progress was necessarily slow. As he was struggling up the ladder the vessel began to move towards the quay wall and someone shouted to Hopkins to let the man go and save himself. Hopkins replied "I have got him now and will bring him up." As soon as the fireman was within reach of men standing on the quay they hauled him into safety; Hopkins had barely managed himself to get up to the quay when the vessel closed with the wall. If he had been a few seconds later there is no doubt that he and the man he rescued would have been crushed to death.

Hopkins could have made sure of his own safety if he had given up his hold of the fireman. He knew quite well the risk he was running and knowing it saved the man.

Frank Hopkins was awarded the **Albert Medal (Sea)**, which was presented to him by the King at Buckingham Palace on February 16, 1928. He also received £20 from the Carnegie Hero Fund Trust. Frank Hopkins was born in 1899 in Newport, Monmouthshire (now Gwent). One of sixteen children, he was the son of William Hopkins, a soldier stationed in Ireland, and Katherine Hopkins (née Riley). He enlisted during WWI but did not serve overseas, thus receiving no medals. He was demobilised on April 8, 1919 as a Private in the Royal Defence Corps, though he had previously served with the Cheshire Regiment. He re-enlisted into the Royal Artillery on May 30, 1919. Most of his service was spent in India between 1919 and 1926 but he did not qualify for any campaign medal. After Reserve service, he was finally discharged on May 29, 1939. He was married to Rose Conlin of Liverpool and they had one daughter, who was only three years old when he died. He had been unemployed for about twenty months by August, 1927, when he performed the act of gallantry which was to earn him the Albert

Medal. The Royal Humane Society awarded him its Silver Medal for the incident. His AM was the Sea award, officialdom never having decided whether docks were at sea or on land! January, 1941, saw him serving aboard the S.S. *Oropesa*, a ship of 14,118 gross registered tons owned by the Pacific Steam Navigation Company. On January 16, she was torpedoed by the U-96 about 180 miles west of the Isle of Mull and sank with the loss of 113 lives, Frank Hopkins among them. He is commemorated on the Tower Hill Memorial, although curiously his post-nominal initials are omitted. He was entitled to the 1939-45 and Atlantic Stars and the War Medal for his WWII service but it is not known whether these were claimed or issued. The whereabouts of his Albert Medal are unknown but it is possible that it was lost at sea along with its recipient.

ALEXANDER DOCTOR CLARK

Date of Deed: June 24, 1929
Date of Gazette: July 9, 1929

Image: Grandson

Alexander Doctor Clark

On the 24th June, 1929, at about 11.30 p.m., a fire broke out in the premises at 89, Hylton Road, Sunderland, in which three children had been left alone by their parents. On hearing that children were in the building, Mr. Clark, although he knew that previous attempts to effect the rescue had failed, broke a staircase window at the back of the premises, climbed through and in spite of the intense heat and flames made his way to the assistance of the children. From the position in which the bodies were subsequently found it appears that Mr. Clark on gaining entry, rushed up the burning stairway to an upper room and brought the youngest child down to the first floor where unfortunately their escape must have been cut off.

It must have been plain to Mr. Clark that in attempting the rescue of the children he was placing his life in the gravest peril. Both the Coroner and the Jury expressed high commendation of Mr. Clark's heroic conduct.

Mr. Clark leaves a widow and three children.

Alexander Doctor Clark was awarded a posthumous **Albert Medal (Land)**, which was presented to his widow, Mrs Isabella Clark, by the King at Buckingham Palace on March 4, 1930. Mr Clark was born at Sunderland, Co. Durham in October, 1897. He was educated at Hylton Road School, Sunderland. He left school early in 1914, taking up employment as an apprentice plater with Messrs William Doxford & Co Ltd, Shipbuilders of Pallion Shipyard. He enlisted in the 7th Battalion Durham Light Infantry on October 8, 1914. He does not appear to have served overseas but he was assigned to a provisional battalion as a physical training instructor in May, 1915. He was demobilised in the spring of 1918. Unable to complete his apprenticeship due to the war, after a period of unemployment he was engaged as a labourer by the Sunderland Gas Company. He was married in November 1918 to Isabella Botcherby of Gateshead and they had two sons and a daughter. One of his sons was lost at sea with the Merchant Navy in July, 1942. He was buried in Bishopwearmouth Cemetery, Sunderland, after a civic funeral. His family still has his Albert Medal.

ANDRIES MULLER HEYNS

Date of Deed: December 28, 1927
Date of Gazette: October 4, 1929

On the 28th December, 1927, at Little Brak Beach, Mossel Bay, South Africa, a youth named Ockardus Johannes Heyns, aged 17, was bathing with a party of friends when suddenly he was attacked by a man-eating shark, which carried him some distance out to sea and bit off his left leg above the knee.

With the full realisation of the danger he was incurring one of the bathers, Andries Muller Heyns, an uncle of Ockardus Heyns, immediately went out to the assistance of his nephew. The shark, meanwhile, had returned to the attack and had gripped Ockardus Heyns by the right foot and ankle. Andries Heyns got hold of his nephew and tried to free him from the shark; nevertheless the foot and ankle of Ockardus Heyns were severely crushed.

Andries Heyns succeeded in reaching the shore with his nephew, who soon became unconscious and died some hours later in Mossel Bay Hospital.

Andries Muller Heyns was awarded the **Albert Medal (Sea),** which was presented to him by the Governor-General of South Africa at Mossel Bay on April 29, 1930. He was also awarded the Stanhope Gold Medal for 1929 by the Royal Humane Society. His Albert Medal is now in a private collection.

ALEXANDER JOHNSTON and WILLIAM HALL

Date of Deed: February 27, 1929
Date of Gazette: February 28, 1930

The s.s. "Tritonia, of Glasgow, with a general cargo on board and a quantity of explosives in No. 3 hold, arrived at Buenaventura, Columbia, on the 27th February, 1929. On the following day the discharging of the cargo was begun, a shore gang being employed for the purpose. During the afternoon a fire was discovered among the cases of dynamite which were stowed in the bridge space of No. 3 hold; the alarm was at once given, and the shore gang with most of the crew left the ship.

The Master, Officers and a few members of the crew who remained on board immediately took steps to deal with the fire. Unfortunately they were unable to control it and the ship had to be abandoned owing to the intense heat and dense smoke as well as the danger of explosion.

Upon reaching the shore the Master, after consultation with the Port Authorities, decided to try to sink the "Tritonia", because of the danger of serious damage to persons and property in the port if the explosives on the ship blew up. Accordingly the Master and the Chief Engineer and Second Engineer (Mr. A. Johnston and Mr. W. Hall respectively) went back to the burning ship. The two Engineer Officers went on board for the purpose of opening the sea cocks. The launch drew off and waited until it was seen that the two Engineers were approaching the ship's side in readiness to leave again. The launch was about to proceed to the "Tritonia" to take off the two officers when the ship blew up and both Engineers were killed.

The launch was severely damaged and those on board were taken on to another launch which cruised about for some time in a vain search for the missing Engineers before returning to the shore.

The two Engineers, fully aware of the very serious risk they ran, sacrificed their lives in a heroic attempt to prevent the explosion.

Alexander Johnston and William Hall were each awarded the **Albert Medal (Sea)** posthumously, which were presented by the King at Buckingham Palace on March 4, 1930 to Mr. Johnston's brother and Mr Hall's father. William Hall was born on July 19, 1901 at Mid Calder, Midlothian. The whereabouts of their Albert Medals are unknown.

HENRY JAMES LEECH

Henry James Leech

Image: Unknown

Date of Deed: October 5, 1930
Date of Gazette: October 31, 1930

Despite terrifying experiences in extricating himself from the blazing wreckage (of Airship R101), Mr. Leech immediately at grave risk re-entered the burning mass and succeeded in disentangling a companion from the network of red-hot girders and hauled him into safety, himself sustaining burns in the process.

Henry James Leech was awarded the **Albert Medal (Land),** which was presented to him by the King at Buckingham, Palace on June 25, 1931. He was born in 1890 at Dudley (now West Midlands) and served in the RNAS from 1916 to 1919. He was awarded the Air Force Medal in the *London Gazette* of February 8, 1919, for bravery while bringing an airship back from Italy to the United Kingdom. He was awarded the British War and Victory Medals for his WWI service. His medals are now in a private collection.

LEONARD PEMBERTON

Date of Deed: November 14, 1930
Date of Gazette: March 6, 1931

On the 14th November, 1930, a number of children were bathing in the Zambezi River at Livingstone, Northern Rhodesia, at a point where a wire enclosure, no longer crocodile proof, had been made some time ago. One of the boys was seen suddenly to disappear. Mr. Pemberton, who was sitting on the bank, dived in fully clothed and despite the fact that he was convalescing from a recent illness, made repeated attempts to save the boy from a crocodile which was holding him under water. Mr. Pemberton was fully aware that he was close to a man-eating crocodile which might at any moment have turned and attacked him and in acting as he did displayed courage of a very high degree.

Mr. Pemberton was unfortunately unsuccessful in his efforts to bring the victim to the surface.

Leonard Pemberton was awarded the **Albert Medal (Land),** which was presented to him at Livingstone on June 3, 1932, though it is not known by whom. He served in the South African War of 1899-1902 and the Great War 1914-1918 and died in Johannesburg on April 29, 1952. He and his wife gave a talk entitled "Dodging the Albert Medal" on National Station 2FC (Australia) which was broadcast on May 17, 1938. His Albert Medal is now in the Albany Museum, Grahamstown, RSA.

WILLIAM GEORGE JOHNSON

Date of Deed: March 15, 1931
Date of Gazette: April 26, 1932

On the night of 15th March, 1931, the "Viking" was in the ice some nine miles from Horse Islands, White Bay, Newfoundland, when an explosion occurred in the magazine causing a large part of the stern to be torn away, and setting the ship on fire. The men in the cabin, galley and engine room and on the bridge were either killed or badly injured, but the majority of the crew, whose quarters were forward, were able to get out on the ice and after the first shock to return to the ship and provide themselves with clothing and some food. The "Viking" carried a crew of 153 men all told, and of these 27 lost their lives. The great majority of those saved were able to reach Horse Islands and were eventually taken off by a relief ship.

After the explosion, Johnson started for the land with a party of about twenty men hauling a dory containing the mate of the "Viking" and a passenger, both of whom had been seriously injured. The party proceeded, hauling the dory through "marshy" ice, until 4 p.m. next day, when Johnson sent all the men in the party except three to Horse Islands for assistance.

At daylight on 17th March no assistance had arrived; Johnson and the men with him had then been for a day and two nights without food or water, and they were still several miles from land. No vessel was in sight, nor was there any sign of assistance, and they were in field ice which at any moment with a change of weather conditions might become a mass of disintegrating pans. In these circumstances Johnson persuaded the three uninjured men remaining with him to make for land, but refused himself to leave the two injured men in the dory.

That afternoon seven men from Horse Islands bringing food with them reached the dory, but it was so badly damaged that they were unable to drag it over the ice and they returned to Horse Islands. Johnson remained standing by the two injured men. About two hours later, he saw the smoke of a steamer, and this proved to be the s.s. "Beothic" searching for survivors. A party of men were landed from the vessel on to the ice, but darkness overtook them before they could reach Johnson and they were compelled to return to the ship. At daylight on the following morning, a rescue party was again landed from the "Beothic", and, this party finding it impossible to convey the injured men across the ice in the damaged dory, returned to the ship for another dory, and eventually succeeded in getting Johnson and the two injured men on board the "Beothic" at 11 a.m. on the 18th March.

The ice conditions prevailing at the time were very treacherous, and the ice was of the type which has very little stability in fog, rain or snow, and might break up rapidly. A sudden change of wind from an off-shore direction would probably have loosened all the pack ice very quickly and sent it out to sea, and Johnson, with his knowledge of ice and weather conditions, must have realised the grave risk he was running in remaining with the injured men.

William George Johnson, First Master Watch, was awarded the **Albert Medal (Sea),** which was presented to him by the Governor of Newfoundland at St. John's, Newfoundland, on June 3, 1932. He was born in Newfoundland on August 17, 1908. He seems to have remained at sea until the middle of 1941 but after that all trace of him is lost. The whereabouts of his Albert Medal are unknown.

HENRY HARTLEY WADSWORTH

Date of Deed: November 5, 1933
Date of Gazette: December 18, 1934

Henry Hartley Wadsworth

Image: Family

On the 5th November, 1933, an explosion occurred in the boiler room of the s.s. "City of Cairo" while she was in the Mediterranean Sea.

The Second Engineer, and Mr. Wadsworth the Sixth Engineer, were in charge of the watch, and immediately the explosion occurred the Second Engineer rushed out of the stokehold and informed the First Engineer, who was off duty, of the mishap.

The First Engineer and the Second Engineer then went below. The Second Engineer went through the engine room and opened the door of the stokehold, but scalding steam drove him back. In returning he passed Mr. Wadsworth making his way towards the stokehold where it was known that some lascar firemen had been trapped at the time of the explosion. Mr. Wadsworth went into the stokehold; and when the steam had cleared away he was found dead in the port wing, close to the lascar firemen whom he had tried to rescue.

Mr. Wadsworth must have known that in entering the steam-filled stokehold in an endeavour to save the lascar firemen he was running a very great risk of losing his own life.

Henry Hartley Wadsworth was posthumously awarded the **Albert Medal (Sea),** which was presented by the King to his mother at Buckingham Palace on February 20, 1935. He was born on December 29, 1908 at West Derby, a suburb of Liverpool. He joined the Merchant Navy as an Assistant Engineer on May 31, 1930. He joined the *City of Cairo* as Sixth Engineer on January 9, 1930. In addition to his AM, he was awarded an "In Memoriam" medallion by the Liverpool Shipwreck and Humane Society. His Albert Medal is now in a private collection.

THOMAS GIBSON

Date of Deed: December 14, 1934
Date of Gazette: June 25, 1935

In December, 1934, the s.s. "Usworth" of Newcastle was in distress in the North Atlantic Ocean while on a voyage from Montreal to Queenstown with a cargo of grain.

Attempts were made to save the vessel but at about midnight on 13/14th December it became clear that she would have to be abandoned by her crew. Very gallant efforts were then made by the Belgian s.s. "Jean Jadot" and the s.s. "Ascania" of Liverpool to take off the crew. In the course of these efforts the "Ascania" manoeuvred as close as was possible to the "Usworth", and about 2 p.m. on 14th December, sent away a lifeboat to her. There had been a whole gale from the west-north-west which at this time had slightly moderated, but there were still frequent heavy squalls and high seas; oil was being pumped on the sea. The lifeboat from the "Ascania" got under the lee of the "Usworth" about fifteen feet away from her, with the crew ready to pull away as the

"Usworth" drifted down on to the lifeboat.

Those on the "Usworth" were told to jump one at a time into the lifeboat, but in the excitement three members of the "Usworth's" crew jumped into the water together. One of the men who jumped from the "Usworth" was the cook, T. Gibson. He was a strong swimmer and would probably have reached the "Ascania's" lifeboat in another two or three strokes, but the messroom boy, L. Jones, who had got into difficulties, shouted for help and Gibson was seen to tread water and then to turn back. Unfortunately he was unable, in the oil-coated sea, to swim with the boy to the "Ascania's" lifeboat, and, notwithstanding attempts made to save them by those remaining in the "Usworth", they were swept under the "Usworth's" stern and both drowned.

There is no doubt that Mr. Gibson sacrificed his life in attempting to save the messroom boy.

Thomas Gibson was awarded a posthumous **Albert Medal (Sea)**, which was presented to his widow, Mrs M.A. Gibson of 218 Marsden Street, South Shields. He was born in South Shields on August 8, 1908 and first went to sea in 1926. Eleven Sea Gallantry Medals in Silver were given to the crew of s.s. "Ascania" and ten Sea Gallantry Medals in Silver (Foreign Services) were given to the crew of the s.s. "Jean Jadot" for their gallant rescue attempts. The whereabouts of Gibson's Albert Medal are unknown.

ANDRÉ JOHN MESNARD MELLY

Date of Deed: May 4, 1936
Date of Gazette: June 23, 1936

His Majesty The King has been graciously pleased to approve that the **Albert Medal in Gold (Land)** *be awarded posthumously to André John Mesnard Melly, Esq., M.C., F.R.C.S., in recognition of the conspicuous gallantry which he displayed during the disorders in Addis Ababa in May, 1936, in his efforts to rescue British and other foreign nationals and wounded Abyssinians, in the course of which he received injuries from which he has since died.*

Image: Unknown

André John Mesnard Melly

The Albert Medal in Gold was presented to his mother, Mrs Eleanor Lawrence Melly, by the King (Edward VIII) at Buckingham Palace on July 14, 1936. He was born on October 9, 1898 in Aigburth, Liverpool, the son of Colonel Hugh Melly. He was educated at Marlborough, Oxford and Bart's, qualifying as MRCS, LRCP in 1926 and further qualified as BM, BCh (Oxon) and FRCS (Edin) in 1929 and 1931 respectively. He went to Abyssinia in 1934. During WWI, he served as a Lieutenant in the Royal Field Artillery, being commissioned on February 23, 1917. He was awarded the Military Cross on September 18, 1918. He died on May 6, 1936. For his WWI service he was awarded the British War and Victory Medals. He was unmarried. He lies buried in the Legation Cemetery, Addis Ababa, Ethiopia and there is a memorial to him at Marlborough College. This was the last Albert Medal in Gold to be awarded to a civilian and its whereabouts are presently unknown.

1940 – 1945

Of the 45 Albert Medals awarded during WWII, only thirteen went to civilians and of these, nine were Merchant seamen. Of the thirteen, five subsequently became George Cross holders in 1971.

SYDNEY OWEN

Date of Deed: January 23, 1940
Date of Gazette: October 22, 1940

On the morning of the 23rd January, 1940, Maxwell Arthur Farrin, a boy of 13 years of age was bathing at Brighton-le-Sands, Botany Bay, New South Wales, about fifty yards from the shore, when he was attacked by a shark which severed his left leg and inflicted serious abdominal injuries. His plight was observed from the shore and Sydney Owen, although warned of the presence of the shark, which was still close to Farrin, unhesitatingly swam out to the boy and brought him back to the shore. Farrin, however, succumbed to the injuries he had sustained.

Sydney Owen was awarded the **Albert Medal (Sea),** which was presented to him by the Governor of New South Wales at Sydney on March 5, 1941. Mr Owen, who was also awarded the Clarke Gold Medal (Australia), is believed to have died on March 17, 1967. The whereabouts of the Albert Medal are unknown.

ROBERT ALLAN FINLAYSON and

RICHARD HAMILTON

Date of Deed: May 31, 1941
Date of Gazette: January 16, 1942

Image: Family

Richard Hamilton

Their vessel was in port undergoing repairs and two members of the crew were engaged in removing plugs from the bulkhead of the port deep tank, when both suddenly collapsed, having been overcome by unsuspected gas which had generated from damaged cargo in the hold. The Second Officer, Mr. Robert Allan Finlayson, observing the occurrence and realising the immediate need for assistance, promptly fastened his shirt around his nose and mouth and, with Able Seaman Richard Hamilton, entered the tank with a rope in an attempt to save the two men.

This brave action on the part of Second Officer Finlayson and Able Seaman Hamilton, unfortunately cost them their lives. Mr. Finlayson was just able to make the rope fast around the body of one of the men before he himself collapsed and died. Able Seaman Hamilton, who had immediately followed him, did not reach the bottom of the tank but collapsed off the ladder when about half way down.

Although they must have known the very great risk they ran in entering the tank, Second Officer Finlayson and Able Seaman Hamilton completely disregarded their personal safety in their gallant endeavour to save the lives of their shipmates.

Robert Allan Finlayson and Richard Hamilton were each awarded a posthumous **Albert Medal (Sea)**. The incident took place on May 31, 1941 on board the MV *Scottish Prince,* which had been damaged by enemy action and was in Alexandria for repairs. Robert Finlayson was born on May 13, 1916 at Newton-le-Willows, Lancashire. He was entitled to the 1939-45, Atlantic and Africa Stars and the War Medal for his service in WWII but it is not known whether these were ever claimed. Richard Hamilton was born on October 21, 1912 at Dalhousie, New Brunswick, Canada. Because their deaths were not as a result of enemy action, neither man is commemorated in the CWGC records. The whereabouts of both these Albert Medals are presently unknown.

TANBUK IRANG

Date of Deed: June 3, 1942
Date of Gazette: September 8, 1942

On June 3rd, 1942, Tanbuk Irang, an Abor volunteer carrier working on the Ledo refugee route, found an Anglo-Indian woman and child in great distress at Shamlung on the Burma side of the Patkoi range. He carried the child over the range up a track most of which was knee deep in mud. The woman was too exhausted to follow, so he put the child down by the side of the path and went back and carried the mother up. He laid her down and went on with the child, and so continued carrying them alternately till he reached Pahari, six miles from where he had found them. There he did not find the assistance he had hoped for and continued in the same manner another four miles to the camp at Nampung. Tanbuk Irang, on his trips backwards and forwards, covered 30 miles of appalling track, for 20 miles of which he was carrying either the mother or the child. All the parties in this area have been working at considerable personal risk; the majority of them have succumbed to sickness and in considerable numbers have died. By this feat of gallantry and endurance, and at great risk of himself dropping from exhaustion and being lost, Tanbuk Irang undoubtedly saved two lives.

Tanbuk Irang was awarded the **Albert Medal (Land)**, which was presented to him at Marghenta on March 10, 1943, although it is not known by whom. The whereabouts of his Albert Medal are likewise unknown.

GEORGE WALTER NEWBERY

Date of Deed: March 17, 1942
Date of Gazette: September 29, 1942

For gallantry in attempting to save life at sea.

Third Engineer George Walter Newbery, aged 23, was awarded a posthumous **Albert Medal (Sea),** which was presented by the King to his mother at Buckingham Palace on October 20, 1942. This was the first of two citations for the Albert Medal of the utmost brevity (but see that for Albert Shearing below). The award was for attempting to save life after his ship, the *M.V. Crista* (Anglo-Saxon Petroleum Company) was torpedoed by

U-83 in the Mediterranean Sea on March 17, 1942, on the Libyan-Egyptian border. Born in 1919, he was the son of Henry and Daisy Newbery of Brentwood, Essex. He was awarded the 1939-45 and Africa Stars and the War Medal for his WWII service. He is commemorated on Panel 33 of the Tower Hill Memorial. The whereabouts of the Albert Medal are unknown.

ALBERT SHEARING

Date of Deed: April 16, 1942
Date of Gazette: January 5, 1943

Albert Shearing

Image: G. May

For great bravery in saving life at sea.

This has to be by far the shortest citation for the Albert Medal, even eclipsing the briefest of the announcements in Queen Victoria's reign. However, Don Henderson noted down an account of the service rendered in his notes for "Heroic Endeavour" and these are given here, with acknowledgement.

On 16th April, 1942, the S.S. Caspia (Overseas Oil & Transport Co. Ltd.) was sailing in the Mediterranean some ten miles south of Beirut, Lebanon, with a cargo of about 7,000 tons of benzine. The ship was torpedoed and orders were given to abandon ship. Most of the crew were in the starboard lifeboat when three more torpedoes struck the ship, which burst into flames. Benzine poured out on to the water and caught fire. The strong current swept the blazing spirit around the ship to where the lifeboat was lying alongside and the crew jumped overboard. There was one small, clear channel through the flames and eleven of the crew made for it. They had to swim 400 yards through the flames and were all badly burned. The ship's carpenter had his eyes badly burned and started swimming in the wrong direction towards the flames. A.B. Shearing went to his rescue, towed him clear of the flames and then kept him afloat for one and a half hours before they were picked up. Had it not been for his gallantry the carpenter must have lost his life in the flames.

Albert Shearing was awarded the **Albert Medal (Sea)**, which was presented to him by the King at Buckingham Palace on October 31, 1944. He was born in Great Ormsby, Norfolk, on June 9, 1916 and appears to have first gone to sea as a Deck Boy in 1934. He then served right through until the end of the war, when he was discharged with a disability pension, due to his experiences on the *Caspia*. He went to live at 65 Victoria Street, Southwold, Suffolk, where he died, aged 34, on May 31, 1950. He is buried in Southwold churchyard. He was entitled to the 1939-45, Atlantic, Africa and Pacific Stars and the War Medal for his WWII service. It is understood that his wife was from the Middle East and may have taken his medals abroad with her after his death.

WILLIAM CHISHOLM

Date of Deed: October 27, 1942
Date of Gazette: April 27, 1943

Image: TNA MN Records

William Chisholm

The ship in which Mr. Chisholm was serving was torpedoed in darkness and immediately began to sink. A fire broke out, which enveloped the bridge in flames and orders were given to abandon the vessel. She sank within eight minutes. One of the Senior Officers, who was on the bridge, was badly injured. He was taken to the surgery where Mr, Chisholm immediately attended to him and afterward, as he was helpless, helped him to the deck in order to get him away from the sinking ship. Mr. Chisholm's efforts, however, were unsuccessful and neither he nor the Officer was seen again.

Although the ship was sinking rapidly, Mr. Chisholm remained and deliberately sacrificed his chance of safety in a gallant attempt to save the life of another.

William Chisholm was awarded a posthumous **Albert Medal (Sea)**, which was presented to his father (his nominated next-of-kin) by the King at Buckingham Palace on June 8, 1943. He had been married but was separated in 1933, although he was not divorced. There followed some acrimonious exchanges between his father and his wife over who should have the AM, which was finally sent to his wife by his father. The vessel involved was the *M. V. Stentor*, which was on charter to Elder Dempster Lines and she was torpedoed 120 miles west of Madeira on October 27, 1942. William Chisholm was born at Findhorn, Morayshire, on May 24, 1899, the son of Alexander Chisholm, a manager of salmon fishings. He married Fanny Bissett Mackintosh, BSc, the daughter of C.S.M. Mackintosh of Waterloo, Dingwall, on September 29, 1930, in King's College Chapel. Before joining the Merchant Navy he had been a Medical Officer on the West African Medical Staff. For his WWII service, he was awarded the 1939-45 and Atlantic Stars and the War Medal. He also received Lloyd's War Medal for Bravery at Sea. All his medals are now in a private collection. He served in the Seaforth Highlanders in WWI from October 5, 1917, at home for nine months and in France for six months. He was awarded the British War and Victory Medals, although these are not with his WWII medals.

DAVID MCRAE

Date of Deed: July 3, 1943
Date of Gazette: December 7, 1943

Image: Edinburgh Evening News

David McRae

The ship in which McRae was serving was lying in a United Kingdom port when the boatswain entered the deep tank to obtain some oil. This tank had previously contained ground nut oil and the residue, having decomposed, had deprived the air in the tank of oxygen. As the boatswain was ascending the ladder from the bottom of the tank he collapsed. A stevedore went to his assistance but he was forced to return and had to be helped out of the tank in a dazed condition. McRae, wearing a civilian duty respirator, then descended the ladder into the tank and he was able to secure a line around the boatswain before he, too, collapsed. The boatswain was hoisted to safety from the tank but when Able Seaman McRae was brought up later he failed to respond to first-aid treatment and died before reaching hospital.

McRae, having seen the boatswain collapse and the stevedore driven back, well knew the risks he was taking in entering the tank. By his very gallant action he saved the life of his shipmate but he sacrificed his own.

David McRae was awarded a posthumous **Albert Medal (Sea),** which was presented to his mother, Mrs. Catherine McRae, by the King at Buckingham Palace on February 22, 1944. Because his death was not as a result of enemy action, David McRae is not commemorated on any CWGC memorial. The vessel involved was the S.S. *Broughty* and the incident took place in the Humber Dock, Hull on July 3, 1943. David McRae was single and lived with his mother and two half-sisters, aged 8 and 6. His brother, Ernest, was killed in action c1943 serving with the Royal Marines. He was born in Edinburgh on September 21, 1919 and educated at David Kilpatrick's School. He had been a member of the 3rd Leith Boys' Brigade. Having done his preliminary sea training at Prince of Wales' Sea Training Hostel in London, he went to sea at 16. His father had also been a Merchant seaman. For his WWII service, he was awarded the 1939-45 and Atlantic Stars and the War Medal. The whereabouts of his Albert Medal are unknown but it is probably with the family.

ELIZABETH ANNE EVERITT

Date of Deed: May 27, 1944
Date of Gazette: July 21, 1944

Image: ACM Everitt, Esq (Son)

Elizabeth Anne Everitt

*The KING has been pleased to approve that the **Albert Medal (Land)** be awarded posthumously to Mrs. Elizabeth Anne Everitt in recognition of the conspicuous gallantry which she displayed in her efforts to rescue the crew of a burning aircraft which crashed, loaded with bombs, into a field near her home. Two of the bombs subsequently exploded, killing her instantly.*

Mrs. Everitt, aged 39, of Puddlewharf Farm, Ashdon, near Saffron Walden, Essex, had been a widow for three months. She observed the collision in mid-air between a Havoc A20, piloted by Captain R.D. Dunlop, USAAF, and a Mustang P51B, piloted by Lieutenant Robert L. Dickens, Jnr, at 1900 hours on Saturday May 27, 1944. The Havoc, loaded with bombs for a mission, caught fire and crashed in a field on Street Farm, Ashdon. Four of the crew were killed and one, Staff Sergeant Mattei, the rear gunner, was injured. Mrs Everitt arrived on the scene and asked another passer-by to go for medical supplies and phone the emergency services. Mrs Everitt and a Sergeant Hartman, USAAF, then went to the aircraft to see if any others could be helped. There were four 500 lb bombs on board and two exploded. Mrs Everitt and her dog died instantly and Sergeant Hartman died later. Sergeant Hartman was posthumously awarded the Soldiers' Medal. The Albert Medal was presented to Mrs Everitt's son, Tony, aged 4, by the King at Buckingham Palace on February 20, 1945. Tony was accompanied by his uncle, Alfred George of Bright's Farm. He still lives on the same farm as his mother and the family is still in proud possession of the Albert Medal.

1946 – 1949

Only one Albert Medal was awarded to a civilian who did not survive to become a GC holder between the end of the war and the end of 1949.

JOHN HOWARD DAVIES

Date of Deed: May 28, 1949
Date of Gazette: November 1, 1949

On May 28th, 1949, a party of Scouts, aged between 11 and 15 years, visiting Sully Island were cut off by the rising tide from a causeway which led to the mainland. Most of the boys got safely across, but two of them were forced off the causeway by the strong tide. The leader of the party returned to help the elder boy but in the struggle he too became exhausted. Margaret Vaughan (aged 14 years) saw from the beach the difficulties they were in. She undressed and swam towards them over a distance of some 30 yards in cold, rough water and against strong currents due to the rising tide. On reaching them she towed the boy to the shore while he supported himself by grasping the straps of her costume and his leader's coat. At about ten feet from the shore a life belt was thrown in which the boy was placed by the other two and the three reached the shore safely. Margaret Vaughan's action probably saved the life of the Scout leader as well as that of the elder boy.

Meanwhile, John Howard Davies (aged 13 years) had safely reached the mainland when he saw that his friend, who was unable to swim, was being forced away from the causeway into deep water. He stripped to the waist and went back along the causeway to help him. By swimming out he was able to grasp his friend and hold him up in the water. Both boys shouted for help and it was obvious that they would not get ashore unaided. By this time a rescue boat had put out from the shore but Davies became exhausted by his efforts and before the boat could reach them he was forced to release his hold on his friend and they drifted apart. The boat rescued the friend but no further sign of Davies was seen. His body was subsequently recovered. There is no doubt that in returning to the aid of his friend after he himself had reached safety Davies gave his life in this rescue attempt.

John Howard Davies was awarded a posthumous **Albert Medal (Land)**. Margaret Vaughan was also awarded the Albert Medal for this incident. She exchanged her AM for the George Cross and is still, happily, alive and living in retirement in Wiltshire at the time of writing. She is the only lady now wearing the George Cross. Despite much effort, it has not been possible to discover anything about John Howard Davies, although it is believed the Scouts awarded him a posthumous Bronze Cross for his gallantry. He is buried in Cathays Cemetery. John Davies' Albert Medal is probably still with his family.

1949 – 1971

By the end of 1949, there were at least nine awards which might be given for 'civilian' gallantry and in some cases it had become difficult to decide on the most appropriate award. Consequently, a purely administrative decision was made, never legitimised by any Statute or Royal Warrant, that the Albert Medal in Gold (and the Edward Medal in Silver) would no longer be awarded and that the Albert Medal (and Edward Medal) would only be awarded posthumously. For some quite inexplicable reason, upon its institution, no provision was made for the posthumous award of the George Medal; indeed such a provision was only made in 1977. Consequently, the Albert Medal was used, quite improperly, as a posthumous George Medal until 1971, when all surviving holders of the AM were invited to exchange their original awards for the GC and the Albert (and Edward) Medal was abolished altogether. This decision was to be the cause of much bad feeling over the years, as those who had not survived to exchange their awards, for whatever reason, were not to be accorded the status of the GC and it especially rankled with those where there were multiple AM awards and one person had fortuitously survived to exchange, whereas their fellow recipient(s) had had no such good fortune. The whole business was a complete dog's breakfast, set in train by the fatuous decision in 1940 to exchange the EGM for the GC. The EGM had always been considered to rank third after the EM and there had been instances where the AM and the EGM had been awarded for the same incident, notably the Quetta earthquake in 1935, when presumably the nine persons awarded the AM were considered to have performed a braver deed than the eight awarded the EGM. This had the effect of elevating those with the lesser award above those with the greater, which again caused some bad feeling. A supreme irony was that two men recommended for the AM and refused, subsequently to be awarded the EGM instead, went on to become GCs in 1940! Of the 25 posthumous awards of the Albert Medal between 1949 and 1971, eighteen went to civilians.

JOHN JOSEPH AHIER

Date of Deed: May 14, 1950
Date of Gazette: August 1, 1950

Image: Family

John Joseph Ahier

On the afternoon of Sunday, 14th May last, three girls were bathing near the rocks on the west side of Caswell Bay, Gower, when two of them were swept out to sea. John Joseph Ahier, aged 18, who was swimming nearby, heard cries of distress from the two girls and immediately went to their assistance. After trying to assist one girl he swam to the other, who had been carried further out to sea. All three were then carried away towards the rocks in the direction of Pwlldu. One of the girls was later rescued by another man, but neither John Ahier nor the second girl were saved. Although he was only a moderately good swimmer and must have been aware of the risk he ran in the treacherous current and so near the rocks, John Ahier did not hesitate to go to the girls' assistance, and gave his life in an unavailing attempt to rescue them.

John Joseph Ahier was awarded a posthumous **Albert Medal (Land).** He was also awarded the Bronze Cross of the Boy Scouts and a Certificate of the Carnegie Hero Fund Trust. His family still proudly hold his Albert Medal and other awards. He was born on August 28, 1931 and educated at Plasmarl School, Swansea. He attended St Paul's Church, Landore, Swansea and was a member of the St Paul's Scout Troop. After leaving school, he became a laboratory assistant in the biology department of Swansea University, afterwards becoming an assistant steward with the Anglo-Saxon Petroleum Company. He was a bachelor. He is buried in Morriston Cemetery, Swansea.

KENNETH JOHN WILSON

Date of Deed: December 1, 1949
Date of Gazette: October 17, 1950

On 1st December, 1949, the oil tanker "Nassarius" was at sea off Port Sudan on a voyage from Beirut to Mena al Ahmeda. At about 2.30 p.m. the Bosun entered a tank in which dangerous gas fumes were present, intending to wash it out with a hose. He was twice forced by the fumes to leave the tank and while attempting to enter it for the third time was overcome by them and collapsed on the top ladder.

Senior Ordinary Seaman Kenneth John Wilson, aged 19 years, was called to help by a pumpman who had been working with the bosun, and the two men climbed down the ladder to try to support the bosun on the ladder until a life line could be obtained. Wilson immediately straddled himself over the bosun's feet, but the pumpman began to lose consciousness and was forced to climb out of the tank again. Wilson remained alone, and a line was passed down to him which he attempted to place around the bosun's shoulders. Before he could do this, however, he was overcome by gas. Realising that he would not be able to climb out unaided, he went to the first landing to await help. Here he collapsed and fell to the bottom of the tank.

He was brought up after about 10 minutes by the Chief Engineer who was wearing a smoke helmet, and was found to have serious head injuries. His breathing was restored by artificial respiration, but because of his injuries this had to be suspended, and he died half an hour later. Wilson displayed great gallantry in entering the tank without a protective helmet or life line, and his courage in remaining to secure a line about the collapsed man when another man had already been forced by the fumes to leave the tank was of the highest order.

Kenneth John Wilson was awarded a posthumous **Albert Medal (Sea),** which was presented by the King to his mother, Mrs Mary Elizabeth Wilson, at Buckingham Palace on November 14, 1951. He was born in Lambeth, London, on January 1, 1930 and joined the Merchant Navy as a Deck Boy in 1948. The whereabouts of his Albert Medal are not known.

HENRY CHARLES MORRIS

Date of Deed: June 11, 1950
Date of Gazette: October 17, 1950

On Sunday, 11th June 1950, a man bathing in the sea at Anderby Creek, Lincolnshire, was carried out of his depth and got into difficulties. Henry Charles Morris, age 67 years, heard his cries for help and immediately ran towards the water undressing as he went. Despite his daughter's warning that he should wait to get a lifebelt, he plunged into the water naked and swam out to the man in difficulties. On reaching him he grasped his hand and began to swim back to shore with him. Almost immediately a heavy breaker struck them both and separated them, and Morris was not seen again. His body was recovered three hours later. After Morris had been swept away it required the combined efforts of several other men to rescue the man in difficulties.

The incident occurred at a point on the Lincolnshire coast which at high tide is dangerous for swimmers at any time. On this occasion the tide was flowing and conditions were particularly bad. Morris was a frequent visitor to Anderby Creek and was well aware of its dangers. He had been a strong swimmer but had done very little swimming for some years. His prompt and determined action displayed courage of a high order and he lost his life after a gallant attempt to rescue a younger man in difficulties

Henry Charles Morris was awarded a posthumous **Albert Medal (Land),** the oldest person to ever receive it. He was a married man from Nottingham and the whereabouts of his medal are unknown, though it is probably still with the family.

HARRY CHARLES EDWARDS

Date of Deed: June 11, 1950
Date of Gazette: October 17, 1950

On Sunday, 11th June, a girl of 14 who was bathing in the breakers at Mablethorpe was carried out to sea by a receding wave and called for help.

Harry Charles Edwards, who was paddling with his small nephew at the water's edge at the time, and was wearing a bathing costume, saw the girl's danger and immediately went through the breakers and swam strongly out to her. On reaching her, he told her to take hold of him and then began to swim back towards the shore with her. A large wave, however, struck them and parted them, and after it had passed Edwards was seen to be floating motionless on the water and being carried further out to sea. He was not seen again until his body was recovered from the sea three hours later.

At this point on the shore a large outfall tunnel enters the sea, and the rising tide creates a very strong current into the mouth of the tunnel. Swimmers are warned of the danger by a large notice. At the time the incident took place the tide was coming in strongly and the sea was at its most dangerous.

Edwards' action displayed the highest courage. He was a strong and experienced swimmer, and must have realised the extreme danger of swimming out beyond the breakers in such a sea. He nevertheless went without hesitation to the girl's assistance and gave his life in an attempt to rescue her.

Harry Charles Edwards, a 41 year old married man from Leicester was awarded a posthumous **Albert Medal (Land)** the whereabouts of which are presently unknown. Edwards had been in the Royal Navy for 14 years and held a number of Life Saving Certificates,

MORRIS RICHARD ELLIS

Date of Deed: July 4, 1950
Date of Gazette: January 23, 1951

On the 4th July, 1950, during tank cleaning on board R.F.A. WAVE COMMANDER, the Boatswain entered No. 6 tank to complete cleaning by hose. The nozzle dropped from the hose into the tank and the Boatswain descended to try to locate it. He was three-quarters of the way up the ladder when he was overcome by gas. Able Seaman Ellis immediately went to his assistance and managed to lash the Boatswain to the ladder with a rope passed down to him. Able Seaman Ellis, who was well aware of the danger and risk involved, was himself overcome by gas, lost his grip of the ladder and fell to the bottom of the tank and was killed.

Morris Richard Ellis

Image: Family

Able Seaman Ellis gave his life to save the Boatswain and largely through his prompt action the Boatswain was brought on deck and recovered.

Morris Richard Ellis was awarded a posthumous **Albert Medal (Sea)**. He was born on July 18, 1926 in Preston, Lancashire, although he seems to have been brought up by grandparents in Holyhead, North Wales. He was educated at the Kingsland School and later the Cybi School, which became Holyhead County School. He was in the Sea Cadets before joining the Royal Fleet Auxiliary. He had an older sister called Lavinia, whose married name was Hughes. He began work as a telegram boy, delivering telegrams from the Post Office in Holyhead before joining the RFA. He is buried in Gibraltar. His Albert Medal is probably still with his family.

ABDUL RAHMAN X MOHD ASKAR

Date of Deed: July 5, 1950
Date of Gazette: July 25, 1952

Fumigation was carried out in m.v. "Cheshire" while the ship was in dock at Birkenhead preparatory to sailing on her next voyage. After the ship had been declared to be clear of gas, members of the crew, with a number of shore workers, boarded her to commence duty. Some time later, at about 10.30 a.m., men working in the engine room began to be affected by fumes of cyanide gas, which were liberated from the bilge water when the compressors were started. More than forty men were affected. Realising the danger to his men if they did not escape quickly Abdul Rahman took up a position of vantage on the middle platform of the engine room and began shouting orders to the men, thus enabling a number of them to escape to safety. His own position was one of great danger, as the concentration of gas at that point was very high, but despite this he carried on giving instructions and helping the men to regain the deck, until he collapsed.

Rescuers were rapidly on the scene, helping the men on the deck, where most of them quickly revived in the open air. Abdul Rahman was brought out by the rescuers and taken to hospital, where he died.

Abdul Rahman x Mohammed Askar, Engine Room Serang, was awarded a posthumous **Albert Medal (Sea)**, which was presented to his widow at Sylhet, Pakistan, by the High Commissioner for the United Kingdom on September 2, 1952. Abdul Rahman was 50 years old at the time of this incident. The whereabouts of the Albert Medal are unknown.

CHARLES WILLIAM GREENWOOD

Date of Deed: October 2, 1952
Date of Gazette: March 31, 1953

On 2nd October, 1952, Mr. Greenwood, a plumber employed by a firm engaged on contract work, was working on board H.M.S. Mull of Galloway, which was undergoing a refit at a Glasgow Shipyard. Whilst in a store room he glanced down an access hatch to a tank below and saw a Naval rating lying unconscious on the deck. Without further thought, Mr. Greenwood took off his jacket and went straight down to the unconscious man, at the same time calling for assistance. A rope was lowered for Greenwood to secure to the Naval rating, but before this could be achieved, Greenwood was overcome by fumes and collapsed.

Two other workmen and a Naval Officer attempted to rescue the two victims, but were unable to reach them before they themselves felt the effects of the fumes and had to retire quickly. They were finally rescued by an ambulance squad equipped with oxygen masks but all efforts to resuscitate them were unsuccessful.

This gallant attempt on the part of Greenwood is worthy of the highest praise. With his experience he must have known the risks of gas and asphyxiation in normally closed compartments, but without heed to any possible danger, he sacrificed his life in trying to save another man.

Charles William Greenwood was awarded a posthumous **Albert Medal (Land)** the whereabouts of which are unknown.

PETER BECKERTON

Date of Deed: January 31, 1953
Date of Gazette: April 28, 1953

Image: E. Daily Press

Peter Beckerton

Shortly after 6 p.m, on the night of the 31st January last, Peter Beckerton, aged 19, who lived with his parents at Snettisham Beach, informed them that the sea was coming over the sea wall. The weather and tide conditions were well known, and Peter Beckerton and his father started off to go to a bungalow at the other end of the beach to fetch a neighbour who lived there and who was ill. On the way there, Peter, realising the danger caused by the inrush of the sea, which was then waist deep, and still rushing in, shouted to his father to go back and that he would take the neighbour to a safer place. He then battled his way some 200 yards to the bungalow where he was last seen near the door. The bungalow was swept away by the tide.

This gallant attempt by Peter Beckerton is worthy of the highest praise as he must have realised the danger to which he was exposing himself and, after sending his father back, deliberately faced the overwhelming odds in an attempt to save a neighbour.

Peter Beckerton was awarded a posthumous **Albert Medal (Land)**, which was presented to his parents in a private ceremony at Buckingham Palace. His mother, Mrs Vera Beckerton, was awarded the British Empire Medal (Civil) for her part in rescuing others from the same disastrous East Coast floods of that year. Peter was also awarded the Bronze Medallion of the Carnegie Hero Fund Trust. He is buried in Snettisham churchyard and his grave was unmarked until 1988. His mother always refused to have a headstone on his grave until after her own death in June, 1985, aged 78, when she was buried with him. The Albert Medal and Carnegie Hero Fund Trust Medallion are still with his family.

HENRY ERIC WILKINSON

Date of Deed: January 5, 1953
Date of Gazette: July 21, 1953

Image: Unknown

Henry Eric Wilkinson

At 1.10 a.m. on 5th January, 1953, at the 5th mile Kuala Lumpur-Klang Road, Malaya, Mr. Wilkinson was driving a station wagon with four passengers when it ran off the road into an old mining pool. At the time of the accident there was a heavy mist making the road slippery and visibility poor.

Mr. Wilkinson and three of the passengers succeeded in reaching the bank safely, but the fourth passenger, an Indian Clerk, was lost in the water. Mr. Wilkinson dived back into the pool three times in an effort to save the missing man but on the third occasion he himself failed to reappear.

The water was very muddy and the bottom was covered with thick weed. The search continued till morning for the two men and when eventually they were brought to the surface it was found that Mr. Wilkinson had succeeded in reaching the other man and had obviously been bringing him towards the surface when he himself was overcome, as his arms were still clasped around him in a lifesaving grip.

Mr. Wilkinson lost his life in an extremely gallant endeavour, under very difficult conditions, to save the life of his passenger.

Henry Eric Wilkinson was awarded a posthumous **Albert Medal (Land)**. He was born in Ulverston, Lancashire (now Cumbria) in 1925 but very little is known about his life. A single man, he went to Malaya as a chemist to work for a rubber company; however, he is not known to the professional chemistry bodies, either industrial or medical, in the United Kingdom. He was a keen footballer. He is buried in Cheras cemetery, just south of Kuala Lumpur. The whereabouts of his Albert Medal are not known.

JOHN ROBERT WALSH

Date of Deed: February 8, 1953
Date of Gazette: July 24, 1953

On the afternoon of 8th February, 1953, a 10 year old boy went on to an ice-covered pond to recover a stick; the ice was about one inch thick, snow was falling and a bitterly cold wind was blowing. When the boy was about 12 yards from the bank, the ice gave way and he fell into the water, which was some 30 feet deep. John Robert Walsh, a resident of the district, was walking on the far side of the pond and at once ran to the scene. After removing his outer clothing and his shoes and socks he walked over the ice to where the boy had fallen through, and from a kneeling position he attempted to rescue the boy, but the ice broke under him. As he entered the water he grabbed the boy and held him up. The ice, although too thin to support him, was thick enough to prevent his making a passage to swim back to the bank, and while he was waiting for aid from the bank he lost his hold on the boy and they were both drowned.

In the appalling weather conditions, and with his knowledge of the depth of the pond, Walsh must have known he was risking his life when he went to the boy's rescue. It was the act of a very brave man.

John Robert Walsh was awarded a posthumous **Albert Medal (Land)**. Mr Walsh was a 48-year-old caretaker of 21 Spendmore Lane, Coppull, which is about half way between Wigan and Chorley in Lancashire. He was the father of six children. The pond in question was a clay pit off Park Road in Coppull. The boy who drowned was Frank Tite of 27 Chapel Street, Coppull, a non-swimmer.

A collection taken up after the incident raised over £1,000, including £100 from the National Union of Public Employees, of which Mr Walsh had been a member. The whereabouts of his Albert Medal are unknown.

MARK GREGORY BAKER and THOMAS WILEMAN

Image: Leicester Murcury

Mark Gregory Baker

Image: Leicester Murcury

Thomas Wileman

Date of Deed: August 17, 1955
Date of Gazette: February 7, 1956

About 8.30 on the morning of the 17th August, 1955, two workmen, William Ward and Thomas Wileman, arrived at a farm near Ticknall in Derbyshire, to continue pumping out foul water from a well; a small pump driven by a petrol engine had been placed on a platform 40 feet down the well a few days before and had been set in motion. Ward went down the well but was rapidly overcome by the fumes from the pump and his mate Wileman, after shouting for help, went down the well to his aid but was also overcome.

Shortly afterwards Dr. Mark Gregory Baker of Ashby de la Zouch arrived on the farm in response to a telephone call from a neighbour for help. Tying a rope round his waist and giving one end to two women to hold, he descended the well to a distance of about 25 feet but beginning to be overcome by the fumes he shouted to be hauled up. Unfortunately the rope became entangled with the cross supports of the well ladder some 20 feet below the surface and he could not be got out until members of the Derbyshire and Leicestershire fire services arrived about 9 o'clock with breathing apparatus. Dr. Baker's body was recovered and artificial respiration applied but was unsuccessful; the other two men were dead before their bodies were extricated. Both Thomas Wileman and Mark Gregory Baker were aware of the risk they ran in going down a deep well at the foot of which a petrol driven pump had been running and the courage of each was of the highest order.

Dr Mark Gregory Baker and Thomas Wileman were each awarded a posthumous **Albert Medal (Land).** Mark Gregory Baker was born on December 10, 1913 and was educated at Wrekin College and Sheffield University. He qualified as MRCS and LRCP in 1938. He held appointments in a practice in Leeds and the Children's Hospital at Sheffield before settling in a practice at Ashby-de-la-Zouch in 1939. He married Miss Ailsa Atkinson, also a doctor, in 1939 and she survived him with a son and a daughter, aged nine and eight at the time of his death. He was a keen car rally driver and model engineering enthusiast, being particularly skilled in building model railway locomotives. His name was inscribed on its Roll of Heroes by the Carnegie Hero Fund Trust and the Ashby Urban Council opened a memorial fund to provide a medical scholarship or bursary tenable at Sheffield University in his memory. The Albert Medal is still with the family. Thomas Wileman was a 63-year-old bricklayer's labourer of South Street, Ashby. He was a single man. His Albert Medal is now in a private collection.

WILLIAM JOHN COLES

Date of Deed: August 10, 1956
Date of Gazette: May 7, 1957

A man who had been digging a well, the shaft of which was 30 feet deep but only 2 ft. 6 ins. wide, was missing. Mr. Coles was called and volunteered to make a search. Later, other searchers heard groans coming from the well and it was then discovered that Mr. Coles, without safety equipment or other assistance, had descended the well in an attempt to find the missing man. Both men were brought to the surface eventually and despite artificial respiration, Mr. Coles died soon afterwards.

William John Coles was awarded a posthumous **Albert Medal (Land).** He was a 45-year-old farmer, married with three daughters, of Higher Sminhay Farm, Marshwood, Dorset. It is about five miles north of Lyme Regis. He is buried in the family grave at St Witte's churchyard, Whitchurch Canonicorum, Dorset. The whereabouts of his Albert Medal are unknown but it is probably still held by the family.

COLIN MURPHY

Date of Deed: June 22, 1960
Date of Gazette: March 10, 1961

Image: Family

Colin Murphy

On 22 June, 1960, he was engaged in modifying equipment installed in a large department store when fire broke out on the premises. Realising that the continued working of ventilating fans might help to spread the fire he began to make his way to the roof to switch them off. On reaching the fourth floor, however, he found the fans had stopped. Then he made his way through the smoke-laden atmosphere to the front of the building where he helped a girl to safety along an eighteen inch ledge outside the premises. He retraced his steps and after helping another girl to escape, he was overcome by smoke and flames and fell on to a canopy on the ground floor. He died of multiple injuries.

Colin Murphy was awarded a posthumous **Albert Medal (Land)**. He was born in November, 1931, at Houghton-le-Spring, Co. Durham, the son of John Murphy, a miner. He had two brothers and two sisters. Baptised at St Michael's Roman Catholic Church, he was an altar boy from the age of seven. He was educated at St Michael's RC School, Houghton from 1936 to 1942, afterwards attending Houghton Grammar School from 1942 to 1947. After school, he worked for a small firm in Sunderland and then joined the RAF as a trainee cadet officer. He passed all his pilot's exams but failed the medical as he had a perforated eardrum. In 1956, he went to work at Cammell Laird's shipyard at Birkenhead as a sheet metal worker and boiler maker; he had learnt sheet metal work in the RAF. By June, 1960, he was working as a sheet metal worker for the Liverpool Ventilation Company, who were engaged in a contract at Henderson's department store in Church Street, Liverpool. Colin Murphy left a widow, Mary, who was a nurse at Victoria Central Hospital, and two sons, Colin and John. He was buried at Landican cemetery, Birkenhead. His widow was presented with the Albert Medal by the Queen on July 5, 1961 at Buckingham Palace. He was awarded their Bronze Medallion posthumously by the Carnegie Hero Fund Trust and his name appears on the Roll of Honour at his old school, Houghton Grammar. His family still proudly possesses his Albert Medal.

STANLEY CHARLES LOGAN

Date of Deed: October 17, 1960
Date of Gazette: September 11, 1962

Image: TNA MN Records

Stanley Charles Logan

When the "Capetown Castle" was approaching Las Palmas in the course of a voyage from Cape Town to Southampton there was a violent explosion in the engine room, which resulted in serious injuries to a number of the engine room staff: two of them died in the ship and five others, including Mr. Logan, died in hospital ashore.

At the time of the explosion Mr. Logan was at the starboard engine controls and he received the full force of the blast and the sheet of flame that accompanied it, and his clothes were burned from his body.

In spite of the intense pain, he stayed at his post. The explosion set off a number of fires in the engine room and in the diesel generating room. Some machinery was still running, which meant that flames were playing on pipes full of oil under pressure, and the fires were being fed by air blown in by fans. If this had continued more fires would have broken out and the whole ship would have been in danger.

Mr. Logan's only thought was to save the ship and the lives of those aboard her by seeing to it that the machinery was shut down. He then caused a report on the situation to be made to the bridge. After that, while refusing assistance to himself, he organised the removal of the other injured members of his staff. He was ultimately persuaded to leave the engine room, but after receiving some medical treatment he tried to enter it again and was only prevented by the smoke being too dense.

After he had returned to the sick bay the ship's lights failed and he tried to get up from his bed and go below to have them seen to. He eventually left the ship about 3½ hours after the explosion and was taken to hospital where he died soon after.

Chief Engineer Stanley Charles Logan was awarded a posthumous **Albert Medal (Sea)**. He was born in East Ham, London on April 28, 1905 and died in hospital at Las Palmas on October 17, 1960. He joined the Merchant Navy as an Engineer Officer about 1931 and served throughout WWII, being awarded the 1939-45, Atlantic and Italy Stars and the War Medal for his service. He spent his whole career with the Union Castle Line. He was married with one daughter and lived in Margate. He was buried in Margate cemetery, grave number 20. His Albert Medal and other medals are thought to be still with his family.

NANETTE HANSON

Date of Deed: November 1, 1967
Date of Gazette: May 14, 1968

Nanette Hanson

Image: Wg Col F. G. Cassoll (RAF Retd)

Mrs. Hanson was taking a needlework class of twelve girls at St. John's School (Dundee) when a soldier, armed with a shot gun, entered the classroom, ordered her and the girls to barricade the doors, and then herded them into a small fitting room which adjoined. During the period that followed the man fired several blasts from the shot gun at the classroom door, on the other side of which the headmaster and members of the staff had gathered. Mrs. Hanson was then brought out of the fitting room and showing complete calm, engaged the man in conversation, during which he expressed a wish to see a young nurse and agreed that if she could be brought the children would be set free. Mrs. Hanson persuaded those outside to leave her to handle the situation; this despite the fact that the soldier had already once attempted to shoot her at point blank range and would have done so had the gun not misfired. The nurse had meanwhile been brought to the school, and quite voluntarily entered the room in an attempt to pacify the man and secure the release of the girls. This was eventually accomplished through the joint efforts of Mrs. Hanson and the nurse who were then left alone in the room with the man trying to persuade him to give himself up. Before he did so, however, he shot Mrs. Hanson in the back killing her instantly.

Mrs. Nanette Hanson was awarded a posthumous **Albert Medal (Land)**, which was subsequently presented to her husband, who by then had moved back to Keighley in Yorkshire. Nanette had come from Ilkley. She was only 26 at the time of the incident and before she went to Dundee she had taught at Ilkley Secondary School, now called Bolling Road First School. She was highly regarded by her colleagues as an expert seamstress and good teacher. The man responsible for her murder, a 19-year-old Private in the Gordon Highlanders, Robert Mone, was subsequently put on trial but was adjudged insane and unfit to plead through suffering from schizophrenia. He was a native of Dundee and was committed to the State Mental Hospital at Carstairs. The nurse involved was Miss Marion Young and she was awarded the George Medal for her part in the incident. She was only 18 years old. Nanette Hanson's funeral was held at St John's Church, Ben Rhydding, Ilkley and was attended by several teachers and pupils from her previous school, Ilkley Secondary. There was a brass plaque at the end of one of the pews in this church dedicated to her memory, which read: "Dedicated to the memory of Nanette Hanson who gave her life in defence of her pupils Nov 1st, 1967. Donated by St John's School Dundee". Unfortunately, this memorial was destroyed by fire some years ago. She was the last citizen of the United Kingdom to be awarded the Albert Medal. The whereabouts of her Albert Medal are unknown but it is probably with her widower.

GEOFFREY CLIFFORD BYE

Date of Deed: May 3, 1968
Date of Gazette: March 31, 1970

Image: Lyne Radley

Geoffrey Clifford Bye

Geoffrey Clifford Bye was First Officer aboard the M.V. Frisia which was moored in Rabaul Harbour on the night of 2nd-3rd May 1968. He was asleep in his cabin below deck when a fire broke out at approximately 4 a.m. and rapidly spread throughout the ship, completely cutting off the approaches to the sleeping quarters of the officers and crew and finally destroying the ship with the loss of three lives.

Being awoken by the heat Bye, instead of taking advantage of two escape routes which were then available to him, by-passed these to go to the aid of the elderly Chief Engineer whom he knew to be asleep in another part of the ship and not to be very agile. When he reached the Chief Engineer's cabin, Bye realised that because of the spread of the fire the only possible means of escape was through the small 12 inch portholes of the cabin. Bye made several attempts to force the Chief Engineer through a porthole until he was overcome by smoke and flames. The bodies of the Chief Engineer and Bye were later found jammed in adjacent portholes.

The late First Officer Bye displayed great personal courage, cool headedness and a complete disregard for his own safety in attempting to save the life of a fellow crew member.

Geoffrey Clifford Bye was awarded a posthumous **Albert Medal (Sea)**. He was born at Merewether in 1945, the son of Arthur Reginald Bye and Flora Rae Bye (née Bruderlin). He was a single man, resident at Boolaroo at the time of his death, aged 22 years. He began his Merchant Navy service in 1963. The whereabouts of his Albert Medal are unknown.

KENNETH OWEN MCINTYRE

Date of Deed: August 25, 1969
Date of Gazette: August 11, 1970

Image: Unknown

Kenneth Owen McIntyre

On the morning of 25th August 1969, the coastal freighter M.V. "Noongah" (1,673 deadweight tons) was lost off Nambucca Heads, New South Wales, with the loss of 21 lives.

The late Kenneth Owen McIntyre was a Greaser aboard the M.V. "Noongah" at the time of the tragedy. Shortly before the foundering of the ship he was seen with other crew members on the poop deck wearing his life jacket but was then seen to remove it and informed the other crew members present that he was returning to the engine room to see if he could render any assistance.

It was not clearly established before the Court of Marine Inquiry into the loss of the ship whether Mr. McIntyre later entered the water wearing his life jacket.

However, after the foundering, the members of the ship's crew who were clinging to a plank saw Mr. McIntyre without a life jacket supporting the Chief Cook. Having dragged the Chief Cook to the comparative safety of the plank, Mr. McIntyre heard someone else calling for help and left the plank to attempt to render assistance. He did not return to the plank and was not seen again although his life jacket was among the debris recovered from the sea.

The late Mr. McIntyre displayed great personal courage and a complete disregard for his own safety in saving the life of a fellow member of the crew and later attempting to render assistance to a further crew member in difficulty.

Kenneth Owen McIntyre was awarded a posthumous **Albert Medal (Sea)**. In addition, he also received a posthumous Bronze Medal of the Royal Humane Society of New South Wales. He was born at Woolongong, New South Wales, on October 7, 1942, being educated at Coniston Public School, Fairy Meadow Public School and Mount Kerra Boys' High School. He had been at sea since 1964. His residence at his death was noted as Fairy Meadow, New South Wales. He was the last person to be awarded the Albert Medal prior to it being superseded by the George Cross in October, 1971. The whereabouts of the Albert Medal are unknown.

Other Awards

Two other recommendations for the Albert Medal, both Land awards of the Second Class, remain to be considered. The first is mentioned in Don Henderson's book "Heroic Endeavour" and refers to a man called **Richard Rice**. He is said to have attempted to save the lives of two men overcome by gas in a large tank in East Greenwich, London, on December 8, 1900. He was a workman with the Telegraph Construction and Maintenance Co. Ltd. The award was apparently approved by King Edward VII on February 22, 1901 but there is no evidence that a notice ever appeared in the *London Gazette* and similarly, no evidence of its presentation, unlike the three ungazetted Service awards of the AM of which there is evidence of their supply and, indeed, the existence of one of them (Sullivan) is known. Rice's would have been a Land award.

In 1911, Nurse **Edith Eileen Reynolds** was recommended for the **Albert Medal** for attempting to restrain a patient in Bristol General Hospital for whom she was responsible from falling from a roof thirty-five feet from the ground. She was unfortunately unsuccessful in her attempt, which took place at 1.40 a.m. on February 6, 1911. The award was approved by the King on March 29, 1911 but she requested that she might decline the award on the ground that the circumstances described had been very much exaggerated. To this the King agreed, expressing admiration for her modesty and self-abnegation.

Two men were inadvertently omitted from *Heroes of the Albert Medal*. This is due to the fact that the first was not a regular army officer but an officer in the Militia. It is proposed to remedy this omission here.

EDWARD DENMAN THORNBURGH-CROPPER

Date of Deed: August 6, 1878
Date of Gazette: June 6, 1879

At 11 A.M., on 6th August, 1878, as the steamship "Idaho", belonging to the Pacific Coast Steamship Company, was in the act of crossing the bar of San Francisco Bay, outward bound, about two miles from the shore, Thomas Nolan, a coloured waiter, threw himself overboard.

Immediately there was a cry of "a man overboard", and Captain CROPPER, a passenger, without a moment's hesitation, threw off his coat and waistcoat, rushed to the stern, and jumped overboard. Although Captain CROPPER made a most gallant and determined attempt to reach the drowning man, Nolan sank before he was reached.

Captain CROPPER was subsequently picked up by the steamer's lifeboat, after being in the water five-and-twenty minutes. The steamship was going eight knots at the time, and there was a high sea running with a westerly wind.

Edward Denman Thornburgh-Cropper was awarded the **Albert Medal of the Second Class (Sea).** He was also awarded the Bronze Medal of the Royal Humane Society. Edward Cropper was born on May 23, 1854, the only son of Edward and Margaret Cropper (née Denman) of Swaylands, Kent. He was educated at Eton College. Although not a regular officer, he was first commissioned into the West Kent Militia, with whom he was serving when he was awarded the Albert Medal. He does not appear to have had any kind of civilian occupation, probably being a gentleman of some leisure, since he spent a good deal of his time serving in various wars and skirmishes with various militia units, including the Welsh Division of the Militia Brigade, Royal Artillery, the Pembroke Yeomanry Cavalry and 30 Company, 9 Battalion, Imperial Yeomanry Cavalry. He served in South Africa during the Zulu War, being awarded the South Africa Medal 1877-79 with clasp *1879* and Mentioned in Despatches. Later, he was to serve in the South African War 1899-1902, being awarded the DSO and Mentioned in Despatches, gaining the Queen's South Africa Medal with clasps *Cape Colony* and *Orange Free State*. He was also awarded the 1897 Diamond Jubilee Medal in Silver and the Bronze Medal of the RHS. He died in London on March 29, 1901, aged only 46. His medals are now in a private collection.

The last man appears to have been both a soldier and a diplomat simultaneously. He was omitted from the first volume on this basis, so he is inserted here, since if he is not, he will have been omitted altogether.

ROBERT WALTER EDMUND KNOLLYS, MUHAMMAD ALI and HASIL

Date of Deed: December 19, 1905
Date of Gazette: January 11, 1907

Robert Walter Edmund Knollys

Image: Unknown

On the 19th December, 1905, Captain Knollys, who was returning from Peshawar, left Dir in order to cross the Lowarai Pass, with him being the Native Assistant, Chitral, a Government Clerk, Captain Knollys' Chitrali Orderly (Hasil) and two or three servants, also a few villagers and Dir Levies.

Having reached a point beyond Mirga, the snow was found to be too deep to allow of the Pass being crossed that day, and it was decided to stop at Gujar Levy Post, about five miles from the top of the Pass.

The snow was about six or seven feet deep and was still falling. About half a mile from Gujar Post, the last four of the party, including Captain Knollys and the Subedar Major of the Dir Levies, were suddenly caught and buried in an avalanche, which fell from a hill on the right. Captain Knollys' Chitrali orderly (Hasil) and a villager of Dir, named Muhammad Ali, who were in front, immediately rushed back, and succeeded in pulling Captain Knollys out, who with their help, at once set to work to find the other three men, who were completely buried.

After about half an hour's hard work in several directions, the three men were found and extricated from the snow, one in an unconscious condition, the others conscious but very exhausted. During this half hour the three rescuers were in imminent peril of their lives, as the spot is notorious for the frequency of the avalanches which fall upon it, and it is moreover well known that when one avalanche has fallen at this place it is almost invariably followed in a very short time by a second. In remaining in the danger zone during the whole of this time, removing the snow with their hands only, and eventually rescuing all the three buried men, Captain Knollys and his two companions undoubtedly showed conspicuous courage and self-devotion.

On the day before this occurrence a succession of avalanches had fallen at another point in the same Pass, and overwhelmed a number of men who were bringing over ponies, 22 men and 11 ponies being killed; and during the 13 months preceding the end of December, 1905, there had been four avalanche accidents on the Lowarai Pass, involving a total loss of 36 lives and 15 ponies.

Muhammad Ali of Dir and Hasil of Chitral are also to be decorated with the Albert Medal of the Second Class for their gallantry. The Medals will be presented in due course.

Robert Walter Edmund Knollys was awarded the **Albert Medal of the Second Class (Land),** which was presented to him by the King at Buckingham Palace on January 8, 1907. Muhammad Ali and Hasil were presented with their medals by the Political Agent of Dir, Swat and Chitral at Drosh on October 14, 1907. Robert Knollys was born on November 10, 1872, the heir to 8th Earl of Banbury and a direct relative of 3rd Viscount Knollys. He became a barrister of Middle Temple and served in the Indian Army, being commissioned as a Second Lieutenant on the Unattached List on January 28, 1893 and appointed to the Indian Staff Corps on March 28, 1894. He was promoted to Lieutenant on April 28, 1895, Captain on January 28, 1902 and Major in 1911. He was promoted to Lieutenant-Colonel on January 28, 1919. He married on October 24, 1908, Etheldred Mary, MBE, who died on April 30, 1955. He died on July 17, 1941. In addition to the Albert Medal, he was also awarded the Kaisar-i-Hind Medal in Silver (VRI) and the India Medal 1895-1902 with clasps *Punjab Frontier 1897-98*, *Samana 1897* and *Tirah 1897-98*, all of which are now in the National Army Museum. At the time of his AM, he was Assistant Political Agent, Chitral. The whereabouts of the AMs of Muhammad Ali and Hasil are unknown.

After Note

During the preparation of this book, evidence has emerged to the effect that three Albert Medallists described in the original volume *Heroes of the Albert Medal* did, in fact, survive to be considered as holders of the George Cross. They are: Victor Brookes (page 31) who died in Stockport, Greater Manchester, on October 16, 1974; Frederick Leonard Houghton (page 95) who died in Aylesbury on December 21, 1980 and William Herbert Meredith (page 122) who died in Folkestone on September 20, 1974. There may be others still to be discovered.

Note On Photographs

It will be appreciated that in a work such as this, the quality of the photographs may well on occasions be less than might be desired. This is inevitable, as the researcher has to do the best he can with what is available. Every effort has been made to ensure that the reproduction is as good as can be achieved. Establishing copyright in the case of photographs is often difficult in this age of frequent photocopying. Attribution has been made wherever possible and apologies are offered for any omissions or incorrect attribution.

Photographs which have come to hand since the first volume

ANNIS, Percy Fairborn (Page 13)

ATKINSON, Edward Leicester (Page 14)

BATTYE, Col B. C. (Page 20)

BELBEN, George Devereux (Page 25)

BROOKES, Victor (Page 31)

CAMPBELL, John Dudley Pitts (Page 37)

CORSCADDEN, Arthur Latimer (Page 44)

CUTHBERTSON, James (Page 49)

FELDWICK, Arthur Edward (Page 60)

GALBRAITH, Ian William (Page 69)

HALLARAN, Charles Francis George Thomas
(Page 79)

HALSTEAD, Arthur (Page 79)

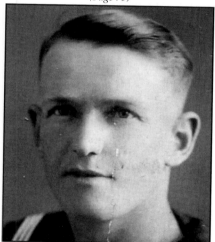

HAMBLY, Cyril (Page 80)

HARVEY, William Fryer (Page 84)

HOSKYN, Charles Reginald (Page 94)

HOUGHTON, Frederick Leonard (Page 95)

LEACH, Grey de Leche (Page 103)

McDOWELL, George Patrick (Page 113)

McHARDY, George (Page 113)

MEREDITH, William (Page 122)

MORGAN, William Marychurch (Page 124)

NEILSON, William (Page 125)

NICHOLL, *Thomas (Page 128)*

PAFFETT, *Frederick (Page 131)*

POOLEY, *Ernest Alfred (Page 135)*

REVELL-SMITH, *William Revell (Page 162)*

RHODES, *Charles Eric (Page 141)*

SCURFIELD, *Bryan Gouthwaite (Page 152)*

SIMMONS, Edward Arthur (Page 158)

SMITH, Fredrick William (Page 159)

STARTIN, Sir James (Page 164)

SULLIVAN, John (Page 171)

Known Locations Of
Albert Medals To Civilians
(at the time of writing)

ABLETT, George	Private collection
ADDY, Mark	Salford Museum and Art Gallery
AHIER, John	Family
ALLAN, John	Private collection
BAKER, Mark Gregory	Family
BATIST, John	Private collection
BATT, Alice	Family
BECKERTON, Peter	Family
BEITH, William	National Museum of Wales
BELL, Edward	Private collection
BILOCCA, Giovanni	Family
BONNICI, Paolo	Family
BROWN, Thomas William	Private collection
CARNE, Charles John	Family
CARNEY, James	Private collection
CHAPMAN, James Kennedy	Private collection
CHISHOLM, William	Private collection
CLARK, Ambrose	Private collection
CLARK, Alexander Doctor	Family
COLE, William	House of Commons collection
COOPER, Alfred John	Private collection
COSTELLO, Edwin	Hull City Museum
DAVID, Edward	Private collection
DIAMOND, Frank	Private collection
DODD, John	Private collection
DONOVAN, John	RN Museum, Portsmouth
DRABBLE, Robert	Private collection
ECCLESHALL, Arthur	Private collection
EMMITT, Florence Amy	Private collection
EVERITT, Elizabeth Anne	Family
EWINGTON, Herbert Frederick	Private collection
FURNEAUX, Alfred William	Private collection
GRAY, Robert	Private collection
HAINES, Samuel James	Private collection
HARDIMENT, Arthur	Private collection
HARRIS, John	Private collection
HAYWARD, Victor George	Private collection
HENNESSEY, Lawrence	Private collection
HIGSON, George	Private collection
HOWELLS, Richard	Private collection
IRISH, George Frederick	Family
KNOLLYS, Robert Walter Edmund	National Army Museum, London

LEECH, Henry James	Private collection
LEWIS, Thomas	Family
LISTER, Maurice	Private collection
MACGREGOR, William	Marischal Museum, University of Aberdeen
MACLEAN, Ronald	East London Museum, RSA
MANN, Algernon Edward	Family
MARCH, Edward B.	Private collection
MARGARY, Augustus Raymond	Lost at sea
MARTIN, William Francis Gordon	Private collection
MATHERS, William	Private collection
MOTTRAM, Thomas Henry	Private collection
MOULDER, James	Family
MUNRO, Robert	Family
MURPHY, Colin	Family
NEIGHBOUR	National Library of Australia
NUTMAN, William John	Private collection
OWENS, Ernest William	Private collection
PEARCE, William Henry	Private collection
PRIDE, Isaac	National Museum of Wales
REED, James Vivian	The Mansion House, Cardiff
ROBINSON, Charles Wood	Private collection
ROLLESTON, William	Glenbow Museum, Calgary
ROSBOTHAM, Hannah	Private collection
SHARP, Peter	National Maritime Museum
SHUTTLEWORTH, Allen Thompson	Private collection
SIMPSON, William	Private collection
SMITH, George Henry	Private collection
SMITH, William	Private collection
SPRANKLING, Charles	Private collection
SPRUCE, Samuel	Private collection
THOMAS, Daniel	Family
THOMAS, Edmund	National Museum of Wales
THOMAS, Isaiah	National Museum of Wales
THOMAS, Rees	National Museum of Wales
THOMAS, William	Private collection
THOMSON, Peter	Castle Museum, Edinburgh
THORNBURGH-CROPPER, Edward Denman	Private collection
WADSWORTH, Henry Hartley	Private Collection
WAGNER, Charles	Durban Museum, RSA
WALTERS, William	Private collection
WESLEY, Henry	Private collection
WILEMAN, Thomas	Private collection
WILLIAMS, Robert Ralph	National Museum of Wales
WILLIAMS, Thomas	Family
WRIGHT, Frederick	Private collection

YEARS WHEN NO AWARDS WERE MADE IN LONDON GAZETTE

1873, 1894, 1899, 1904, 1924, 1933, 1946, 1954, 1958, 1959, 1960, 1963, 1964, 1967, 1969, 1971.

Heroes of the Albert Medal
Addenda & Errata

Page 1	Line 17. Amend *darke* to read *dark*
Page 3	Amend photo caption to read "The grave of H. Fitzsimmons AM (q.v) in Gauhali War Cemetery."
Page 4	Amend upper photo caption to read "...and..."
Page 9	Under ALLAN A.D.H Add at the end of citation: "When they were within a few yards of the ship two or three men in the forepart jumped into the sea and were rescued; the third, who had climbed up the mast, was saved later when the mast fell.
Page 16	Line 14. Insert after *Vivid*).
Page 19	Line 21. Delete hypen in *February*
Page 21	Line 27. Amend to read "Royal Canadian Naval Volunteer Reserve"
Page 28	Last Line. Amend to read "... Medals, 1939-45..."
Page 32	Line 15. Amend to read *dropped*
Page 37	Line 22. Insert brackets round LG and date
Page 47	Line 8. Add at the end of line *1938*
Page 50	Line 37. Delete hyphen in *recognition*
Page 57	Line 13. Add to **Remarks** " A Fanconi Cup in his memory is still awarded by the Red Cross in Somerset."
Line 33	Amend *witnesses* to read *witnessed*
Page 62	Line 38 Insert) after second *1916*
Page 68	Photo caption should read **H.C. FRENCH**. Line 37 Amend *oft* to read *of*
Page 71	Line 8. Amend *is* to read *his*
Page 86	Line 12. **Town / county connections** should be on next line
Page 91	Line 41. Delete *J* at the end of line
Page 95	Line 28 Delete at *BP*
Page 110	Line 13 Amend *boliers* to read *boilers*
Page 113	Line 26 Add to **Remarks:** Also awarded 1939-45. Atlantic and Africa Stars and War Medal
Page 118	Line 34. before *1854* insert *IGS*. Delete *bars*
Page 128	Line 29 delete hyphen from *recognition*
Page 139	RATH, Nicholas. Died Balbriggan, Co. Dublin Jan 8, 1960
Page 142	Source of photo should read "J. D. O' Malley"
Page 150	Line 1. Amend surname to read *de Sausmarez*
Page 152	Line 29 After *1914* add)
Page 159	Line 2 Delete) after *H*
Page 160	Line 25 Delete *(No. 5)*.
Page 171	Under *SULLIVAN, John.* Against **Place / date of birth** insert *Cork Ireland 1877*. Against **Place /date of death** insert *Plymouth Devon 1940* Against **Place of memorial** insert *Weston Hill Cemetery, Plymouth.* Against Remarks add: Joined RN aged 16 and served in WWI at th battle of Jutland. Married Edith Callaway in 1910 at St Josephs Church, Devonport. Two sons, one RN the other MN, one daughter. His AM is now on show in the RN Museum, Portsmouth

Page 173	Line 21 Amend Pembroake to read Pembroke
	Line 21 Amend Elanor to read Eleanor
Page 177	Line 23 Insert *was* before *only*
Page 178	Source of photo should read *Reveille*
Page 180	Line 12. Second word should read *also*
Page 183	Remove source from photo caption
Page 186	Line 29 Amend *Railwaymen* to read *Railwayman*
Page 188	Line 6 Amend *diaplayed* to read *displayed*. Photo is allegedly of Wild's brother!
Page 191	Line 24 Amend *than* to read *then*

Back cover Under **The Author.** Line 9 Amend *maintainind* to read *maintaning*

Index

Bibliography

ABBOTT, P.E. and TAMPLIN, J.M.A., British Gallantry Awards, Nimrod Dix, 1981

ABELA, A.E., Malta's George Cross and War Gallantry Awards, Progress Press Company Ltd, 1989

BATT, A.L. (Ed), The Diary of Alice, 1993

BESLY, Edward, For those in Peril, National Museums & Galleries of Wales, 2004

CARPENTER, D.J., Clydach Vale Flood Disaster, Rhondda Borough Council, 1995

COX, Barry (Ed), Lifeboat Gallantry, Spink, 1998

HENDERSON, Major D.V., GM, Heroic Endeavour, J.B. Hayward, 1988

LLOYD, W.G. Tales of Torfaen, Published by the Author, 2000

O'SHEA, P.P. CNZM, LVO, An Unknown Few, P.D. Hasselberg, Government Printer, Wellington, New Zealand, 1981

STANISTREET, Allan, 'Gainst All Disaster, Picton Publishing, 1986

STANISTREET, Allan, Brave Railwaymen, Token Publishing, 1989

STANISTREET, Allan, Heroes of the Albert Medal, Token Publishing, 2002

WILSON, Sir Arnold, MP and McEwen, Captain J.H.F., MP, Gallantry, Oxford University Press, 1939

British Medical Journal, various obituaries

Strand Magazine

Journal of the Orders and Medals Research Society, various articles

Medal News, various articles

London Gazette, citations, HMSO Crown Copyright

The National Archives (various)

Who was Who (Various)